'PATAPHILOLOGY

Before you start to read this book, take this moment to think about making a donation to punctum books, an independent non-profit press,

@ https://punctumbooks.com/support/

If you're reading the e-book, you can click on the image below to go directly to our donations site. Any amount, no matter the size, is appreciated and will help us to keep our ship of fools afloat. Contributions from dedicated readers will also help us to keep our commons open and to cultivate new work that can't find a welcoming port elsewhere. Our adventure is not possible without your support.

Vive la Open Access.

Fig. 1. Hieronymus Bosch, *Ship of Fools* (1490–1500)

'PATAPHILOLOGY: AN IRREADER. Copyright © 2018 by editors and authors. This work carries a Creative Commons BY-NC-SA 4.0 International license, which means that you are free to copy and redistribute the material in any medium or format, and you may also remix, transform and build upon the material, as long as you clearly attribute the work to the authors (but not in a way that suggests the authors or punctum books endorses you and your work), you do not use this work for commercial gain in any form whatsoever, and that for any remixing and transformation, you distribute your rebuild under the same license. http://creativecommons.org/licenses/by-nc-sa/4.0/

First published in 2018 by punctum books, Earth, Milky Way.
https://punctumbooks.com

ISBN-13: 978-1-947447-81-3 (print)
ISBN-13: 978-1-947447-82-0 (ePDF)

LCCN: 2018954815
Library of Congress Cataloging Data is available from the Library of Congress

Book design: Vincent W.J. van Gerven Oei
Cover image: After Albrecht Dürer, "Saint Jerome Extracting a Thorn from the Lion's Foot, Lyons, 1508 (copy)," n.d., woodcut. The Metropolitan Museum of Art, acc. no. 31.54.43.

HIC SVNT MONSTRA

'Pataphilology
An Irreader

Edited by Sean Gurd &
Vincent W.J. van Gerven Oei

Contents

Preamble
Steve McCaffery
The Papyrus of Ani: *Egyptian Book of the Dead:*
A Prototype of Ekphrastic Translation of Plate 1, Chapters 1–5
(Along with a Brief Note to Explain Its Rudiments)

11

Introduction
Sean Gurd
Elements of 'Pataphilology

21

• • •

One
Michael D. Gordin and Joshua T. Katz
The Walker and the Wake:
Analysis of Non-Intrinsic Philological Isolates

61

Two
James I. Porter
"On Epic Naïveté":
Adorno's Allegory of Philology

93

Three
Sean Braune
'Pataphilological Lacan
117

Four
Paul Allen Miller
Going Soft on Canidia:
The Epodes, *an Unappreciated Classic*
139

Five
Erik Gunderson
The Paraphilologist as 'Pataphysician
167

• • •

Bibliography
217

Contributors
235

Preamble

The Papyrus of Ani: Egyptian Book of the Dead: A Prototype of Ekphrastic Translation of Plate 1, Chapters 1–5 (Along with a Brief Note to Explain Its Rudiments)

Steve McCaffery

The Pataphysical premise for ekphrastic translation is simple. Meaning (core) is the epiphenomenon of Sign (surface). Under the rubric of this premise, translation becomes subject to the following clinamen: a swerve of translation to the level of description.

Such an attempt to establish a system of verbal linear correspondence as a studied *description* of what is *seen* (i.e., by a treatment of hieroglyph as phenotype, hence a new code), will of necessity be partly a subjective response, cf. *Tender Buttons*. Ekphrastic translation liberates the latter from the domain of service, of utility, into the realm of creativity. "HA HA," doubtlessly Bosse-de-Nage would exclaim/explain.

Fig. 1. E.A. Wallis Budge (ed.), *The Papyrus of Ani: A Reproduction in Facsimile,* 3 vols. (London: The Medici Society Ltd. & New York: G.P. Putnam's Sons, 1913), 2:339–41, Pl. 1.

The Papyrus of Ani

An ekphrastic translation of Plate 1 Chapters 1–5

   this   I guess is
       the man who
   moves with
          the star in his
   armpit
        black   with a band
   a page across from
   the column
         black

   disc and the oval end
   spotted
         who lines up and sits like
   a snail or a
   stone round the dark

   kick of a bird.

                fuck the snail
   circle a bit
   (more)
       larger and wave

   bend it.

   who blocks (not blocks)
   blocks circles.
          yes.   who circles a
   bit.

    who puts the line across and
          above the feather puts the pen and
    the helmet he puts with
            the line and the helmet
across
      and the pen up

seated as he is where
      the eye was
larger
    where the pillar was and still is
a line to his arms
            and (perhaps)
is held
      holding a pen up when
this happened.
          well
the flag blew way at least
if the flag was
    near to the circle
(it was and)
        it squared up the bit
of the circle well
        half of it
bended a loop band and
      wiggled it

then as a wave
was a
    wave came   & it
wiggled it
wiggled.

at three flags
        three flags dripping
   in a bowl

not three bowls
    in a bowl near an ibis
and separate
             defined in
the next text
              his wave
dripped.

                  what has this to do with
two feathers.
a pen.
a hen.
not   a hen.   a man

crouched

over his hand (or his arm) where
the serpent   is
              (not)
the snail where

look at a band
              just
above it.

one long horizon and
       the feathers underneath it
                           (rattles): that
serpent
       again when
the head drips
              frontal

the dish missed.

how not to do this:
                    taking a feather for a walk next
taking a feather   standing it up
right
     moving the legs into rain
with a pouch and
a feather.

feathers come to be pens from
inward hawks
              its horns are
a scarab's mandibles
                      oval
a feather alone where
the man sits
seated beside it
                the beetle the dish again
(is it)
     the man takes the feather or:
the feather in front of the man in

front of the hawk

suddenly
one thin wafer one
triangle in
one swift sickle the hawk looks
the line bends.

there are three flags which mean
there is a helmet hovering
above his arm

cup resting above the k-
for kukoo
 (a little bird comes.

no.   k's for kick
i'll kick it up the ass
a wave of
 ripples from my knee below
the circle in
 side the dot.

  .

what has this
 to do with

two feathers
a pen
a hen

not a hen
a man

and a crouch.

  .

over the hand
where the serpent is
 (not)
 the snail where

look at a band
 just
above it

Addendum

The following is an earlier version of part of the same plate.

put-the-line-on-across-it a
bove and
the featherpenhelmet-and
put-the-line-across
helmet.
both helmet-and pen.

seated where the eye (is)
larger-on-the
pillarline.

an arm perhaps.
holding a pen.
a pen.
happened.

flag blows away
it is away now
flag-is-not
the circle (bit)
square and square beside-it
(circle) bit
overaband a
loopa (band).

wiggle-a-bit.
bit.
wave.

three flags now and then
and dripping bowl where
ibis comes separate
defines the next text

the wave
drips.

two feathersand
a pen is a hen
not a hen is a mancrouch.

over the hand where
serpent is
(not)
snail. where. bandisaboveit

Introduction

Elements of 'Pataphilology

Sean Gurd

1

I began to think with the word 'pataphilology around 2001, as a way of grouping a dossier of very strange texts that ranged in date of origin from the 1860s through the 1990s and in genre from avant-garde literature through the work of outsiders, hallucinators, schizophrenics, and principled refuseniks to normal (and normative) language practices. Sometimes these texts (many of which are gathered in the epoch-marking 1998 anthology *Imagining Langugae,* edited by Jed Rasula and Steve McCaffery) deploy perfectly respectable philological methodologies, but in a manner which leads to bizarre and even otherworldly results; at other times new philologies are invented, then deployed to produce remarkable and moving documents. Reading these works, I felt as though I had entered an alternate world in which everything I knew had somehow been subtly changed, where everything was itself and yet unsettlingly different at the same time.

My interest in this 'pataphilological file, as I came to think of it, was surely sustained by my fascination with, and even my love for, the philology practiced in the classics departments where

I worked and studied. I didn't know what 'pataphilology said about philology, or even if it said anything at all about it; I had not done much beyond recognizing that 'pataphilology seemed to share a set of gestures with its more well-known counterpart. But I am certain that that little file (to which, from time to time, I added a new work, a new name, a new idea) contributed to my engagement with classical philology. So I was delighted when the neologism, which I had never even said out loud, appeared in print in 2013, in an article by James Zetzel called "The Bride of Mercury: Confessions of a 'Pataphilologist."[1] Surveying Roman textual scholarship in later antiquity, Zetzel imagined that it was practically impossible to tell philology and 'pataphilology apart. I wouldn't say that about *my* 'pataphilologists — what they do is very different from philology as I know it — but Zetzel's argument is entirely concerned with scholarly practices that belong to the "mainstream," even to the Grand Tradition of European literary learning. Although our 'pataphilological dossiers were different, it intrigued me that the work done by my artists and outsiders might resonate with what happens in professional (or at least professorial) philology. Perhaps the line separating the two was less rigid than I thought. Here was an invitation, finally, to get to work on 'pataphilology, to figure out what problem, fictional or not, it sought to solve.

Why 'pataphilology? — I mean, why the word? Because of 'pataphysics, of course, that well-known discovery of Alfred Jarry. In *Exploits and Opinions of Dr. Faustroll, Pataphysician*, Jarry offered the following discussion, which has now become canonical.

> An epiphenomenon is that which is superinduced upon a phenomenon.
>
> Pataphysics, whose etymological spelling should be ἔπι (μετὰ τὰ φυσικά) and actual orthography 'pataphysics, pre-

[1] James E.G. Zetzel, "The Bride of Mercury: Confessions of a 'Pataphilologist," in *World Philology*, eds. Sheldon Pollock, Benjamin Elman, and Kuming Kevin Chang, 45–62 (Cambridge: Harvard University Press, 2014), 46.

ceded by an apostrophe so as to avoid a simple pun, is the science of that which is superinduced upon metaphysics, whether within or beyond the latter's limitations, extending as far beyond metaphysics as the latter extends beyond physics. Ex: an epiphenomenon being often accidental, pataphysics will be, above all, the science of the particular, despite the common opinion that the only science is that of the general. Pataphysics will examine the laws governing exceptions, and will explain the universe supplementary to this one; or, less ambitiously, will describe a universe which can be — and perhaps should be — envisaged in the place of the traditional one, since the laws that are supposed to have been discovered in the traditional universe are also correlations of exceptions, albeit more frequent ones, but in any case accidental data which, reduced to the status of unexceptional exceptions, possess no longer even the virtue of originality.

DEFINITION. Pataphysics is the science of imaginary solutions, which symbolically attributes the properties of objects, described by their virtuality, to their lineaments.[2]

'Pataphysics is the extension of an intellectual series that begins in physics and proceeds through metaphysics (thus it is ἔπι [μετὰ τὰ φυσικά], [supervenient] upon [what comes after physics]). Metaphysics and physics are not, says Jarry, a science of generalities; rather, they are concerned with exceptions that have become commonplace, even banal (they "possess no longer even the virtue of originality"). Whatever brings us beyond metaphysics, then, must be able to discover something vivid and compelling within the field of common exceptions: it would be a capacity to focus on the luminous detail, but also a refusal to treat that detail as just an example of some broader set or general category. In the simplest terms, it's clear that what accomplishes

---

2 Alfred Jarry, *Exploits and Opinions of Doctor Faustroll, Pataphysician: A Neo-Scientific Novel*, trans. Simon Watson Taylor (Boston: Exact, 1996), 21–22. (Alfred Jarry, *Œuvres* [Paris: Robert Laffont, 2004], 492).

the transition from meta- to 'pata-physics is just Jarry's text: 'pataphysics is, above all, the result of a certain way of writing. But *Faustroll* (as I will try to show shortly) is pervasively and palpably philological; so much so that one could claim, simply, that the operation that achieves 'pataphysics is a kind of philology. Call it 'pataphilology, and give it credit for the emergence, as Jarry puts it, of "a universe which can be — and perhaps should be — envisaged in the place of the traditional one."

Jarry was born in 1873 to a bourgeois family, once prosperous but undergoing a gradual economic decline.[3] His talents with French, Latin, and Greek promised a significant academic career, but his love for literature and art was not matched by his enthusiasm for schoolwork, and he failed to gain entrance to the École normale supérieure. Instead, he turned to the theatre and the press. Poverty was a constant companion, because he lacked the financial patrimony that, then as now, was so often the needed complement to a literary career. Nonetheless there was a breakthrough in 1897, when the Théâtre de l'œuvre produced a five-act play, *Ubu Roi*. The play was a success — *de scandale,* anyway; in the short term it may have been most famous for introducing the nonce word or modified obscenity *merdre*. *Ubu Roi* did not lift Jarry out of poverty, but it did secure his position as a significant figure on the literary scene. It was to Ubu that Jarry first attributed the possession of a new science, *la pataphysique*. In *Ubu Cocu,* Ubu is a *docteur en pataphysique,* which is explained as "a science which we have invented and whose need is broadly felt."[4] Linda Klieger Stillman describes Ubu as "the supreme scientist, capable of pataphysically resolving all oppositions, much as a mirror contains simultaneously two inverted worlds. Equal but, and because, opposite."[5] The instrument of Ubu's pataphysics was a scepter or wand with which the physical world could be bent and transformed at will. Jarry

3 Alistair Brotchie, *Alfred Jarry: A Pataphysical Life* (Cambridge: MIT Press, 2011), 7–26.
4 Cited from Linda Klieger Stillman, "The Morphophonetic Universe of Ubu," *The French Review* 50, no. 4 (March 1977): 586–95, at 595.
5 Ibid.

calls it a *baton à physique,* an appellation behind which one does not need a great deal of energy to hear *pataphysique*.[6]

Jarry's first drafts of 'pataphysical theory may have been written in 1894, under the title *Éléments de pataphysique*.[7] Perhaps by 1895 he had sketched out some more analytical components. These early attempts show every sign of being heavily theoretical, technical descriptions.[8] But at some point it became clear that the indicative mood was not appropriate to the subject and that the whole project needed to be wrapped or encapsulated in narrative form. That led to the manuscript of what we know today as the *Gestes et opinions du docteur Faustroll pataphysicien.* The bulk of the text was written rapidly in 1897–98; it was in sufficiently good condition for an excerpt to be published in the *Mercure de France* in the spring of 1898.[9]

Learned consensus is that "'Faustroll' is an amalgamation of 'Faust' and 'troll,' familiar to Jarry, who had played the role of the king of trolls in *Peer Gynt*."[10] That etymology requires the removal of a *t* to make the compound: Faust-troll becomes Faust'roll. Another explanation for the name arises from the end of the *Gestes et opinions,* when this Faust, this über-scientist, dies and unfurls himself into the ocean: "[A]nd behold, the wallpaper of Faustroll's body was unrolled by the saliva and teeth of the water."[11] Written on the unscrolled sheet is a telepathic letter from Faustroll to the British physicist Lord Kelvin containing a detailed overview of the founding principles of pataphysics. Thus, in the end, the novel's hero turns out to be a book-roll. FaustROLL or Faust[SC]ROLL or — better — Faust"roll.

We could take that as the first sign of how important philology is to the operations of 'pataphysics. There are others. The

6   But see below.
7   Alfred Jarry, *Gestes et opinions du docteur Faustroll pataphysicien,* édition annotée (Paris: La Différence, 2010), 9.
8   Ibid.
9   Ibid., 10.
10 Ibid., 45.
11 Jarry, *Exploits and Opinions of Doctor Faustroll, Pataphysician,* 99 (Jarry, *Œuvres,* 532).

basic premise of the novel is this: Faustroll travels through the streets of Paris, which has become a vast archipelago of islands; each island is a tribute or response to one of Jarry's contemporaries on the Paris literary and artistic scene. Jarry's habitual procedure in the description of islands in the Paris archipelago is to compile a topography out of details drawn from the honorand's oeuvre, much in the matter of post-impressionist painting, where the canvas is filled with fragments of color and form and the "picture" is best described as an epiphenomenon emerging from their collocation.[12] In this way the book is a *summa* of reading, a sort of précis of the work of his colleagues in literature and art. But transforming Paris into an archipelago also makes the novel a *periplous,* a fictional voyage around the known world. Here Jarry invokes the *Odyssey* (we will see momentarily just how deeply his knowledge of Greek extends), but also Rabelais, whose fourth and fifth books narrated an equally fantastic naval adventure. For Patricia Murphy, 'pataphysics is ultimately a Rabelaisian enterprise:

> The explanation that *pataphysique* "étudiera les lois qui régissent les exceptions" calls to mind Rabelais' elaborate pseudo-scientific constructions at the beginning of *Pantagruel.* Faustroll experiments with changing his size, making himself extra small. The results are similar to some of the experiences of "Alcofribas Nasier" in the mouth of Pantagruel. Pantagruel is accompanied by Panurge, Faustroll by Panmufle. Even dissimilarities may point to a connection. The content of Jarry's description of the *île sonnante* is far removed from the content of Rabelais' *île sonnante.* But Jarry is imitating Rabelais by using a favorite device of his model, taking literally and rendering concrete an expression intended as metaphor or metonymy.[13]

12 See, for example, Jarry, *Gestes et opinions du docteur Faustroll pataphysicien,* 192–95.
13 Patricia Murphy, "Rabelais and Jarry," *The French Review* 51, no. 1 (October 1977): 29–36, at 30.

Nor is it merely a matter of shared detail or spiritual inspiration: Jarry's language is replete with Rabelaisian borrowings,[14] as deeply rooted in the history of French as, say, *Finnegan's Wake* is rooted in the history of English.

Philology thus practically constitutes the project of *Faustroll*. When Jarry claims that pataphysics' "etymological spelling should be ἔπι (μετὰ τὰ φυσικά) and actual orthography *'pataphysics*, preceded by an apostrophe so as to avoid a simple pun," he provides a treasure chest of philological exploits, introducing important concepts such as "etymological spelling," "actual" orthographies, and puns. Just what pun Jarry was trying to avoid remains unarticulated. But Christian Bök runs through some possibilities:

> Ubu, for example, is a slapstick comedian (*pataud physique*) of unhealthy obesity (*pateux physique*), whose bodily language (*patois physique*) foments an astounded physics (*épatée physique*) that is not your physics (*pas ta physique*). Pataphysics embodies a polysemic fusion of both poetry and science, insofar as the French idiom for the English word "flair," *la patte* (the hand of the artist, the "paw" of the style) appears in the homophonic phrase *patte physique* — the flair of physics.[15]

Any way you cut it, pataphysics is a physics that demands — or, better, that relies on — the utmost sensitivity to language and textuality. Indeed, the work is inseparable from a text-critical tradition which has restored and explained it. Jarry died in 1907 without seeing the complete work in print; the first edition was published in 1911 by the Bibliothèque Charpentier. Five editions later, Jarry's collected works were published as part of the

14 According to Taylor, his expressions are "calqués en grande partie sur le quart livre et le cinquième livre de Rabelais." (M.A. Carey Taylor, "Le Vocabulaire d'Alfred Jarry," *Cahiers de l'Association Internationale des Études Françaises* 11 [1959]: 320.)
15 Christian Bök, *'Pataphysics: The Poetics of an Imaginary Science* (Evanston: Northwestern University Press, 2002), 27.

Bibliothèque de la Pléiade in 1972, as much of an acknowledgement as any that he had achieved canonical status. By that time, the Collège de 'Pataphysique had become one of Paris's most prestigious literary societies. Founded in 1948 and occulted between 1975 and 2000, the Collège produced a commentary on Faustroll in five issues of the *Organographe* of the *Cymbalum Pataphysicum* between 1982 and 1985. This commentary was collected as a single volume in 1986,[16] then republished in expanded form with a new edition of the text in 2010.[17] I quote the preface to the commentary:

THE MASTER BOOK

"Everything is in *Faustroll*," claims Satrap Boris Vian. And many Optimates of the College of 'Pataphysics draw a literal conclusion from this fact, finding answers to all questions by the method of opening the Master Book at random: thus for the 'pataphysician the *sortes faustrollianae* replace the *sortes biblicae, homericae* or *vergilianae*. Election of a small number and embarkation in an ark like in the Bible, navigation like in the *Odyssey*, descent to the kingdom of the unknown dimension as in the VIth book of the *Aeneid*; *Faustroll* transcends these illustrious models, which it expropriates (like a repoman) following the example of the Rabelaisian Pentateuch and without even trying to compete with them. It places itself, to the degree that doing so has any meaning, beyond all literature. [...]

Everything is in *Faustroll*, clearly, because Jarry took care to put it all in there.[18]

Readers will surely notice that *Faustroll*, in this reverent description, obeys some of the signal laws of 'pataphysics: it effortlessly exceeds literature (as 'pataphysics exceeds metaphysics, as meta-

---

16 Alfred Jarry, *Gestes et opinions du docteur Faustroll, pataphysicien: Roman neo-scientifique*, édition annotée (Paris: Cymbalum Pataphysicum, 1986).

17 Jarry, *Gestes et opinions du docteur Faustroll pataphysicien*.

18 Ibid., 7–8. All translations from this edition are my own.

physics exceeds physics), and yet it does so by being nothing *but* literature. The totality of *Faustroll,* we might say, is epiphenomenal on the totality of literature.

The Collège's commentary proceeds, carefully and with extreme sobriety (out of which emerges, quite naturally, an incredible delirium), to "place, date, draw back disguises, articulate allusions and people, clarify contexts, unravel interferences and sources."[19] But it also takes upon itself the task of "speculation," which here means something like what its etymology implies; stepping through the looking glass and "treating places, characters, itineraries, acts, and options like real beings, acts, and places, seeing this world itself (the common place where mediocrity is comfortable) in the place of another world, treating *Faustroll* as though it were reducible to glosses like a common Bible."[20]

Clearly, the commentary on *Faustroll* is not a joke. If it is true that 'pataphysics is "the revelation of laughter" (*la révelation du rire*),[21] that means that 'pataphysics attends to the truth disclosed therein. Only thus can the commentary write of *Faustroll* that it is "not hermetic, but so concise, so dense with allusions and borrowings, inviting the imagination and speculation so vividly, without ever letting itself be worn out in 'meaning,' that it seems, if you will, to make exegesis an exigency [*exiger l'exégese*]."[22] *Faustroll* makes an infinite demand on the reader. The commentary's overriding imperative is to respond to this demand by following up every citation and allusion it contains. All of this bespeaks real philological labor. So, too, does the attempt, in evidence throughout the commentary, to establish the geography of Faustroll's travels. When *Faustroll* reports, for example, that they rowed for six hours between L'île de Bran and the Pays du Dentelles, the commentary remarks that, without knowing the *speed* of the rowing, it is impossible to determine

---

19 Ibid., 21–22.
20 Ibid., 23.
21 See Ruy Launoir, *Clés pour la 'pataphysique* (Paris: Seghers, 1969). This has grounding in textual authority. See below.
22 Jarry, *Gestes et opinions du docteur Faustroll pataphysicien,* 19.

the exact distance between the two regions.[23] Nonetheless, and despite sometimes strenuous efforts to establish the geographical coordinates (efforts which recall the ancient and ongoing attempts to connect Odysseus' travels to real-world places, still very much in evidence during the centuries of the Grand Tour), the commentary also recognizes that these coordinates are only "anchors in the real" of verbal derivations[24] — puns producing geography (L'île de Bran = Hildebrand) — or, to put this differently, fictional topography functioning as "the revelation of laughter."

One of the things revealed by the Collège's commentary is that Jarry brought to his writing a virtuosic sense of language and an extensive knowledge of the classical heritage. Again and again, the *Gestes et opinions* rests on a Rabelasian base that itself, in turn, emerges from a Greek substrate. For example: when Faustroll takes essential supplies from each of his cherished books, he takes from the *Odyssey* "the joyful walk of the irreproachable son of Peleus in the meadow of asphodels."[25] The reference passes through Rabelais, who made an offhand reference to the asphodels in the Elysian fields in *Gargantua* 13.[26] The commentary assumes a reference here, too, to *Odyssey* XI.538–540, remarking that

> [Ulysses] summons (in the strong sense, as Faustroll "summons" the twenty-seven beings from their paginary space) the shadow of the dead and speaks with the famous ones, including Achilles who says, as Jean Giono would do later, that he would rather be a farm-hand than a dead hero in the Elysian fields.[27]

---

23 Ibid., 122.
24 Ibid., 20–21.
25 Jarry, *Exploits and Opinions of Doctor Faustroll, Pataphysician,* 19 (Jarry, *Œuvres,* 490).
26 Jarry, *Gestes et opinions du docteur Faustroll pataphysicien,* ad loc.
27 Ibid., 125.

References to the *Odyssey* are hardly surprising, given the fact that the *Gestes et opinions* is the tale of a naval adventure in which the hero travels from marvelous place to marvelous place. Nor is the invocation of a happy afterworld entirely incongruous in a novel which culminates with its main character passing on to the next dimension — and then writing a theoretical treatise about it.

But Jarry's investment in Greek provides more than what we must admit is, after all, an easy set of references to the *Odyssey*. Some sophisticated details emerge from this side of his education. Thus, for example, in chapter XII Faustroll opens and reads from his copy of *éléments de pataphysique*, "Livre N, chapitre ς." It does not require extraordinarily deep knowledge to know that Greek systems of numeration use alphabetic symbols. But the editors of the commentary report that this reading is found only in the later MS version of the *Gestes et opinions* (MS F):

> In revising the MS F, he reminded himself that, in fact, the Greeks added in this place the *wau* or the numerical digamma (the digamma is the old sixth letter of the alphabet, long vanished from writing) and he corrected it.[28]

Of course, the non-numerical form of the digamma was F, and so it is fitting that the MS in which Jarry made this correction has come to be known as the F MS (this is not, in fact *why*, it has this name, however; the association between the digamma and the bibliographical record is as 'pataphilological as anything you could imagine). We remark as well that the sound *w*, which the digamma originally notated, disappeared from most dialects of Greek before the historical period, and though it was pronounced in early Homeric epic, it is not notated in Homeric texts, nor was it likely pronounced in most performances. The Homeric text is shot through, we might say, by hidden apostrophes which conceal a lost letter. How appropriate that it should

---

28 Ibid., ad loc.

be used for the chapter of a non-extant work on the elements of pataphysics.

I offer this abbreviated discussion of Jarry's novel — it could be extended *ad infinitum* — to make it clear that 'pataphysics depends rather profoundly on 'pataphilology. To characterize it briefly, this 'pataphilology is a singular way of working with language that revivifies singularities or exceptions. As such, there is no *one* 'pataphilology; like vice, 'pataphilology has an infinite variety of forms. Each 'pataphilological undertaking is radically and uniquely itself. Nor can there be a generalized 'pataphilology *as such* or *per se*: each is always, and necessarily, bound to the object whose singularity it resuscitates and celebrates.

11

Before offering a brief overview of some of the work that has gathered in my little 'pataphilological file, let me insist again that 'pataphilology (like 'pataphysics) is not a joke. We are talking here about language practices that are deadly serious. 'Pataphilologists work hard, perhaps harder than traditional philologists, and their personal sacrifice is far greater. So is their ambition: 'pataphilologists reach back to the dawn of language and conjure with the most vital elements of human existence. This work is most definitely not orthodox, but it may be indispensable.

It is the surface of language, say some 'pataphilologists, that matters: if there is meaning, it can only be got at through a form of extreme rigor that begins not from the illusion that words have meanings, but from their sensual appearance. Echoes, rhymes, sonic similarities frequently play an outsized role. In the realm of language, another word for this is "Cratylism." In Plato's *Cratylus*, Socrates glides along the sensual contours of Greek in order to hear what the language seems to whisper.

> It seems to me that Poseidon was so named by the first who called him this because the nature of the sea held him as he walked, and prevented him from making progress, but was

like a bond (δεσμός) for his feet (ποδῶν). So he called the god who governed this capacity Poseidon, because he "bound the feet" (ποσί-δεσμον). But he added the ε for the sake of making the word more attractive. Or maybe he didn't say this, but instead of the first σ he said λλ (πολλείδων), to indicate that the god knew (εἰδότος) much (πολλά). Or maybe he was called "the shaker" (ὁ σείων) because of the earthquakes, and the π and the σ were added later.[29]

This might be called a "rhyming method." "Rhyme" channels the ancient Greek word ῥύσμος or ῥύθμος. The word eventually came to mean "rhythm," but in fifth-century physical theory it had a more technical meaning: it meant something like "form."[30] In Democritus, rhythm designated the specific configuration of elementary particles or elements, στοιχεῖα, which gave a thing its appearance and being.[31] To put this a different way, "rhythm" named the object's singular material configuration — a historical conglomeration of concrete elements reducible to no abstract paradigm. To demonstrate how atomic elements (στοιχεῖα) combined to create rhythms or forms, Democritus used the example of words, which are changed when their letters are changed or moved about.[32] In the *Cratylus* too, στοιχεῖον designates both "element" and "letter." And yet ῥύθμος also rhymes, obscurely, with ῥέω, "flow," so that what names form is also closely connected to flux.[33] Adding to the complication is the fact that the Greek word for "flow," ῥέω, sounds very much like one of the Greek words for "speech," ῥῆσις, which could punningly be described as a stream from the mouth.[34] The *Cratylus* thus appears

---

29 Plato, *Cratylus* 402e–403a.
30 J.J. Pollitt, *The Ancient View of Greek Art: Criticism, History, and Terminology* (New Haven: Yale University Press, 1974), 218–28; Émile Benveniste, *Problems in General Linguistics* (Coral Gables: University of Miami Press, 1971), 281–88.
31 Usefully gathered in Benveniste, *Problems in General Linguistics*, 283.
32 Aristotle, *Metaphysics* 985b4.
33 Benveniste, *Problems in General Linguistics*, 281.
34 See Plato, *Theaetetus* 206d and 263e.

to be doing some extremely sophisticated conceptual work, establishing a philosophical liaison between Democritean physical theory and the Heraclitean thesis that what is is in a state of perceptual change, and using this liaison to interpret language as a stream of letters/elements (στοιχεῖον) in a constant process of change. Remarking on the surface interaction of letters in Jarry and Joyce, Sean Braune has called this *etymism,* joining atom and etym in a single rhyme, and we might compare the comments of Joshua Katz and Michael Gordin in Chapter One of this collection on the relation between Adam and the atom in *Ridley Walker*.[35] David Melnick's extraordinary homophonic translation of *Iliad* 1–3 shows that this sort of thing is a great deal more than just a parlor game: it belongs to the same poetic tradition that would include the Sanskrit *śleṣa*, a genre of epic poem which tells two stories (for example, the *Ramayana* and the *Mahabharata*) in the same text, at the same time.[36]

Οἳ δ' ἄρα Περκώτην καὶ Πράκτιον ἀμφενέμοντο
καὶ Σηστὸν καὶ Ἄβυδον ἔχον καὶ δῖαν Ἀρίσβην,
τῶν αὖθ' Ὑρτακίδης ἦρχ' Ἄσιος ὄρχαμος ἀνδρῶν,
Ἄσιος Ὑρτακίδης ὃν Ἀρίσβηθεν φέρον ἵπποι
αἴθωνες μεγάλοι ποταμοῦ ἄπο Σελλήεντος.
    Ἱππόθοος δ' ἄγε φῦλα Πελασγῶν ἐγχεσιμώρων
τῶν οἳ Λάρισαν ἐριβώλακα ναιετάασκον·
τῶν ἦρχ' Ἱππόθοός τε Πύλαιός τ' ὄζος Ἄρηος,
υἷε δύω Λήθοιο Πελασγοῦ Τευταμίδαο.
    Αὐτὰρ Θρήϊκας ἦγ' Ἀκάμας καὶ Πείροος ἥρως
ὅσσους Ἑλλήσποντος ἀγάρροος ἐντὸς ἐέργει.
    Εὔφημος δ' ἀρχὸς Κικόνων ἦν αἰχμητάων
υἱὸς Τροιζήνοιο διοτρεφέος Κεάδαο.[37]

---

35 The 'pataphilological operator "etymic" is linked to 'pataphysics by Sean Braune, "From Lucretian Atomic Theory to Joycean Etymic Theory," *Journal of Modern Literature* 33, no. 4 (Summer 2010): 167–81.
36 See Y. Bronner, *Extreme Poetry: the South Asian Movement of Simultaneous Narration* (New York: Columbia University Press, 2010).
37 *Iliad* 2.837–847.

Hide our wrapper coat. Ink I, proct yon amp pain name
                                                              moan to.
Guy Sestos 'n' Guy Abydos neck on Guy Dionne. Airy Spain!
Tune out tour, tacky days. Sir Cassius sore. Come, us sand
                                                                     Ron
As you, Sir Tacky Days, on a respite tempera, nip poi,
Heighten ass, make a leap at a moo up a silly yen: toes.
   Hippo those, dog. A pool, a pale lass goin' ink, kiss a
                                                                    moron.
Tone high? Larissa an air rib, bollock an eye, yet ass scone.
Tone irk? Hip boat host appeal lie. You stows dose, array O's.
We ate due woe. Late, though, you pale us, goo. T' you,
                                                                Tommy Dao.
   Out art! Rake Cossack, gawk a mast. I pare rosy rows.
'Oh sue us, Hellespont! Oh saga!,' Rose sent to Sergei.
   Euphemous dark husk eco-known. In ache mate town.
We owes Troezen, know Yod, Dio. Trap fey husk, ya Dao.[38]

Like the *śleṣa,* Melnick has attempted to create a text in which the same sequence of sounds can be taken either as telling the *Iliad,* or as telling the story of what nearly all of *Men in Aïda*'s commentators have called an ebullient homoerotic orgy. *Men in Aïda* rhymes with the *Iliad,* sharing, if I may put it this way, the same etymic rhythm.

Such projects make meaning *epiphenomenal* to the acoustic substrate. It's hard not to think here of the work of those shadowy figures in Hellenistic literary theory who defined poetry more or less exclusively in terms of its sonic construction and then insisted, in a manner other philosophers found infuriating, that the essence of the poem was epiphenomenal, thus in effect claiming that the defining nature of poetry was to be found in its accidental features.

---

38 David J. Melnick, *Men in Aïda* (San Francisco: Uitgeverij, 2015), with Sean Reynolds, "Hospitality of the Mouth and the Homophonic Kiss: David Melnick's Men in Aïda," *Postmodern Culture* 21, no. 2 (January 2011); Sean Gurd, "David Melnick's Men in Aïda," *Classical Receptions Journal* 8, no. 3 (July 2016): 295–316.

> In practice, the Critic scans an aesthetic artifact for its (phonic) display of material micro-differences [...] as these are arranged by *thesis* and *taxis,* i.e. by *synthesis*. In their ensemble, these differences of quantity and quality — they are in fact positional attributes, and endowed with relational values — constitute aesthetic qualities at a higher level (the "macro-level" of sensation in contact with a *synthesis*), where sound can be seen to be "caused" (the "elements," viz. their positionalities, are literally the "causes," *aitia*), as a surface effect, a sur-plus phenomenon, or to take their own striking terminology, an "epiphenomenon."[39]

That tends to transform linguistic signs into glyphs. Let us make an anachronistic distinction: if in the early modern period hieroglyphs were thought to be pregnant with higher or mystical meanings, a 'pataphilological glyph is the representation of what you would perceive if you could somehow suspend the idea that a sign meant anything determinate: it is, to put this another way, a purely sensual presence.

The *Codex Seraphinianus,* created by Luigi Serafini, a 400-page ersatz encyclopedia in an incomprehensible writing system, appears to be the compendious description of an alien world, covering everything from microbiology to technology and culture. But its hundreds of pages of text mean nothing, and never will, and though some words appear to be made out of the things they describe, there is no way to decipher it. Even its Rosetta Stone is disconcertingly different from ours. The *Codex Seraphinianus* revels in the sheer materialism of the written trace: just as, in one entry, we are shown methods for floating words off the page, as though they had three dimensions and measurable mass, so does the experience of "reading" the codex

---

39 James I. Porter, "Content and Form in Philodemus: The History of an Evasion," in *Philodemus and Poetry,* ed. Dirk Obbink (Oxford: Oxford University Press, 1995), 137.

become a purely sensual one, a kind of delight in graphic surfaces alone.[40]

In the graphic novel *Dicamus et Labyrinthos: A Philologist's Notebook,* the Toronto-area composer, artist, and soundscape theorist R. Murray Schafer tells the story of an unnamed philologist who has set out to decipher some mysterious Cretan tablets. We read the journals of the philologist as he works towards his solution, which turns out to involve the myth of Ariadne and the legend of the labyrinth. This writing system is eminently decipherable, in fact it's only an encipherment of English, with a relatively simple code. But *that* makes the whole thing more bizarre — a philologist deciphers an ancient script that is just a cipher of his own tongue. As though to confound the ourobouric mystery, the philologist disappears into the labyrinth at the end of the book.[41]

The made-up tablets in *Dicamus et Labyrinthos* point towards a second common element in these undertakings: while 'pataphysics is the science of "imaginary solutions,"[42] 'pataphilology often seems to reverse the polarity of this definition, offering very real solutions to imaginary problems. Most notable here are projects like Schafer's that offer translations, or dramas depicting the translation of made-up documents, often in equally made-up languages. Armand Schwerner's *Tablets,* for example, which he began publishing in 1968 and continued to work on through 1991, are a collection of "translations," essays, and typographic fantasies purporting to be based on the project of decyphering some of the oldest writing in human history.[43] Even in the earliest lines of the work, it's easy to appreciate Schwerner's

---

40 Luigi Serafini, *Codex Seraphinianus* (Milan: Franco Mario Ricci), 1993.
41 R. Murray Schafer, *Dicamus et Labyrinthos: A Philologist's Notebook* (Indian River: Arcana, 1984). I met both the *Codex Seraphinianus* and Schafer's *Dicamus et Labyrinthos* in the luminous anthology edited by Jed Rasula and Steve McCaffery, *Imagining Language: An Anthology* (Cambridge: MIT Press, 1998).
42 Jarry, *Exploits and Opinions of Doctor Faustroll, Pataphysician,* 22.
43 Armand Schwerner, *The Tablets* (Orono: National Poetry Foundation, 1999).

virtuosity with scholarly gestures. I cite the first four verses of the first table, each of which has a line of commentary added by an unnamed "scholar-translator":

All that's left is pattern* (shoes?)

   *doubtful reconstruction

I rooted about . . . like a . . . . sow* for her pleasure

   *atavism: a hieroglyph: perhaps 'a fetal pig,' 'a small pig,' 'goddess'

the (power)* for all of [us]!

   *perhaps 'damage,' if a borrowing; cf. cognate in N. Akkadian: 'skin-burn'

I made a mistake. The small path was barely muddy. Little squush;
   And wet socks.* it is (scholarship?)(meditation?)

   *modernism. Specificity of attire a problem. Possibly 'underwear' (dryness?)[44]

Let me start at the end of this passage and work backwards. The translator's indecision between scholarship or meditation in trying to decide what "it is" is, on the face of it, a ludic invocation of something many of us know all too well: the original words are poorly attested, or inherently ambiguous, and that leads to a bivalent translation. But by the end of his life Schwerner was writing tablets which set up a conflict between meditative translation methods and scholarly ones, and so the two possible meanings turn out to be a commentary on the commentators' methods (see below). The same verse evokes an issue common to many 'pataphilological tablets: there is a radical anachronism in which present and deep past seem to coalesce and combine uncomfortably, in which subject (translator) and object weirdly

---

44 Ibid., 13.

coincide. "Little squush; and wet socks" receives the comment "modernism. Specificity of attire a problem." Indeed — because the word might be underwear, not socks. Both are jarring, however, not merely because ancients didn't wear underwear or socks, but also because something about these items of clothing is too intimate to appear in a text so purportedly other and archaic. The clothes we wear against our skin are, in a way, symbols for how private, tactile, and personal our contemporary predicament can be.

The second line invokes a similar anachronism with the note on "sow," the original of which is a "hieroglyph," and therefore an "atavism," reaching back into older strata of written language. The lacunae Schwerner put in this line seem to have been one of the primary attractions for using the tablet form in his original conception of the project: his early working notes evince a repeated concern with the limitations of the English tense system and an interest in developing poetic means to express what the tense system forecloses as expressive possibility. "Attention must be paid," he writes, "to the necessary, unavailable, tenses between the few tenses that we have in English, those that tempt us into believing that grammatical orders of reality have anything to do with our experience."[45] The tablet form with its gaps and discontinuities allows him to impose a fragmentary status that breaks and can even refuse the false continuity of syntax and tense. Eventually, Schwerner would supplement the rhetoric of lacunary translation with a fictive invocation of languages that existed "before" there was inflection, "when" the time-sense itself was linguistically dispensable. The "atavism" of the hieroglyph for "sow" figures the temporal impurity, or maybe it is the omni-temporality, of the *Tablets*' imagined ur-language.

Last, let's look at the first verse. On the one hand, it seems like a joke. "All that's left is pattern" might be a quite important expression of poetics, a translation (as it were) of Eliot's "these fragments I have shored against my ruin," a verse that is certainly relevant to the *Tablets*. But then the translator's "doubtful

---

45 Ibid., 133.

reconstruction" suggests that the word isn't pattern but "shoes." That would appear to seriously undermine the profundity of the first line. No pattern: just shoes. There are few more 'pataphilological first lines in modern poetry, except perhaps for B.P. Nichol's "purpose is a porpoise."[46] The grin you might be grinning at this point will turn to horror and regret, however, when you recognize that "all that's left are shoes" is also a grim recollection of the shoes that remained when the Nazi gas chambers had done their terrible work. Schwerner's "scholar-translator" has what can best be described as a fraught relationship with philology's anti-Semitic heritage; the scholarly voice fantasizes about an originary speech that is not Semitic,[47] and chillingly reflects on the difficulty of his undertaking with the ill-omened comment "but work makes freedom."[48]

Schwerner's last *Tablets* move into questions about the origins of language and its difficult relationship with experience. In these late works, he imagines a script that includes determinatives that, for example, establish the posture a body takes when a word or a phrase is said, or prescribe the state of mind of the speaker (Schwerner calls them "Mind/Texture/Determinatives" [M/T/Ds]).[49] Different M/T/Ds connected to the same phrase lead to radically different meanings (and therefore translations).

He is someone else, perhaps an animal. He lives inside plant names.
He races inside his messages of fleet means. He is the calling voice
Of the names inside the wheat and the barley. He can't say them
Forever. He tells them +
Through the inside of his eyes, he sees
The inside of his eyes and describes the animal nature of plants.

46 B.P. Nichol, *The Martyrology, Books 3 & 4* (Toronto: Coach House Press, 1976).
47 Schwerner, *The Tablets*, 71.
48 Ibid.
49 Ibid., 149.

The same sequence of symbols, differently sized and accompanied by different M/T/Ds, leads to a radically different translation:

He will surely never die. The world is made of his voice.

Where is he, mouth of the ear
Great artificer, perturbed basket of claims
Shoot of roots & shrinker of [retinues]
Making the mazy watery blue one oozing red
Entreating the stutterer in the meaning cave . . . .+ + + + + + +
+ + + [50]

By this point in his work, Schwerner is treading a very fine line between fictionalized translation and sincere, concerted *poie-*

50 Ibid., 94.

sis. He was in fact inventing a way of being-in-the-world that came with its own writing system, language, and methodology of translation, complete with polemics between different interpretations of the same experiences. "Mind/Texture/Determinatives" come, says Schwerner, in two types or flavors: "pure" M/T/Ds are existential or cognitive states, the products of intense, inner searching by a blind, archaic artificer.[51] But there is a second group of M/T/Ds, which Schwerner calls "Utterance/Texture/Indicators," or U/T/Is, which "isolate particular vectors largely related to the external world stage and graft them onto a written expression."[52] Schwerner discusses at length the "U/T/I of solitary reading" (which places the utterance it modifies into the mouth of a person who is reading alone), as well as a set of U/T/Is which designate "body-declensions," that is, the specific postures a body might take while uttering an expression (lying down dying, lying down sick, crouched giving birth, etc). U/T/Is attempt to "publicize or make socially visible" the experiences of the M/T/Ds, but such a project is bound, in at least some degree, to fail, and so Schwerner describes these tablets as "sacred forgeries, or rather forgeries prompted by a dazzled and mournful reconsideration, retrospective as well as perhaps economically profitable, of the sacred."[53] That pretty clearly describes the *Tablets*, too — and so, like R. Murray Schafer's philologist, Schwerner reaches deep into the archaic past only to find himself.

In a move mirroring the difference between the inward-looking M/T/Ds and the socially-visible U/T/Is, Schwerner describes translation as a conflict between "Sympathy-Meditation" and "Insertion/Ingestion."

> [Sympathy-Meditation] refers to a specific translation-process in the light of which the doer com/poses his doings, the objects; the Reception-Attribute signals a major constituent in the very shape-worker, intent on doing his do.

---

51 Ibid., 81–85.
52 Ibid., 97–98.
53 Ibid., 98.

What is the habitus of the world which is borne over to the translator's diagnosis by the liminal ghosts of Utterance — world whose propensities he may perceive as neural, anatomical, style, or sly? He is not quite aware of such intermittent analogical audacities; at some penultimate way-station of speculation, surrender to the delights and perils of Fascination yields to action.

Surprises inhere in the cryptic ground of the translator's thaumaturgical operations. This ground — in the context of the Path of Sympathy-Meditation — exists along with the translator's assumptions that the composition of the world is an ingathering of individual entities characterized by their particulars; these are conceived of as idiosyncratically bounded, each a kind of Platonic idea of its Thingness as it were, all picked, packed and ready, set aside for perceptual collecting and labelling. Residing for the most part far below the shuttling and prehensile elaborations of consciousness, the translator's assumptions do not quite attain to the mettlesome certitudes of a vision of the world. The limits and anxieties of his experiences will lead him to ignore or to suppress his intuitions about the nature of the ground, which he might at best experience as agonist — constrictively or oracularly pythonic, at worst as super-market. The Receiver is actually a Collector.[54]

I don't want to put too fine a point on it, but that is almost a word-for-word importation of Jarry's definition of 'pataphysics. Things are taken to be singular configurations of singularities, "platonic ideas of their own thingness"; compare Jarry's claim that 'pataphysics "attributes the properties of objects, described by their virtuality, to their lineaments."[55] We might ask how such a method of translation could ever adhere to the "letter of a text," but these tablets have no letters to adhere to. Sympathy-meditation leads to an utterance in the vicinity of a text,

---

54 Ibid., 110–11.
55 Jarry, *Exploits and Opinions of Doctor Faustroll, Pataphysician*, 22.

grounded in an awareness of the singularity of things. "Insertion/Injection," on the other hand, directs itself to a world experienced as essentially unitary one which gives rise to "stuffs whose boundaries are established through acts effected by the PI worker's language, or his practice."[56] This is, in other words, a translation method that recasts the original utterance in terms of a "target" language or culture.

The Tablets progressively reveals itself to be rooted in the profound problem of transforming intense experience into language.[57] In addition to the "Mind/Texture/Determinatives," Schwerner also introduces what he calls the "Entrance-Exodus Vibration" (E.-E.V.), which he uses to address the problem of the relationship between words and things. Simply put, the degree of vibration of a glyph is a measure of the dissonance between its semiotic "transparency" and its sensual "presence." One might imagine the vibrating indeterminacy of the relation between word and object as the staging-point for a choice between two philological paths: one in which you trust what words give you, accept an intimacy between what is the case and what one can say, and another in which the discomfort carried by the dehiscence between what is said and what is lived provokes radically unorthodox methodologies: strange etymologies, glyphic surface-rhymes, fictional languages, and imaginary fragments.

Schwerner's *Tablets* points toward a third characteristic of some 'pataphilologies: though they start from the surfaces of language (sound, glyph), they seek to convert that into a search for the most profound origins of human experience. One can compare this impulse with the Epicurean doctrine of the *clinamen*, that atomic swerve thanks to which there is anything at all. For the most part, the twentieth-century reception of the swerve has emphasized its role in the elimination or reduction of fatefulness and the consequent donation of freedom to hu-

56 Schwerner, *The Tablets*, 113.
57 "*Ominacunei* segments are sometimes subject to Entrance-Exodus Vibration (E.-E.V.): the word is *never quite the thing* nor is it ever *quite not-the-thing.* The degree and type of Vibration affecting a particular segment are codified within my diacritical pointers…"; Ibid., 113.

man existence. It functions (in Christian Bök's words) as "the atomic glitch of a microcosmic incertitude — the symbol for a vital poetics, gone awry."[58] The value of such a perspective is, perhaps, rather painfully obvious. The clinamen, a world-generating deviation from physically determinate behavior, is the grounding exception, the non-paradigm or elementary heuristic that serves to organize the entire science.

But within the Collège de 'Pataphysique, the doctrine of the clinamen — necessary because "Clinamen" is the title of a chapter in *Faustroll* — has other resonances. The commentary on Jarry's novel recalls Lucretius's insistence that the swerve must be as slight as possible: just enough to set atoms off on their trajectories, but not enough to violate the natural laws of their movement. One might be tempted to say: the swerve must take place, but not at all. Or: the clinamen doesn't happen, and in doing so it creates the world. The clinamen, the Collège insists, is an imaginary solution to the problem of origins: given the world, whence? Given a word, what led to it? If the vulgar avant-garde emphasizes the swerve as an originary seeding of choice in the universe, hieratic 'pataphysics understands that the clinamen is only a construction, and one so close to being nothing at all that it is guaranteed to have no power over us.

A 'pataphilological drive to uncover impossible origins is more than amply present in *Faustroll* and its commentarial tradition. Consider one of Jarry's greatest literary coups: the portrait of Faustroll's (ba)boon-companion Bosse-de-Nage. Bosse-de-Nage is parodically modelled on Jarry's some-time friend, the Belgian author Christian Beck. Prefacing their remarks with the caveat that "Ubu is not a satire of the bourgeoisie and Bosse-de-Nage is not about a Belgian,"[59] the authors of the commentary nonetheless observe that Beck's nom-de-plume was Joseph *Bossi*. As if comparing Beck to a baboon wasn't enough, the commentary suspects fecality: "*Bosse-de-Nage* is face-of-the-moon [*face-de-lune*]" where *Nage* → *Nache* → *fesse*, in "ancien

---

58 Bök, *'Pataphysics*, 43.
59 Jarry, *Gestes et opinions du docteur Faustroll pataphysicien*, 160.

Français": thus Bosse-de-Nage is "ass-face." The commentary cites another opinion according to which Bosse is a verb, and Bosse-de-Nage = *travail de la fesse*.⁶⁰

Again, let me insist that 'pataphilology is not a joke. In a discussion of the logic of metaphor which is cited at length by the scholar-translator of Schwerner's *Tablets*, Octavio Paz remarks on the very serious work that the ass-face metaphor does:

> There is not much purpose in repeating here everything that psychoanalysis has taught us about the conflict between the face and the ass, the (repressive) reality principle and the (explosive) pleasure principle. I will merely note here that the metaphor that I mentioned, both as it works upward and as it works downward — the ass as a face and the face as an ass — serves each of these principles alternately. At first, the metaphor uncovers a similarity; then, immediately afterward, it covers it up again, either because the first term absorbs the second, or vice versa. In any case, the similarity disappears and the opposition between ass and face reappears, in a form that is now even stronger than before. Here, too, the similarity at first seems unbearable to us — and therefore we either laugh or cry; in the second step, the opposition also becomes unbearable — and therefore we either laugh or cry. When we say that the ass is like another face, we deny the soul-body dualism; we laugh because we have resolved the discord that we are. But the victory of the pleasure principle does not last long; at the same time that our laughter celebrates the reconciliation of the soul and the body, it dissolves it and makes it laughable once again.⁶¹

"Ass-face" Bosse-de-Nage has only one expression in his vocabulary: HA HA. Jarry remarks that the correct spelling should be AA, "because the aspiration was not written in the world's

---

60 Ibid., 162.
61 Octavio Paz, *Conjunctions and Disjunctions*, trans. Helen R. Lane (New York: Viking, 1974), 5.

ancient language."[62] This looks at first like a throwaway riff on the role played in French orthography and pronunciation by the history of the language; could it be more than accidental that from the Hellenistic period on the Greek aspiration (*h*) was notated in written texts by a diacritic, '? Jarry elevates his reflection on Bosse-de-Nage's HA HA into a tour-de-force of almost neo-Platonic sophistication.

> A juxtaposed to A, with the former obviously equal to the latter, is the formula of the principle of identity: a thing is itself. It is at the same time the most excellent refutation of this very proposition, since two A's differ in space, when we write them, if not indeed in time, just as two twins are never born together — even when issuing from the obscene hiatus of the mouth of Bosse-de-Nage.
>
> The first A was perhaps congruent to the second, and we will therefore willingly write thus: $A \cong A$.
>
> Pronounced quickly enough, until the letters become confounded, it is the idea of unity.
>
> Pronounced slowly, it is the idea of duality, of echo, of distance, of symmetry, of greatness and duration, of the two principles of good and evil.[63]

From mathematical equation, through geometry, through a reconstruction of the basic components of space and time: this is, in effect, a mini-Timaeus, a mathematical cosmology drawn in the sound of the baboon's voice.

Not so crypto-Platonic, either. Chapter ten offers a series of translations of Bosse-de-Nage's little vocal object (h)a:

— Ἀληθῆ λέγεις, ἔφη
— Ἀληθῆ
— Ἀληθέστατα.
— Δῆλα γάρ, ἔφη, καὶ τυφλῷ

---

62 Jarry, *Gestes et opinions du docteur Faustroll pataphysicien*, 345.
63 Jarry, *Exploits and Opinions of Doctor Faustroll, Pataphysician*, 74–75.

— Δῆλα δή.
— Δῆλον δή.
— Δίκαιον γοῦν.
— Εἰκός.
—Ἔμοιγε
κτλ.

— You speak truth, he said.
— True.
— Most True.
— Clear things, he said, even to a blind man.
— Clear things.
— Clear.
— Indeed, it is just.
— Seems right.
— Seems that way to me.
Etc.[64]

These are, for those of you who haven't checked your Plato recently, the affirmative replies to Socratic questions in the Platonic corpus. "Systematically compiled (or re-copied from a compilation by Jarry), following the alphabetical order, the Platonic has are 42 in number, but in the MS L Jarry scratched out the last, reducing their number to coincide with the number of chapters in the *Life and Opinions*." So says the commentary.[65] Which, for its part, would like to know what language is the "ancient" one Jarry seems to imply is spoken by Bosse-de-Nage when he says (h)a (h)a (or 'a'a). Hebrew and Egyptian are possibilities, but the commentary ultimately decides that the most plausible answer is the language before Babel. Alluding to the robust tradition of pataphilologists described by Queneau (among others) as *les fous littéraires*, the commentary comments:

64 Ibid., 28–29.
65 Jarry, *Gestes et opinions du docteur Faustroll pataphysicien*, 164.

Jarry was interested in the "primitive" language which so excites linguists — or "crazy linguists," some would say. In Chapter XVI, he mentions the "language of paradise" intelligible even to the animals which is, certainly, the oldest there is.[66]

Compellingly, the commentary refers to Jarry's essay in *La Chandelle Vert*, *"Ceux pour qui il n'y eut point de Babel,"* in which Jarry seems to espouse the idea, proposed by Victor Fournié in *Introduction à l'histoire ancienne*, that "the same sound or the same syllable has the same meaning in all languages."[67] The "stone-age professor" called his students to attention by saying

Hein

(cf. ha ha): this can then be found in *in-cipere*, etc. Even more to the point, the echos of the original sonic language can be found in laughter (ha! ha!):

We believe that laughter is not only what M. Bergson, our excellent professor of philosophy at the *lycée Henri-IV* called it — the sentiment of surprise. We think we should add: it is the impression of truth revealed [*l'impression de la vérité révélée*].[68]

Ha Ha: the revelation of the truth (unity, duality, dimensionality, space and time…). Following widely accepted contemporary geological thought, Fournier called this primal (and yet still with us) language, the language spoken by the primate Bosse-de-Nage, *Lemurien*.[69]

The resolute philological pursuit of a necessary and impossible origin — also animal, as it happens — is most extraordinarily

---

66 Ibid.
67 Jarry, *Œuvres*, 1015. My translation.
68 Ibid., 1016.
69 Jarry, *Gestes et opinions du docteur Faustroll pataphysicien*, 350.

present in the work of Jean Brisset (1837–1919), whose lifetime project was to deduce the origins of humankind from extensive etymological investigations into French vocabulary. His method was the pun. Puns, insisted Brisset, are not jokes. When we laugh at them, he says, that is a god-given defense designed to prevent us from realizing what they reveal.

> The iron sword which guards the way to the tree of life is called "pun" or "word-play." The idea that there could be something hidden beneath the pun could never occur to any one, because such an idea was forbidden the human spirit. It was imposed on us only to laugh stupidly. [...]
>
> It was by [divine] revelation and on the appointed day that we were led to formulate the following law:
>
> The study of the relationship which exists between different ideas, expressed by a sound or a series of identical sounds, naturally leads the spirit to discover the nature of the creation of speech, which co-occurs with the creation of man, who is himself the Word.[70]

He himself has realized the truth of language "at the appointed time" and "by revelation." He will teach us to read the book that lies open on our lips. Literally: writing of etymology as "the key which opens the book of speech," Brisset comments, "you can see perfectly well that the books are open, because the first books [*livres*] are lips [*lèvres*]."[71] Typically, Brisset guides us simply by presenting his etymologies with minimal commentary: "the words speak for themselves," and meditating on them will lead to illumination.[72]

There is no more radical application of the 'pataphilological principle of sensualism than what we find in Brisset: to understand an expression you have not only to listen to it but also feel

---

70 Jean-Pierre Brisset, *Les origines humaines* (Paris: Baudouin, 1980), 16–17. All translations of Brisset are my own.
71 Ibid., 147.
72 Ibid.

it in your mouth and on your lips, massage it until it reveals its truth to you.

> If I say; teeth, mouth [*les dents, la bouche*], that evokes only ideas that are very familiar: the teeth are in the mouth.
> [...]
> The teeth seal [*bouchent*] the entrance of the mouth [*la bouche*] and the mouth helps [*aide*] and contributes to that closure: *the teeth close it* [*les dents la bouchent*], *helping the mouth* [*l'aidant la bouche*].
>
> The teeth are the help [*l'aide*], the assistance *in the mouth* [*en la bouche*] and they are also too often *ugly in the mouth* [*laides en la bouche*] [...] At other times, it's *milk* [*lait*]: they are white like *milk in the mouth* [*lait dans la bouche*].[73]

Here Brisset invites us to chew on our speech, to cut it up and roll it around on our tongues until our persistent mastication reveals a whole series of hitherto unexpected truths.

And what we discover, if we listen closely enough, is that humankind's earliest ancestors were frogs. As the upright, landgoing form gradually emerged from its watery progenitor, his language evolved at the same time.

> Like man, the frog lives in all climates, on earth and in the water. Frogs are diurnal and nocturnal, they love musical evenings, but in the morning they stay in bed, which is the earth. Frogs are quite friendly and like to live close to men, to the point of coming and sitting far from water, close to someone who watches them — so long as he remains reassuringly still.
>
> Our frogs speak our language. I have made a note of their cries: *coaque, coéque, quéquête, que re r'ai haut, cara, cara, cate, cate,* and also *couique*. People say they say *ololo* and *brekekex* as well, but I haven't heard those.

---

[73] Jean-Pierre Brisset, *La grammaire logique. Suivi de la science de Dieu* (Paris: Tchou, 1970), 146.

> *Qu'ai haut, co* = come [*viens*]. What matters is the *co*, which is the origin of "again" [*encore*]. I've *co*, have you *co?* etc. Nothing could be more familiar. *A que* = *au cul*, to [my] behind. *Co ac* also means "have access": it's a call to "act together," and the male obeys it. [...]
>
> The cries of the frog are the origins of human language. When they sing together, from afar it sounds like the brouhaha of the human crowd. Their actual language cannot do otherwise than give an imperfect idea of what it was like when the spirit which animates all of humanity moved on the surface of the waters and was concentrated in these animals who transformed themselves slowly into men by a chain whose links were united for a long time, before the all-powerful destroyed the intermediaries.[74]

Brisset's etymologies eventually reveal a complicated history. The evolution of humankind from its froggy ancestry left traces not only in language but also in myth and religion. More or less (Brisset is hard to understand, and the story is long), frogs emerged from spawn produced autonomously by the waters. They then developed genitals and thumbs (in which form they are recognizable as Uranus ("*Urahn* [fore-father] and Uranus are certainly the same word [...] in *Urahn* and Uranus we also find the word *rane,* frog"[75]). When the species achieved human form, that was Saturn, or the devil (*Saturnus* = *Satan*). Brisset provides an extensive account of the evolution of anatomically modern humans on the basis of etymologies of our parts. He also vividly imagines the emotional and behavioral consequences of these anatomical changes.

The ancestors, we are told, had a very hard life. They ate each other alive, and even felt them still living within themselves.

> Le mot *beu* ou *boeuf* désigne la bouche. *Le beu haut* = lève le bec = *le beau*. [...] Par consequent, beau = bouche ou bec.

74 Ibid., 203.
75 Ibid.

Dans le ton beau = dans le tombeau. [...] La première *tombe* et le premier *tombeau* sont donc dans la bouche et c'est là que les mots ont été mis *dans la tombe, au tombeau, au ton beau.*[76]

From this ancestral practice of living cannibalism Brisset derives the practice of etymology.

> The true life is in the word. It is the spirit which gives life, says Jesus: the flesh has no purpose. The words which I say to you are spirit and truth. As creatures, we no longer eat our dead, but spiritually we always eat them, because we speak of them in the same terms used by those who did eat them and invented speech. [...] The spirits which speak in us and through which it is given us to think and control ourselves, these spirits are connected to the words which they made: it is, therefore, really the spirits of the ancestors who speak and live, immortal, in our mortal bodies.[77]

Behind the Christian veneer, here, we discern a deeper, darker vision: speech is the remnant of an originary cannibalism thanks to which the past continues to live in us. But the opposite is also true: we are the host for the past, which lives in us like a parasite. Etymology, in Brisset, is the becoming-conscious of this eternal form of ancestor worship.

• • •

Let me face an objection. Schwerner, Schafer, and Melnick are all self-conscious artists, working with the forms and gestures of traditional philology, while Brisset is seriously attempting, in however misguided a fashion, to produce orthodox philology. If Schwerner (et al.) can be taken as pursuing a moment of authenticity — for example, the experience of the sacred — that somehow goes beyond what "normal" philology does, and thus

---

76 Ibid., 193.
77 Ibid., 195.

at least implies a critique of the latter, Brisset seems to do everything he can to be just as dry-as-dust as his philological counterparts. There is surely something to this objection: Brisset and the poets are different from each other. But the difference, I think, doesn't lie in the goal. Brisset's ambition is, in fact, far greater than any orthodox philologist working today. He wants nothing other than a reconstruction of the evolutionary origins of humanity on the basis of the etymology of French; and in that, he is much more like Schwerner than like (say) Émile Benveniste. The true difference between poets like Schwerner and figures like Brisset, I think, lies in the fact that the poets are self-conscious about the singularities of their procedures, while Brisset is not; in fact, Brisset insists quite vehemently that anyone who proceeds honestly and vigorously would produce the same results as him.

The difference, to put it otherwise, lies in the '. Jarry almost never wrote *'pataphysics*; his usual spelling was simply *pataphysics*. The Collège, elaborating on Jarry's argument that the generality of science is in fact only a collection of exceptions that have become unoriginal, made a doctrinal claim: everything is pataphysical, and everyone is a pataphysician. Those who know this and embrace it are 'pataphysicians ("the College of 'Pataphysics uses the apostrophe to distinguish between voluntary 'pataphysics and involuntary pataphysics").[78] Exactly that seems to be what distinguishes Brisset from Schwerner (et al.): he is a pataphilologist, while the poets are 'pataphilologists.

III

Each of the essays that follow addresses 'pataphilology in a different way: it is in the nature of the topic that we will find resonances and points of contact but no over-arching hypothesis or argument. What we do find, however, is a recurrent inter-plaiting of the methods of Jarry during the composition of *Faustroll* with the high seriousness of "classical" philol-

---

78 Jarry, *Gestes et opinions du docteur Faustroll pataphysicien*, 146.

ogy. There is also a recurrent concern with sound — the audible glyph of language, one might say — as the basic material of the linguistic attractions perpetrated in puns, etymologies, and new-language formation, or as the noise of the singular or the subject. Indeed, there is also a recurrent preoccupation with the subject: what is it? How can it be freed? Is it, perhaps, a 'pataphysical object, secured through strange new forms of language practice? And there is a consistent engagement with forms of time that, like the strange loops of Schwerner and Schafer and the odd origins of Brisset, seem to defy orthodox chronology, to tie the line of history into a knot or a Möbius strip.

Examining a series of "non-intrinsic philological isolates" — languages, more or less, forged for a single use (often literary) and not generally spoken beyond that one application — Joshua T. Katz and Michael D. Gordin make the case that what we call "philology" is better treated as an assemblage of language practices that can occur in different combinations in different contexts and that can be variously analyzed apart, and partly legitimated or delegitimated, by different scholars working in different disciplines at different times. One corollary of this viewpoint is that it becomes harder to tell what is "good" or "real" philology and what is pseudo- or pata-philology. Given a broad and neutral enough perspective, they suggest, it may not be possible to tell the difference. Faustroll's games with language are as philological as anything produced by the Académie Française. While Katz and Gordin study the extraordinary languages to be found in a number of modern novels — *Ridley Walker, The Wake, Clockwork Orange* attract most of their attention — their argument asks whether far more conventional works of literature shouldn't also be treated in a similar way. How close to their non-intrinsic philological isolates is the Latin of the grammarians, or that of Vergil for that matter? These are questions that will be taken up in detail by Erik Gunderson at the very end of the collection (see below).

James Porter's contribution attends to one of the modern age's strongest readers of Homer: Theodor Adorno, whose essay on "epic naïveté" exposes a philological anachrony of the profoundest nature. Adorno and Jarry have more in common than a sober reading of either might initially suggest. Both were virtuosos at creating compelling texts by collocating fragments. In his greatest works, Adorno created "constellations" of textual fragments meant to explode the present and its ideologies; these constellations could also be read as allegories (this was a strategy he adapted from Walter Benjamin). Porter shows that Adorno's reading of Homer projects the "method of fragments" back onto the epic itself, whose language "disintegrates" into fragments held together by little more than convention, and which as a result becomes an allegory of history. Jarry, too — at least in *Faustroll* — proceeded in a similar way: images, glimpses, gestures drawn from the work of each chapter's *honorandum* are brought together to produce something wholly new. And Adorno's emphasis on the sound of epic, its perpetually frustrated ambition to become noise, comes close to the essentially 'pataphysical ambition to "symbolically attribute the properties of objects, described by their virtuality, to their lineaments." Porter's reading of Adorno's reading of Homer's curiously multivalent particle ἤ shows Adorno contemplating a sound that rhymes uncannily with Bosse-de-Nage's Platonic HA. But Porter juxtaposes Adorno and Jarry: if there is an "ethics of ludic disobedience" in Jarry, Adorno "mimics the object of his critique in order to subvert it from within."

Beginning from a reconstruction of some of Jacques Lacan's connections with surrealism, Dadaism, and the French avantgarde, Sean Braune argues that Lacan's discourse on the subject is, in the final analysis, a kind of 'pataphysics, and that his notorious way of communicating represented a rigorous form of 'pataphilology. Indeed, not just his writings and his seminars, but also his clinical practices emerge, in Braune's analysis, as "a 'pataphilological laboratory of *lalangue* and mathemes." Braune's 'pataphilological ontology of the subject suggests that subjectivity may be the solution to an imaginary problem, one that emerges in the fictive space of the psychoanalytical encounter.

Existing in ethernity, Braune's Lacanian subject seems to resonate with the walled-off (barred) subject analyzed by Paul

Allen Miller in his contribution. Reading a series of Horace's *Epodes,* Miller proposes that the distinguishing feature of philology is its disciplined attention to what is said and what is meant. Philology struggles, however, with forms of discourse like irony which, he claims, rely on the mysterious presence of an unspoken and sometimes even unmeant component of the communication, an element that somehow manages to suggest the existence of a distinction between the said and the meant. For Miller, 'pataphilology emerges at the moment when one begins to attend to this moment of unmeaning. Now, someone might object (and indeed, this someone might be a philologist) that the mysterious thing that brings us to understand that an utterance does not mean what it says is, in fact, a communication, and therefore a meaning — that, to put this another way, an ironic communication *intends* its irony, and says so. Knowing that a sentence is ironic (this philological perspective might imply) either entails that you have been told so or that you haven't, and in the latter case you can't really say that you know the sentence is ironic. To which a 'pataphilological reader would reply: if a sentence says it's ironic, if it directly signals its irony to you using signs you understand, it's not really all that ironic. "Knowing" irony isn't exactly knowing, if we're being honest about it. It's more like something that just happens, as it were; when it happens, or why it happens, and to whom, would be quite unpredictable, ultimately dependent on a one-off interaction between a reader and a text.

'Pataphysics' trajectory from Ubu to Faustroll isn't without political implications (or quite a bit of irony): what began as the instrumental science of an overweening king figure ends as a mode of language play connected to the dispossessed, nomadic man of learning, in whose hands it becomes capable of deflating the pretentions of power. (There is an unwritten *Faustroll contra Ubu* written beneath the lines of Jarry's novellistic work.) Erik Gunderson's closing contribution to the volume, "The Paraphilologist as 'Pataphysician," begins to articulate the polemical and political implications of 'pataphilology. The first part of his essay is a profound reading of Priscian's account of the anatomy of language, reaching from the voice to the word, and showing in detail that this discourse has been exquisitely crafted to establish a full and fully signifying presence. There is, in Priscian's account, no room for the arbitrary or the radically meaningless. But, as Gunderson demonstrates, the rule-governed linguistic purity theorized and celebrated by late-antique grammarians is in fact beset and surrounded by exceptions and variations: poets violate the rules all the time, and so too do the grammarians themselves. The fact that they seem to enforce linguistic lawfulness while palpitating with anomalous singularities reminds me of Jarry's insistence that science is not the study of laws but the study of exceptions that have become banal, that have lost the distinction of being original. Gunderson describes the grammarian as "a paraphilologist who attaches himself to language as its guardian." This paraphilologist, who could also be called a pataphilologist (note the absence of an '), was countered in antiquity by writers like Lucian, Petronius, and Apuleius, whose playful inversions of grammatical authority Gunderson finds to be 'pataphilological in the most orthodox sense. They embrace willingly what the paraphilologists do in ellipses or in the context of a disavowal.

Perhaps it might be appropriate to close this lengthy introduction with a return to the question with which I began: what is the difference, or *is* there a difference, between philology and 'pataphilology? The answers to this question vary across the book, but it does seem to me that in important ways each contribution tends towards *eliding* the difference more than towards emphasizing or defining it. In this sense, Katz and Gordin, with their assertion that pataphilology *is* philology, line up well with Gunderson's observation that grammatical enforcements of language's lawfulness tend to coincide with an ever-shifting and anomic field of linguistic singularities. There is nothing but the *clinamen* and its consequences. This is, in a sense, just what was implied by the Collège de 'Pataphysique when it defined the difference between pataphysics and 'pataphysics as the difference between voluntary and involuntary: philology and pataphilology would, on this model, be more or less synonyms, while 'pataphilology would be little more than the self-conscious, willing embrace of the practice and all its implications.

One question we are left with concerns tactics. How should we proceed? Via the ludic abandonment of sense, as Porter observes relative to Jarry? Or should one adopt the gestures and style of philology in order to explode it from within? Perhaps the answer to that question lies in the first contribution to this volume, which I have not yet mentioned: Steve McCaffery's ecphrastic translation of the *Papyrus of Ani*. Here we have, I would suggest, as classical a presentation of 'pataphilological procedure as one could imagine. Evoking a return to the most archaic of origins, McCaffery "reads" the hieroglyphic script as a series of images to be named ecphrastically. He quite literally (not literally at all, actually; there are no letters here) transforms them into glyphs, in a move analogous to Melnick's homophonic translations of *Iliad* 1–3. One could interpret this undertaking as a parodic refusal of sense, a finger in the eye of philology and its grandest pretensions. Look again, though, and I think you will find something else. McCaffery's is a movingly honest and close reading of the papyrus — the voice of this poem takes seriously the difficulties of scrutinizing such a text, and the translation's fabric has a compelling unity and pathos that do not derive from any kind of facile flippancy. In a way, what McCaffery does is evoke the (non)sense of the hieroglyph in the moment before it is deciphered. And that, we would do well to recall, is not a joke: it evokes the verge or the cusp of comprehension, a site I would propose to be analogous with the 'pataphysical subject in Lacan as it is discussed by Braune, the free subject concealed behind irony pointed to by Miller, or even the truth hidden behind the gates of the earthly paradise imagined by Brisset. What we find in McCaffery's translation, I propose, is an approach that combines "parodic philology" with the ludic refusal of sense. And that (as Cavafy said somewhere) may be some kind of a solution.

One

The Walker and the Wake: Analysis of Non-Intrinsic Philological Isolates

Michael D. Gordin and Joshua T. Katz

for David Bellos

This paper has two points of departure. The first is the use of marginal phenomena to elucidate complex core conceptual questions, an approach that has been used to good effect in a wide variety of disciplines.[1] One such question is "What is language?," where one not uncontroversial research program looks at animal behavior that arguably resembles human communication (e.g., bee dances, whale songs).[2] Another question — which we insist on distinguishing sharply from the

---

1 E.g., Émile Durkheim, *Suicide: A Study in Sociology,* trans. John A. Spaulding and George Simpson (New York: Free Press, 1951 [1897]); Mikhail Bakhtin, *Rabelais and His World,* trans. Hélène Iswolsky (Bloomington: Indiana University Press, 1984 [1965]); Clifford Geertz, *The Interpretation of Cultures* (New York: Basic Books, 1973).
2 Tania Munz, *The Dancing Bees: Karl von Frisch and the Discovery of the Honeybee Language* (Chicago: University of Chicago Press, 2016); D. Graham Burnett, *The Sounding of the Whale: Science & Cetaceans in the Twentieth Century* (Chicago: University of Chicago Press, 2012). For the nineteenth-century precursors to these debates, see Gregory Radick, *The Simian*

former — is "What is *a* language?" By this we refer both to the determination of the place at which one language stops and another begins (e.g., Danish/Norwegian, Kazakh/Kyrgyz) and to the potential distinction between a language and a dialect (e.g., *Hochdeutsch/Bairisch,* Modern Standard Arabic/Maghrebi).[3] We confine ourselves to this latter question.

The second point of departure, more common in anthropology and history of science, is the categorization of intellectual concepts or disciplines into collections of practices. To take an example from the history of physics, certain theories (e.g., classical electromagnetism, quantum field theory) are only clearly definable in retrospect; in the process of research, what physicists actually do is solve problems using specific, often heterogeneous, sets of calculating practices (e.g., partial differential equations, Feynman diagrams) that frequently transcend highly policed intradisciplinary borders. Different physicists retrospectively group together particular calculating practices and call the resulting conglomeration "thermodynamics" or "string theory."[4] Our proposal is that "philology" — and therefore also *pata*philology — is amenable to the same sort of analysis: it can be treated as a set of practices (e.g., collation of manuscripts, hermeneutics) that individual scholars, and communities of scholars, aggregate in various combinations and deploy with different emphases.[5]

> *Tongue: The Long Debate about Animal Language* (Chicago: University of Chicago Press, 2007).
>
> 3 For a good general discussion of what is involved in discriminating among languages, see Stephen R. Anderson, *Languages: A Very Short Introduction* (Oxford: Oxford University Press, 2012).
>
> 4 Andrew Warwick, *Masters of Theory: Cambridge and the Rise of Mathematical Physics* (Chicago: University of Chicago Press, 2003); David Kaiser, *Drawing Theories Apart: The Dispersion of Feynman Diagrams in Postwar Physics* (Chicago: University of Chicago Press, 2005).
>
> 5 For a large-scale history of philology, see James Turner, *Philology: The Forgotten Origins of the Modern Humanities* (Princeton: Princeton University Press, 2014). See also the essays in Sheldon Pollock, Benjamin Elman, and Ku-ming Kevin Chang, eds., *World Philology* (Cambridge: Harvard University Press, 2014).

These combinations and emphases may at times seem peculiar. The question is, to whom? Our point is quite general. In any domain of knowledge (science, medicine, the humanities), the boundary between the legitimate and the anathema is contentious, in terms of both where it should be drawn and whether the drawing of such a line is even permissible. The allegation that something is pseudoscientific is notoriously problematic, for a variety of reasons.[6] First, people never attribute quackery to themselves; the term thus cannot be separated from polemic. Second, since the definition of controversy is that specialists in a discipline do not yet know what the right answer is, disciplines cannot definitively label a position valid or erroneous (e.g., string theory or the innateness hypothesis, today).[7] And third, theories that were once mainstream (e.g., astrology) become demonized, while ones that were demonized (e.g., atomism) become conventional wisdom. The point has been most extensively explored in the natural sciences but is equally applicable to other areas of *Wissenschaft,* such as philology.[8]

There are more and less helpful ways of making the extension. One strand of scholarship, drawing extensively on the sociology of deviance, explores the less respectable neighborhoods of language use (thieves' cant, *Rotwelsch,* Pig Latin) as

6   Michael D. Gordin, *The Pseudoscience Wars: Immanuel Velikovsky and the Birth of the Modern Fringe* (Chicago: University of Chicago Press, 2012). See also Michael Hagner, "Bye-Bye Science, Welcome Pseudoscience? Reflexionen über einen beschädigten Status," in *Pseudowissenschaft: Konzeptionen von Nichtwissenschaftlichkeit in der Wissenschaftsgeschichte,* eds. Dirk Rupnow, Veronika Lipphardt, Jens Thiel, and Christina Wessely, 21–50 (Frankfurt am Main: Suhrkamp, 2008).

7   On string theory, contrast Brian Greene, *The Elegant Universe: Superstrings, Hidden Dimensions, and the Quest for the Ultimate Theory* (New York: Norton, 1999) with Lee Smolin, *The Trouble with Physics: The Rise of String Theory, the Fall of a Science, and What Comes Next* (Boston: Houghton Mifflin, 2006). On linguistic innateness, contrast Steven Pinker, *The Language Instinct* (New York: Morrow, 1994) with Michael Tomasello, *Constructing a Language: A Usage-Based Theory of Language Acquisition* (Cambridge: Harvard University Press, 2003).

8   Lorraine Daston and Glenn W. Most, "History of Science and History of Philologies," *Isis* 106 (2015): 378–90.

modes of protest against established norms, defined negatively by the absence of some specific properties of the unmarked linguistic variant: in short, as "anti-language."[9] Our difficulty with this framework, which has had the salutary effect of increasing empirical awareness of such widespread phenomena as well as some of their general characteristics, is that it starts from an assumed definition of "language" and then searches for its by-blows. More promising, in our view, is the aforementioned emphasis on practices of language use. A forger, just like a philologist, collates texts and studies, say, the forms of majuscules. Much can be gained by bracketing the intellectual or monetary value of the forgers' fruits and focusing instead on which practices they learn from the philologists — and, conversely, what the philologists learn from the forgers.[10] At the level of practices, there is no need to introduce a notion of deviance. Pataphilology is philology, full stop.[11]

The canonical domain of philology — that is, where philological practices are deployed — is literature. Our entry point is fiction written in what one might call *non-intrinsic philological isolates,* by which we mean unique forms of language (hence, isolates) that could be used outside the confines (hence, non-intrinsic) of the literary works (hence, philological) in which they made their debut — though generally they aren't. A marginal perspective, no doubt, but sometimes the fringe reveals the core.

9   M.A.K. Halliday, "Anti-Languages," *American Anthropologist* 78 (1976): 570–84. See also Daniel Heller-Roazen, *Dark Tongues: The Art of Rogues and Riddlers* (New York: Zone, 2013).

10 Anthony Grafton, *Forgers and Critics: Creativity and Duplicity in Western Scholarship* (Princeton: Princeton University Press, 1990); Carlo Ginzburg, "Clues: Roots of an Evidential Paradigm," in *Clues, Myths, and the Historical Method,* trans. John and Anne C. Tedeschi, 96–125 (Baltimore: Johns Hopkins University Press, 1989 [1986]).

11 Compare James E.G. Zetzel, "The Bride of Mercury: Confessions of a 'Pataphilologist," in *World Philology,* eds. Sheldon Pollock et al., 45–62 (Cambridge: Harvard University Press, 2014). Perhaps because of our focus on practices, we find ourselves closer to Zetzel's identification of pataphilology with philology than to the subtle efforts at demarcation in Sean Gurd's introduction in this volume.

We might classify such literary works along two principal axes: degree of playfulness and attention to rules. Although some elements of wordplay are present in all literature, not to say all language, some literary works strongly emphasize these aspects while others do not. Likewise, language itself is highly rule-governed — as is all literature — yet literary texts differ broadly in the degree to which they, explicitly or implicitly, call attention to the character and pervasiveness of the rules themselves. It is not difficult to find works that illustrate essentially any location along these dimensions. For example, members of Oulipo produce literature that is both extraordinarily ludic and extraordinarily rule-bound, often for the purpose of showing that it is possible to do so (e.g., writing a novel in French without the letter *e*), though in the best cases the emphasis on form enhances the content rather than overshadows it.[12] By contrast, we concentrate on fictional works that highlight the specifically ruled aspects of their construction and therefore set Oulipian writings aside.

The works we will consider are all written in English — or "English," if you prefer, though we aim to convince that the quotation marks make no real difference.[13] For reasons we will address, most are British, postwar, written in the first person, male, and post-apocalyptic. Among other novels, we discuss Anthony Burgess's *A Clockwork Orange,* Russell Hoban's *Riddley Walker,* Paul Kingsnorth's *The Wake,* and James Joyce's *Finnegans Wake.* We begin with Irvine Welsh's English Scottish *Trainspotting,* which — despite appearances — presents the fewest difficulties: "The sweat wis lashing oafay Sick Boy; he wis trembling. Ah wis

12 For a history-*cum*-Bildungsroman of Oulipo, see Daniel Levin Becker, *Many Subtle Channels: In Praise of Potential Literature* (Cambridge: Harvard University Press, 2012). The classic example of the *e*-less novel is Georges Perec's *La Disparition* (1969), translated by Gilbert Adair as *A Void* (1994); a native English example of the same conceit where e-lessness may not enhance content is Ernest Vincent Wright's *Gadsby* (1939).

13 Examples could readily be adduced for other languages. Vladimir Sorokin's *Den' oprichnika* (2006), translated by Jamey Gambrell as *Day of the Oprichnik* (2011), provides a straightforward analogue in Russian, with debts to some of the other novels discussed in this essay.

jist sitting thair, focusing oan the telly, tryin no tae notice the cunt."[14]

• • •

Mark Renton speaks, and the novel begins. Renton is the main character, and often the principal narrator, of *Trainspotting,* the celebrated and controversial 1993 novel by Irvine Welsh (b. 1957). The disputes are multi-layered, and a proper cultural or linguistic analysis (neither of which we will do) would yield substantial insights.[15] Two points about the controversy are worth noting for our account. For one thing, the protagonists are heroin addicts and small-time crooks in the slums of Edinburgh who engage in bar fights, rape, infanticide through neglect, and other activities that are not cricket. For another, the reader is immediately struck by the language. If you are reading this essay with comparative ease, then you probably find the above quotation hard to parse, as you would most of the novel until page 32. There you find, at the start of a new section, this: "Despite the unmistakable resentment she could feel from her mother, Nina could not fathom what she had done wrong." The language is achingly familiar.

Welsh's episodic novel consists mostly of stretches of dialogue or internal monologue in the argot of the underclass, studded with clauses reminiscent of the Nina passage (the first of these comes already in the second paragraph). For those who lack exposure to the nightlife of present-day Edinburgh, Renton's locutions are understandably difficult. His protagonists belong to the sort of population for which the notion of "antilanguage" was developed as a sociological categorization of the dialect of an underprivileged group: in this case, a spectrum of

14 Irvine Welsh, *Trainspotting* (London: Secker & Warburg, 1993), 3.
15 A particularly insightful example is Stacey Mankoff, "Wankers, Burds, and Skag: Heteroglossia in Trainspotting," *Empty Mirror,* http://www.emptymirrorbooks.com/features/literature/wankers-burds-and-skag-heteroglossia-in-trainspotting.html.

language use that ranges from Standard Scottish English all the way to broad Scots.

Scots is a well-known Germanic language that is widely considered a dialect of the well-known Germanic language English and, like most linguistic forms, exhibits a rich heterogeneity across distances both geographic and socioeconomic. Renton's speech may become easier for you if you take it off the page: in the formulation of John Mullan, "As with [Robert] Burns's poetry, if it looks obscure all you have to do is speak the words aloud."[16] The trick works for two reasons. First, as literate people in a society with strict orthographic norms, we find spelling that is aberrant abhorrent, but the very deviations serve admirably to represent "non-standard" dialects in print. And second, variance in speech is expected, and you may well have heard Scots (and Scottish) in your day-to-day life — on the tube, on the telly — for reasons that have nothing to do with Irvine Welsh.[17] Even if you haven't, once you've read a few pages, you notice that the language is for the most part predictable in its diction, rhythms, syntax, and for that matter spelling: it is regular the way our languages are. In the terms we set out in the introduction, *Trainspotting* is low on wordplay but high on regularity. For all that, it falls outside our main purview, for the important reason that its regularity is not what we have called "isolated." Welsh's Scots is regular because Edinburgh's Scots is regular: the regularity was in the world and was then imported into the book. (Pata)philology becomes more interesting when we move from book to world.

It goes almost without saying that the language in which a book is written plays a large role in defining its internal world,

---

16 John Mullan, "So to Speak," *The Guardian,* May 30, 2008, https://www.theguardian.com/books/2008/may/31/irvinewelsh.

17 Conversely, the less exposure an audience has to the idiom, the less this works. The first twenty minutes of the 1996 movie adaptation of the novel were redubbed for American audiences with slightly toned-down Scots (see http://www.imdb.com/title/tt0117951/trivia?ref_=tt_trv_trv). Once they had become accustomed to the rhythm of the dialogue, the average American was presumably able to enjoy the same movie as British viewers.

and it follows from this that the more non-standard the language of a novel is, the more alien its world appears. Consider *A Clockwork Orange*, which Anthony Burgess (1917–1993) published in 1962 and which rocketed to tremendous popularity after the sensational release of Stanley Kubrick's 1971 film. The book's — and to a lesser extent the movie's — evocative dystopia relies heavily on the character of the first-person narration, which never lapses from the protagonist Alex's idiolect.[18] Once again, the quality of the argot, which Burgess later named Nadsat, is visible from the first line and becomes especially strong in the third paragraph:

> Our pockets were full of deng, so there was no real need from the point of view of crasting any more pretty polly to tolchock some old veck in an alley and viddy him swim in his blood while we counted the takings and divided by four, nor to do the ultra-violent on some shivering starry grey-haired ptitsa in a shop and go smecking off with the till's guts. But, as they say, money isn't everything.[19]

Burgess knew what he was doing — his erudition in English, other languages (especially Malay and Russian), and experimental fiction is impressive[20] — and countless critics have produced countless pieces of criticism about him and especially about this particular novel.[21] Without *A Clockwork Orange* we would perhaps not have *Trainspotting*; Welsh's admiration for

---

18 The linguistic behavior of the fictional (and entirely imaginary) gang of which Alex is the leader has been analogized to that of the sorts of real-world hooligans to whom Halliday applied the term "anti-language": see Roger Fowler, "Anti-Language in Fiction," in *Literature as Social Discourse: The Practice of Linguistic Criticism*, 142–61 (London: Batsford, 1981 [1979]).
19 Anthony Burgess, *A Clockwork Orange* (London: Heinemann, 1962), 1–2.
20 See, e.g., Anthony Burgess, *A Mouthful of Air: Language and Languages, especially English* (London: Hutchinson, 1992).
21 A sample of contemporary and later criticism may be found in the Norton Critical Edition, edited by Mark Rawlinson (New York: Norton, 2011).

Burgess's artistry is evident from his introduction to the Folio edition.[22]

Alex's Nadsat works rather differently from Renton's language(s). The most immediately striking feature of the quoted passage is lexical. Words such as *deng* and *veck* do not belong to any dialect or form of English, from 1962 or otherwise. Burgess developed the language, whose name is derived from the Russian suffix used for numbers in the teens (*-nadtsat'*), to convey a placeless and timeless (though future) world in which the Anglophone and Soviet spheres have merged. Indeed, many of the words are themselves lightly modified Russian lexemes: *deng* from *den'gi* "money," for example, and *veck* from the final syllable of *chelovek* "person." These lexical substitutions are almost entirely regular. Wordplay is important too: for instance, *ultra-violent* from *ultraviolet*. Burgess also characteristically blends the Russianesque and the ludic, as with *starry* from Russian *staryi* "old," but a stellar English pun to boot.

Wordplay aside, our pataphilological point is that Alex's language is non-intrinsic: there is no reason why a community could not function entirely in Nadsat, which is, after all, a dialect — albeit invented — of English. The only difference from Scots is that real people happen not to speak it. Any philological practice (pragmatics or etymology, say) that can be applied to a language could be applied to it. Yet *A Clockwork Orange* is atypical compared to the main works discussed in the next section in that, although we do not hear Nadsat on the radio, it is not entirely an isolate. In the second sentence of the novel, Alex describes his fellow gang-members as "my three droogs" — the last word derived from Russian *drug* "friend" — and this particular Burgessism has made it into the *Oxford English Dictionary*.[23] You can't get more standard English than that: we've gone from his book to our world.

---

22 Irvine Welsh, "Introduction," in Anthony Burgess, *A Clockwork Orange* (London: Folio Society, 2014), xi–xix.
23 OED, s.v. *droog*: "Anthony Burgess's word for a member of a gang…; a young ruffian; an accomplice or henchman of a gang-leader."

• • •

Russell Hoban (1925–2011) was born in Pennsylvania and moved in 1969 to London, where he remained until his death. Widely lauded for *The Mouse and His Child* (1968) and such other children's books as the "Frances the Badger" series (1948–1970), he also wrote a large number of novels for adults. Easily the most prominent of these is *Riddley Walker,* first published in 1980 and re-released in an "expanded edition" in 1998. Set a couple thousand years after a nuclear war has thrust the surroundings back (or forward) to the Iron Age, the title character and exclusive narrator, a boy living in the southeastern part of England that we know as Kent, struggles to understand both the world he lives in and how it came to be as it is.[24] Here is the opening:

> On my naming day when I come 12 I gone front spear and kilt a wyld boar he parbly ben the las wyld pig on the Bundel Downs any how there hadnt ben none for a long time befor him nor I aint looking to see none agen. He dint make the groun shake nor nothing like that when he come on to my spear he wernt all that big plus he lookit poorly. He done the reqwyrt he ternt and stood and clattert his teef and made his rush and there we wer then. Him on 1 end of the spear kicking his life out and me on the other end watching him dy. I sayd, 'Your tern now my tern later.' The other spears gone in then and he wer dead and the steam coming up off him in the rain and we all yelt, 'Offert!'[25]

Meet "Riddleyspeak," Hoban's name for this "breaking down and twisting of standard English," a style he began developing through wordplay ("I like to play with sounds, and when

---

24 For an introduction to literary experiments relating to nuclear war, see Michael D. Gordin's three linked essays from 2015–2016, "What to Say after Nuclear War," available at *Histories of the Future* (http://histscifi.com/essays/gordin).

25 Russell Hoban, *Riddley Walker,* exp. edn. (Bloomington: Indiana University Press, 1998 [1980]), 1.

alone in the house I often talk in strange accents and nonsense words"). Although he referred to Riddleyspeak as the product of "grammatical decline," the linguistic construction represents a plausible depiction of a future English once an island in the North Sea (Riddley and his tribe call their environs "Inland") has been cut off from international media and contact with speakers of foreign tongues.[26] The transformations are thus not the product of language contact but of internal developments within an isolated speech community centered on Canterbury ("Cambry").[27]

These transformations encompass all aspects of language: phonology, morphology, syntax, semantics, pragmatics, and (specific to the written rather than the implied spoken form) spelling and punctuation. Sounds have mutated in ways that are familiar to scholars of linguistic change across time and space; as with *Trainspotting*, it helps to read the novel out loud (and the more familiar you are with late-twentieth-century Kentish, the easier comprehension should be). Certain consonants have shifted (*teef* for *teeth*);[28] clusters have been simplified (*las* for *last, groun* for *ground, dint* for *didn't*);[29] and there has been metathesis (*parbly* for *prob'ly,* itself syncopated from *probably*). The past tense and past participial ending *-(i)t* rather than *-(e)d* has largely taken over (*kilt, lookit, reqwyrt, ternt, clattert, yelt*) and auxiliaries have been dropped (*I gone, he done, the steam coming up*). Clauses run together, double negatives are standard (*there hadnt ben none, I aint looking to see none agen*), and some words have a different sense from what we are used to (*come 12, gone front spear, clattert his teef*). Also, periods are used sparingly and there is little other punctuation (commas introduce direct

26 Russell Hoban, "Afterword," in *Riddley Walker,* exp. edn., 225.
27 Readers will find useful *Riddley Walker Annotations* (http://www.errorbar.net/rw), "a collaborative project devoted to analysis of Russell Hoban's very good 1980 novel."
28 So-called "*th*-fronting" is found in a number of dialects today, including Estuary English.
29 We might expect *en* for *end* and, even more, *an* for *and*; Hoban in some places compromised consistency for the sake of readability.

speech). The final word of the quoted paragraph, "Offert!," presumably the phonological and morphological continuation of our word *offered,* owes its *Lord of the Flies*-like pragmatic force in part to its similarity to the German word *opfern* and its past participle *(ge)opfert,* which means "sacrificed."

Sacrifice is the dominant theme of the novel. The picaresque plot chronicles Riddley's encounters and culminates in the rediscovery of gunpowder, thus reproducing in miniature the collapse of the preceding civilization: ours. Riddley has to negotiate with tribal leaders (such as "Goodparley"), parry the manipulations of the titular leader of the non-polity (the "Ardship of Cambry"), and decode the encrypted meanings within folk songs and riddles, not to mention the Punch and Judy-derived religion of the "Eusa show" cult. This cult derives from the wall painting "The Legend of St Eustace," a late-fifteenth-century masterpiece visible to anyone who visits Canterbury Cathedral today. The tale the painting tells has overshadowed even the depicted Jesus ("Littl Man the Addom," a brilliant portmanteau of Adam, the atom, and the image of Christ on the Cross being pulled in two directions until he splits), and the locals have interpreted it as a rich narrative of the collapse and its salvific content.[30] The plot of *Riddley Walker* is not complicated, but Riddley — being twelve and without educational resources — takes a long time to put the pieces together. As in *A Clockwork Orange,* linguistic form serves content, and Hoban put it aptly: "Technically [Riddleyspeak] works well with the story because it slows the reader down to Riddley's rate of comprehension."[31]

The divergence between the reader's rate of comprehension and Riddley's comes to the fore in an especially striking encounter with another language. Midway through the novel,

---

[30] A direct tribute comes in the post-apocalyptic middle section, "Sloosha's Crossin' an' Ev'rythin' After," of David Mitchell's *Cloud Atlas* (2004). Not coincidentally, an essay by Mitchell originally published in 2005 under the title "On Reading *Riddley Walker* in Hiroshima" is appended to a recent edition ("Afterword II," in Russell Hoban, *Riddley Walker* [London: Orion, 2012], 223–25).

[31] Hoban, "Afterword," 225.

Goodparley shows Riddley "a peace of paper" and tells him, "Have a read of this."[32] The document is titled "The Legend of St Eustace" and is written in late-twentieth-century English (very close to the language of this essay); we immediately recognize it as a tourist brochure that describes the wall painting in the Cathedral ("The date of the painting is about 1480; the work is highly skilled in an English tradition and is a magnificent example of wall painting of this date"). Both Goodparley and Riddley have seen the work of art. They do not, however, recognize any relationship between it and the text — or between either one and the Eusa cult — and they in fact have a hard time understanding the text at all:

> Wel soons I begun to read it I had to say, 'I dont even know ½ these words. Whats a Legend? How dyou say a guvner S with a littl t?'
>
> Goodparley said, 'I can as plain the mos of it to you. Some parts is easyer workit out nor others theres bits of it wewl never know for cern jus what they mean. What this writing is its about some kynd of picter or dyergam which we dont have that picter all we have is the writing. Parbly that picter ben some kynd of a seakert thing becaws this here writing (I dont mean the writing youre holding in your han I mean the writing time back way back what this is wrote the same as) its cernly seakert. Its blipful it aint jus only what it seams to be its the syn and foller of some thing else. A Legend thats a picter whats *depicted* which is to say pictert on a wall its done with some kynd of paint callit *fidelity*. St is short for sent. Meaning this bloak Eustace he dint jus tern up he were sent. *A.D. 120* thats the year count they use to have it gone from Year 1 right the way to Bad Time. *A.D.* means All Done. 120 years all done theyre saying thats when they begun this picter in 120 nor they never got it finisht til 1480 is what it says here wel you know there aint no picter cud take 1360

32 Hoban, *Riddley Walker*, 123.

years to do these here year numbers is about some thing else may be wewl never know what.'[33]

What Goodparley and Riddley are doing here with a language they might think of as "old English" is not fundamentally different from what Gordin and Katz did a couple of paragraphs ago with a language we might think of as "postmodern English": both are philological — and pataphilological — practice in action. Goodparley and Riddley are "mis-" or "over-"reading, something Hoban wants contemporary readers to notice; twentieth-century standard English is not an isolate. Similarly, Gordin and Katz may be mis- or over-reading as well, although it is precisely the isolated quality of Riddleyspeak that makes definitive judgments impossible. In our opinion, such "errors" matter little in comparison with the general philological point: results of interpretation are less significant than *techniques* of interpretation, and such techniques, which bring together linguistic change, wordplay, and folk-etymology, are in fact a standard way for people to align their modes of speaking about the world with the world itself.[34]

• • •

---

33 Ibid., 124–25. Riddley copies out, on another "peace of paper" (29), what he considers the canonical version of "The Eusa Story" (chapter 6, 30–36). This long precedes any mention of the painting, and Hoban leaves the connection obscure. It begins: "Wen Mr Clevver wuz Big Man uv Inland thay had evere thing clevver."

34 In the nice words of Derek Attridge, "Word-play [...] is to etymology as synchrony is to diachrony" (in *Peculiar Language: Literature as Difference from the Renaissance to James Joyce* [Ithaca: Cornell University Press, 1988], 109). For the connection between etymology and wordplay, see also, e.g., Joshua T. Katz, "*Nonne lexica etymologica multiplicanda sunt?*" in *Classical Dictionaries: Past, Present and Future,* ed. Christopher Stray, 25–48 (London: Duckworth, 2010), and "Etymological 'Alterity': Depths and Heights," in *Deep Classics: Rethinking Classical Reception,* ed. Shane Butler, 107–26 (London: Bloomsbury, 2016).

Representing future worlds requires — or at least might require — creating non-intrinsic philological isolates simply because we have no firm idea what a future language might be like. But it does not follow that such creations are a matter only for the future. More common are efforts to produce linguistic forms that map onto the past, a past about whose languages we often have greater clarity (thanks to the work of philologists, among others). In English, we need only point to Thomas Pynchon's *Mason & Dixon,* a late-twentieth-century (1997) American novel that seeks to replicate the prosody and general style of Laurence Sterne's eighteenth-century English, and to Anthony Burgess's final novel, *A Dead Man in Deptford* (1993), which does something similar for the life and language of the sixteenth-century playwright Christopher Marlowe. These are attempts to produce — better: *re*produce — premodern linguistic forms with a postmodern plot. One could in principle do the same for the eleventh century and compose a novel in Old English. Such an effort would likely perplex readers today even more than "old English" flummoxes Riddley and Goodparley. What if someone were instead to create a postmodern language for a premodern plot and renew, as it were, Old English?

Here is the beginning of the entry for the year 1066 in the *Peterborough Chronicle,* the so-called E-text of the *Anglo-Saxon Chronicle,* an account of English history from the late ninth century to the middle of the twelfth:

Millesimo.lxvi. On þissum geare man halgode þet mynster æt Westmynstre on Cilda mæssedæg, ⁊ se cyng Eadward forðferde on twelfta mæsseæfen, ⁊ hine mann bebyrgede on twelftan mæssedæg innan þære niwa halgodre circean on Westmynstre. ⁊ Harold eorl feng to Englalandes cynerice swa swa se cyng hit him geuðe, ⁊ eac men hine þærto gecuron, ⁊ wæs gebletsod to cynge on twelftan mæssedæg.

7 þy ilcan geare þe he cyng wæs, he for ut mid sciphere toge-
anes Willelme.³⁵

The reader may appreciate a translation:

> 1066. In this year [1065] the minster at Westminster was consecrated on Holy Innocents' Day, and the king Edward passed away on the eve of Twelfth Night, and was buried on Twelfth Night inside the newly consecrated church in Westminster. And Earl Harold succeeded to the kingdom of England just as the king granted it him — and also men chose him for it — and was blessed as king on Twelfth Night. And the same year in which he became king, he went out against William with a raiding ship-army.³⁶

Now, here is another account of 1066:

> see i had cnawan yfel was cuman when i seen this fugol gli-dan ofer
>   a great blaec fugol it was not of these lands it flown slow ofer the ham one daeg at the time of first ploughan. its necc was long its eages afyr and on the end of its fethra was a mans fingors all this i seen clere this was a fugol of deofuls. in stillness it cum and slow so none may miss it or what it had for us. this was eosturmonth in the year when all was broc
>   what is this fugol i saes to my wifman³⁷

While the reader may appreciate a translation of this as well, it isn't really necessary. A few orthographic substitutions, a little familiarity with another Germanic language (e.g., German *Vo-*

---

35 *The Anglo-Saxon Chronicle: A Collaborative Edition,* vol. 7: *MS. E,* ed. Susan Irvine (Cambridge: Brewer, 2004), 86.
36 *The Anglo-Saxon Chronicle,* trans. and ed. M.J. Swanton (London: Dent, 1996), 195 and 197 (footnotes omitted).
37 Paul Kingsnorth, *The Wake* (London: Unbound, 2014), 9. The *fugol* "bird" occupies the narrator greatly in the early pages, e.g., "i was specan of this fugol i will not spec yet of the frenc" (11).

gel "bird"), some acquaintance with the history of English, and the passage is almost transparent. Almost. What is this?

In 2014, the English writer Paul Kingsnorth (b. 1972), a resident of Ireland known for his journalism, ecological and political activism, and cofounding of the "Dark Mountain Project," published a novel titled *The Wake*[38] about the Norman apocalypse of 1066 and its immediate aftermath as seen through the eyes of Buccmaster of Holland (Lincolnshire), a cantankerous village grandee who loses his family and livelihood after the invasion and assembles a band of what today might be called terrorists that "feohts for angland."[39] In many ways, the language Kingsnorth invents for Buccmaster is Hoban's Riddleyspeak turned on its head: postmodern premodern Once-English rather than premodern postmodern Future-English.[40]

In Riddleyspeak, as we have seen, consonants are dropped and clusters simplified. Perhaps unsurprisingly, in Kingsnorth's language — we will follow Buccmaster in calling it "Anglisc," though we capitalize the word[41] — consonants appear to be added, though from the implied historical point of view they have been restored, for they were there in Old English but have been lost over the course of the millennium: the *g*'s of *fugol, eages,*

---

38 The publication history is atypical. Kingsnorth financed the writing of the book through the crowdfunding publishing website Unbound. Following extremely enthusiastic reviews and longlisting for the Man Booker Prize, the book was taken up by Graywolf Press in the United States, reaching a much broader audience. His latest novel, *Beast* (conceived as the second part in a trilogy begun by *The Wake*), was released in the United Kingdom in July 2016 by Faber & Faber.
39 Kingsnorth, *The Wake*, 247.
40 In his review of *The Wake* for *The Guardian*, Adam Thorpe compares Kingsnorth's language to Hoban's, https://www.theguardian.com/books/2014/apr/02/the-wake-paul-kingsnorth-review-literary-triumph.
41 "[P]seudo-O[ld]E[nglish]" is what Kingsnorth himself calls it, though he means the choice of words, not the structure of the language in general. This is one reason why we have opted for Buccmaster over Kingsnorth. More significant, however, are the loaded implications that come with the prefix "pseudo-" (see above, with footnote 6).

and *daeg* (all words in Old English[42]) have become the glides *w* and *y* (*fowl, eyes,* and *day*),[43] and the etymology of *woman* as a compound of *wif* (cf. *wife*) and *man* becomes visible. Other obvious linguistic features are the marking of verbal forms with a final syllable *-an,* sometimes for a present participle (*was cuman, seen ... glidan, first ploughan*), sometimes for a past one (*had cnawan*), as well as the use (not part of actual Old English) of past participial forms for the simple past (*i seen, it flown, it cum*).[44] Where we would write *v*'s, Anglisc has *f*'s (*yfel, ofer, afyr, deofuls*); there are no capital letters; and there is even less punctuation than in Riddleyspeak (nothing but periods, and these only sparingly). The effect, as in *Riddley Walker,* is to intentionally alienate the reader.

There is, however, an important difference in ontogeny: whereas Hoban began his experimentation through an expressed interest in wordplay and its relationship to the rules of linguistic change, Kingsnorth began from regularity ("I tried to hem it in with some rules"). In fact, Kingsnorth's Buccmaster seems to eschew wordplay entirely. Kingsnorth is explicit in "A Note on Language" (one of two afterwords to the novel) about both the rationale for the language and the method by which he produced it:

> The first and most important rule was that I wanted to use only words which originated in Old English. The vast majority of the vocabulary of this novel consists of words that, in one form or another, existed in English 1000 years ago. The exceptions are cases where words did not exist for what I wanted to say, or where those that did were so obscure today,

---

42 Kingsnorth has taken some liberties: the plural of *eage* would have been *eagan* and the last word written with the ligature known as ash (*dæg*).

43 In actual Old English the verb *plough/plow* did not yet exist, but the noun was *plog*.

44 To simplify slightly, actual Old English present participles ended in *-ende,* past participles in *-en.*

or hard to pronounce or read, that they would have detracted excessively from the flow of the tale.[45]

He goes on to describe two orthographic rules ("I did not use letters which did not exist in Old English" and "I wanted to render as many OE pronunciations as I could on the page"[46]), to comment on "the catholicism of my approach to the language, old and new,"[47] and to stress that "[t]here was one final rule I set myself, and it was this: all of the previous rules could be overridden, if necessary, by a meta-rule, which functioned as a kind of literary thegn: do what the novel needs you to do."[48]

All this speaks to the method but not the rationale. Why, after all, would someone write a novel "in a tongue which no one has ever spoken, but which is intended to project a ghost image of the speech patterns of a long-dead land: a place at once alien and familiar"?[49] In harmony with Kingsnorth's general approach, the logic is both aesthetic and intellectual (though decidedly not practical):

> This novel is not written in Old English — that would be unreadable to anyone except scholars. It is written instead in what might be called a shadow tongue — a pseudo-language intended to convey the feeling of the old language by combining some of its vocabulary and syntax with the English we speak today.[50]

There would be no point in using a non-intrinsic isolate if it did nothing to further the plot of the novel. There are many ways in

---

45 Paul Kingsnorth, "A Note on Language," in *The Wake*, 353. As in actual Old English, there are a very few words in Anglisc that originate in Latin, e.g., *corona* "crown" and *preost* "priest" (from post-Classical Latin *presbyter*, itself a borrowing from Greek).

46 Ibid., 353–54.

47 Ibid., 355.

48 Ibid., 355. Note that Kingsnorth makes explicit, in a way Hoban does not, both the rules and the possibility of bending them for aesthetic purposes.

49 Ibid., 356.

50 Ibid., 353. Once again, we reiterate our reservations about "pseudo-."

which Anglisc does this, but we point to one specific contrast with the premodern postmodern language of *Riddley Walker*. When Riddley and Goodparley discuss the text about St. Eustace, they demonstrate their awareness of linguistic change over historical time. Although Kingsnorth's own immersion in historical sources and scholarship is impressive, his Buccmaster displays no corresponding awareness. He understands languages as mutually exclusive independent entities, as in this passage:

> well now that all this is gan there is yonge folc in this land who is forgettan already how things was. there is yonge folcs in angland now who nefer cnawan a time before there was frenc ofer them nefer cnawan a time when our cyngs and our thegns spac with us in our own tunge nefer cnawan what it is to lif in a land where all the ground is not tacan by one man and this man an ingenga[51]

In Buccmaster's view, the young must speak either Anglisc or Frenc; they will not speak the evolving mixture that will come to be known as English.[52] This either-or framework extends to politics, religion, and all other aspects of life:

> they is afeart i saes all afeart for the eald ways is stronger than their crist
> men from the ham has been lystnan to this and saen naht but now one specs. i can not see his nebb well in the light of the fyr
> this is blaec specan he saes we sceolde not spec lic this no mor
> thu is a wyrm then i saes and no anglisc man
> i is anglisc he saes as anglisc as thu but the eald ways is deorc and if the preost hears of this our ham will be deorc also

[51] Kingsnorth, *The Wake*, 163.
[52] This is not surprising since it took well more than a generation to introduce the massive amount of "French" vocabulary that we now take for granted: see Elaine Treharne, *Living through Conquest: The Politics of Early English, 1020–1220* (Oxford: Oxford University Press, 2012).

> the preost has thy beallucs in his hands then i saes we feohts for angland we will spec as we wolde
>
> but the eald ways the eald gods all of this is gan saes this man. it is all of the eald times the deorc times these is the times of the crist and we is his men. there is no need to spec lic this now[53]

Buccmaster does not know that he is a character in a novel and would probably not call his narrative "The Wake." Nonetheless, there are a number of reasons why Kingsnorth might have chosen this title. The one to which he himself calls attention in "A Note on History" (the second afterword) is the existence of Hereward the Wake, a brigand of the eleventh century. "Hereward was certainly real," Kingsnorth writes, but "there is no evidence that this nickname was." That is no deterrent to using the reference as the title, however, since "[n]ovelists can do that sort of thing."[54]

• • •

To connoisseurs of literature, any reference to a "wake" in a novel that experiments radically with the English language inevitably summons a very specific association: *Finnegans Wake* (1939) by James Joyce (1882–1941). This is the totemic ur-source for any non-intrinsic philological isolate — even though it isn't written in one. Joyce's language is certainly an isolate, but it is quintessentially intrinsic: only Joyce himself commands the idiom, which is extraordinarily high on wordplay but has no rules in the sense that every lexical innovation satisfied his personal — unarticulated and inarticulable — aesthetic judgment.[55] It is easy to imagine another novel written in Nadsat; any new attempt to produce "Wakespeak" would fail.

---

53 Kingsnorth, *The Wake*, 247.
54 Paul Kingsnorth, "A Note on History," in *The Wake*, 359.
55 Illustrative of this point is the fact that the work that in many senses comes closest to bending the language in the manner of *Finnegans Wake* is Joyce's own *Ulysses* (1922).

Take the familiar opening page of the novel:

```
    riverrun, past Eve and Adam's, from swerve of shore to bend
of bay, brings us by a commodius vicus of recirculation back to
Howth Castle and Environs.
    Sir Tristram, violer d'amores, fr'over the short sea, had passen-
core rearrived from North Armorica on this side the scraggy
isthmus of Europe Minor to wielderfight his penisolate war: nor
had topsawyer's rocks by the stream Oconee exaggerated themselse
to Laurens County's gorgios while they went doublin their mumper
all the time: nor avoice from afire bellowsed mishe mishe to
tauftauf thuartpeatrick: not yet, though venissoon after, had a
kidscad buttended a bland old isaac: not yet, though all's fair in
vanessy, were sosie sesthers wroth with twone nathandjoe. Rot a
peck of pa's malt had Jhem or Shen brewed by arclight and rory
end to the regginbrow was to be seen ringsome on the aquaface.
    The fall (bababadalgharaghtakamminarronnkonnbronntonner-
ronntuonnthunntrovarrhounawnskawntoohoohoordenenthur-
nuk!) of a once wallstrait oldparr is retaled early in bed and later
on life down through all christian minstrelsy. The great fall of the
offwall entailed at such short notice the pftjschute of Finnegan,
erse solid man, that the humptyhillhead of humself prumptly sends
an unquiring one well to the west in quest of his tumptytumtoes:
and their upturnpikepointandplace is at the knock out in the park
where oranges have been laid to rust upon the green since dev-
linsfirst loved livvy.
```

This particular version of the text is copied from *Finnegans Wiki*;[56] the gray elements are hyperlinks to interpretations and references, often very philologically elaborate ones. A wide variety of people have inserted references; the important point for us is what does and does not get annotated (at least as of June 28, 2016). You will note that the only elements left unexplained are *after*; *and*; *and their*; *brings us*; *down*; *from*; *his*; *is*; *not yet, though*; *of*; *of a once*; *of his*; *of the*; *on the*; *that the*; *the*; *to*; *to the*; *was to be seen*; *and were*. Every word here is Germanic; every word here is what is sometimes called an Anglo-Saxon monosyllable (though *their* is a borrowing from Scandinavian); and every word here except *brings* and *seen* is a function word or copula, that is to say, an article, preposition, pronoun, or other small lexeme that holds the language together but is not a major vehicle of content. In the eyes of many of his readers, then, Joyce's astonishing inventiveness does not extend to the fundamental building blocks of the language.

Finnegans Wake is the granddaddy of all the works we have discussed (and so many more). Despite the tremendous difficulties it poses to readers, it is indisputably part of the canon

---

56 *FinnegansWiki*, http://finnegansweb.com/wiki/index.php/Main_Page.

of English literature. That such a work occupies a high position in the esteem of critics grants permission, if you will, to writers and publishers to entertain myriad other flights of experimentation. Some are successful (aesthetically or linguistically), many are not; all are Joyce's progeny. In some instances, the debts are publicly recognized, as in Anthony Burgess's wonderful *Re Joyce,* one of the best introductions of the entire œuvre for the lay reader.[57] More often, though, the debts are left even less acknowledged than the gentle nod in Kingsnorth's title.

Obviously there were interesting experiments with English prose before Joyce, but the towering status of *Finnegans Wake* in experimental literature is uncontested. The fact that the particular works we examine take Joyce as their point of departure — explicitly or not — has generic implications. As noted at the start of the paper, most of the works we discuss are British, postwar, written in the first person, male, and post-apocalyptic. Let us begin with the first. The majority of the authors were born British (like Joyce, whose Dublin was a British, as well as Irish, city in those days) or elected Britain as their home. They differ from Joyce in exclusively setting their works in a post-apocalyptic future or past; whatever else it may be, *Finnegans Wake* cannot be characterized as post-apocalyptic (or even set in any particular time). The novel was published only months before the outbreak of the most destructive war in European, and world, history. The trauma of that war, and the permanently looming apocalypse of the nuclear weapons that appeared at the conflict's conclusion, darken all the works in *Finnegans Wake*'s wake.

Explaining the dominance of the first-person voice is straightforward: if you wish to create an idiolect, it is helpful to have an "idiot," that is, a unique voice embodying the language and worldview. (A striking feature of *Finnegans Wake* is that it is a disembodied idiolect.) In our view the characteristic

---

57 Anthony Burgess, *Re Joyce* (New York: Norton, 1968), originally published in the United Kingdom as *Here Comes Everybody: An Introduction to James Joyce for the Ordinary Reader* (London: Faber & Faber, 1965). See also his *Joysprick: An Introduction to the Language of James Joyce* (London: Deutsch, 1973).

masculinity is potentially connected: first, the authors are men, and first-person narratives written by men tend to adopt a male point of view; second, the authors of works set in the future, principally but not exclusively science fiction, have historically been overwhelmingly male; and third, more tentatively, one might identify a certain rhetorical machismo in bravura linguistic performance.[58]

Finnegans Wake is in some sense unreadable — and it is probably the only highly acclaimed English-language work by a major author that cannot be used for a win (or, rather, a loss) in the game "Humiliation," invented by David Lodge in his 1975 campus novel *Changing Places*. This is because, although it is in English, most people would not immediately concede the point. As our final example, we contrast it with a work that is not in English at all — or, indeed, in any other canonical, card-carrying language — and yet is easily understandable to any well-educated person who knows English.[59]

Here is a passage in a short story — we can call it a detective story, though that bends the genre slightly — that deals with a not-too-distant future when China overtakes the administration of the European Union:

> After algunos tiempos, manige manageros from Cabillot schola was enroled por importante jobs. Und presto nomanno coudde los understande. Eine colossale incomprehensione presto blocked alles Chinese administratione in Europa. Der Chinese governor coudde nicht unterstande wat was happeningante. Alles der Chinese power structura was

[58] The last point is often alluded to in literary controversies. See, e.g., the kerfuffle surrounding Jonathan Franzen's essay "Mr. Difficult" in *The New Yorker* 78, no. 29 (September 30, 2002): 100–11. The masculine title is revealing.

[59] We surmise this from an admittedly small and uncontrolled sample of students and colleagues who have read the text. All of them know English, and many of them know another European language as well. It is quite possible that the work would also be straightforwardly understandable to someone who knew two or three European languages *other* than English, but — given the global position of English today and the vagaries of education — the experiment is harder to conduct.

fallingante. Quarrelose disputes erupted porqué superiores
unterstudde nicht inferiores und orders coudde not trans-
mitte. Alles Chinesos in Bruxel speaked perfecte Europanto
und believed dat esse English. From Beijingo commandantes
unterstudde nicht wat lingua was seine Europese manageros
speakante. Rapido, der invasive Chinese machine tilted.[60]

From the text, we know this is "Europanto," but what is that?
As it turns out, the main character, Inspector Cabillot, doesn't
quite know either. When, in another story ("Cabillot versus der
malefiko Finnko"), he takes an obligatory language examination
("examen test"), he "coudde chose nicht" among three options
for "How dixit in Europanto 'I love you'?".[61] If anyone knows the
answer, it is Diego Marani (b. 1959). In 1996, Marani, an Italian who has worked as a translator for the European Union in
Brussels, invented this international auxiliary language, a satirical take on both the most famous such construction, the Esperanto of L.L. Zamenhof (1859–1917), and the macaronic quality
of contemporary European affairs.[62] Perhaps best known for his
novel *Nuova grammatica finlandese* (2000), translated by Judith
Landry as *New Finnish Grammar* (2011),[63] Marani has published
numerous newspaper columns in Europanto, as well as the collection of tales from which the passage above comes, *Las adven-*

---

60 Diego Marani, *Las adventures des Inspector Cabillot* (Sawtry: Dedalus, 2012), 107.
61 The options are: "A. Ich turbo toi[.] B. Ich amorante van toi[.] C. Me palpito por toi" (23–24).
62 In his 1939 novel *The Confidential Agent,* Graham Greene's title character meets his contact, the Kafkaesque "K," at a language school where the latter teaches Entrenationo. Obviously drawn from the model of Esperanto, Entrenationo's resemblance to the not-yet-invented Europanto is striking. This observation and some of the points we make in what follows are also noted in Tim Conley and Stephen Cain, *Encyclopedia of Fictional and Fantastic Languages* (Westport: Greenwood, 2006), 3–4.
63 It will be clear from this paragraph that Marani has a thing about Finnish, a non-Indo-European European language that plays no role in Europanto. If it did, Marani's Europantic excursions would be much less understandable to his likely audiences.

tures des Inspector Cabillot (2012). For reasons that should be obvious, we do not expect ever to see a translation.

In the terms set out above, Marani's argot is evidently high on playfulness and not entirely devoid of rules.[64] For example, Marani generally refrains from juxtaposing two words drawn from the same "source language," though "algunos tiempos" at the beginning of the passage quoted above is an obvious exception. Our point is that such rules are routinely broken, presumably for reasons connected to Marani's aesthetic judgment. Europanto is thus similar to Wakespeak[65] (and distinct from the Anglisc of *The Wake*): it is an isolate — and it stands to reason that a philologically informed reading would be interesting — but it

64 There is in fact a surprising history behind Europanto and its ruledness. While all citations of *Las adventures des Inspector Cabillot* in this essay come from the 2012 British edition, we note that Marani published a book of the same title in France over a dozen years earlier (Paris: Mazarine, 1999). The two works are far from identical: not only do they not have exactly the same chapters in exactly the same order (though there is some overlap), but there are, for reasons never explained, substantial differences in the grammar, lexicon, and orthography of Europanto itself. To select a single example, in the 2012 edition, the eponymous hero is described in the "Introductione" as follows: "Inspector Cabillot esse der autentiquo europeane polizero, fightingante contra der evil por eine Europa van pax und prosperity donde man speake eine unique lingua: Europanto" (7). In 1999, however, the "same sentence" reads: "Inspector Cabillot est el autentiquo europeano polizero qui fighte contra el mal por eine Europa van pax und prosperity donde se speake eine sola lingua: de Europanto" (29). We have already stated that if anyone knows Europanto, then it is Marani, but we cannot determine the validity of the *modus ponens*. Marani's own knowledge has evidently changed substantially, with the later form having a significantly greater English (and also German) component. Thus, while Europanto is not devoid of rules, many of them are observed in the breach. To adapt a fragment of Heraclitus, no one besides Marani can write a book in Europanto — and neither can he.

65 We note a further connection between Marani and Joyce: Trieste. *New Finnish Grammar* takes place in this Italian city, and Marani has written a short book about the city's literary *genius loci*, Italo Svevo (1861–1928): *A Trieste con Svevo* (2003). Svevo, as a side job, tutored an Irish émigré to the city in Italian and the local Triestine dialect; the latter, meanwhile, began composing an important novel in what was then a Habsburg port city. The student, obviously, was James Joyce, the novel *Ulysses*.

is utterly intrinsic. Attempts by others to speak or write Europanto will probably be more successful than analogous efforts with Wakespeak, but we expect that they will quickly degenerate. (Arguably, Marani's own prose degenerates: in our experience, the experiment yields diminishing returns the more pages one reads.) Marani's ear is what makes the language work and also what makes it so readable. Contrast his passage with the following piece written by another Italian, drawn from a similar Eurochimera, but one that is so strongly ruled that it tolerates no exceptions:

> Estis malvarmete ekstere, sed la ĉambro, kie ni sidis, estis agrable varma. Mia plej kara amiko, Ernesto, sidis kontraŭ mi, donante sin plene al sia komforta brakseĝo. Jam dum unu horo ni parolis Esperante kaj pasis de temo al temo. Estis vere instiga plezuro aŭskulti lin; li tiom bone sidis en la lingvo. Ordinare, kiam li parolas per sia gepatra lingvo: la angla, mankas al li la vervo kaj esprimo, — sume, la muziko, kiu montriĝas kiam li parolas Esperanton. Lia Esperanta prozo estas poezio.[66]

These are the first sentences of Cezaro Rossetti's 1950 novel *Kredu min, sinjorino!* (*Believe Me, Miss!*), written in Esperanto. We expect that most readers of this essay will agree that the Rossetti passage is more difficult to comprehend than Marani's idiolect, and yet Esperanto — which has survived for well over a century and continues to have thousands of devotees and even native speakers — is certainly not an isolate.

In a number of ways, *Las adventures des Inspector Cabillot* is an outlier. Though postwar and male, Marani does not have the other properties we have highlighted. His tales are not written in the first person. They are not post-apocalyptic; the detective story is a conservative, largely formulaic genre; and the titular character projects wackiness rather than doom and gloom.

---

66 Cezaro Rossetti, *Kredu min, sinjorino!* ([Scheveningen]: Heroldo de Esperanto, 1950), 7.

Most saliently, Marani is not British. Marani, no less than Europanto itself, represents Europeness, and we cannot fail to mention — writing this essay in Berlin the week after the Brexit vote — that Marani himself winks at the awkwardness of Great Britain's place in Europe:

> Was der jahro 2052. De Europeane Pax sich extended undisturbed from Portugallia zum Slovakkia, from Finlandia zum Cypro. Europa was indeed plus und plus grande. Aber ella was united und dat was essentiale. Germania was der leader country, in second platz come Franza, Nederlanda, Belgica, Luxemburga, Danelanda, Swedelanda, Finlandia, in terza platz come Italia, Espania, Ellenia, Portugallia. Dann come Polanda, Ungaria, Cekia, Slovakkia, Slovenia, Cypro und Turkelandia. Op bench reserva, come Grosse Britannia.[67]

Maybe it is post-apocalyptic after all?

• • •

Answers do not matter so much as questions, said the Good Fairy. A good question is very hard to answer. The better the question the harder the answer. There is no answer at all to a very good question.
— Flann O'Brien[68]

Our paper began with a straightforward question: "What is a language?" In the Good Fairy's terms, this is a good question but perhaps not a very good one. While we have not answered it (and do not propose to do so now), we believe that we have made progress. By concentrating on highly self-conscious linguistic experimentation in fiction — and within that, on the rule-bound rather than the playful — we have shown that the oddity of the subject matter is no barrier to the deployment of standard philological practices. The texts of particular interest

---

67 Marani, *Las adventures des Inspector Cabillot*, 23.
68 Flann O'Brien, *At Swim-Two-Birds* (London: Longmans, Green, 1939), 291.

to us are composed in what we have called non-intrinsic philological isolates. In regard to the animating question, the term to focus on is "philological."

We have not offered a definition of "philology" either, and quite deliberately. Our focus has been on practices of interpretation — used by those who call themselves philologists, but also by many who do not — with the aim to show that practices are where the stuff of any specific language becomes tractable. We would extend the point beyond philology to "a language": just as philology is an abstract construct that denotes a collection of shared practices, so is "a language" (let's take "English") a collection of shared, specifically linguistic, practices. Each speaker of English makes use of particular practices in articulating his or her language, and these idiolects (highly mutually intelligible as a rule, but not utterly: Cambridge and Jamaica and Glasgow and Colombo and Fargo…) are grouped together as the thing we call "a language." Every edge is blurry, but you can still distinguish it, especially if you practice. A non-intrinsic philological isolate is a language; pataphilology is philology.

Philology is pataphilology, but is a language a non-intrinsic philological isolate? That a language is philological is obvious. That it is non-intrinsic is equally obvious. (There is no such thing as a private language.[69]) What, however, about the claim that a language can be an isolate?

The languages we have discussed so far have been mostly fictional. This matters, no doubt, but not in the way you might expect. At issue is the relationship between the adjective "non-intrinsic" and the noun "isolate." When the language in question is largely the product of an individual's imagination, the two can function independently. Consider the isolates Wakespeak (intrinsic) and Riddleyspeak (non-intrinsic). In languages found in the wild, however, the two are strongly correlated, a relationship most visible when they are on the brink of extinction. Take,

---

69 Stewart Candish and George Wrisley, "Private Language," in *The Stanford Encyclopedia of Philosophy*, Fall 2014 edn., ed. Edward N. Zalta, http://plato.stanford.edu/archives/fall2014/entries/private-language.

for example, Apiaká, currently spoken, according to the latest census, by a single person in Brazil.⁷⁰ There is no meaningful way to distinguish Apiaká from a non-intrinsic isolate; more people *could* speak this language, but they just happen not to. The last speaker of Apiaká, whose name the authors of this essay regrettably do not know, occupies the same position now that Dolly Pentreath of Mousehole occupied in the eighteenth century.

Arguably. Pentreath is the best-known candidate for "the last native speaker of Cornish." The laurels for that dispiriting position are hotly contested. Pentreath died in 1777 and was the last person to speak Cornish natively, but she was bilingual in English and purists may (and do) contend that "the last native speaker of Cornish" should therefore be sought earlier, say with the monolingual Chesten Marchant (d. 1676). In any event, after Pentreath, Cornish entered a period when it was not even an isolate — it was simply not. In recent decades, though, there has been a movement underway to make Cornish great again. To be more precise, Southwestern Britain has seen not just what the census-takers call a "reawakening" of Cornish but a surprising number of aspirants to the tongue, with different linguistic necromancers pushing for the acceptance of their own boutique choices in such realms as vocabulary and orthography.⁷¹ Cornish is, of course, not an isolate from the perspective of historical/

70 Gary F. Simons and Charles D. Fennig, eds., *Ethnologue: Languages of the World,* 20th edn. (Dallas: SIL International, 2017), https://www.ethnologue.com/language/api.

71 Simons and Fennig, eds., *Ethnologue,* https://www.ethnologue.com/language/cor: "No known L1 speakers, but emerging L2 speakers." A small taste of the controversy can be had by comparing the following three textbooks, all by Ray Chubb: *Skeul an Tavas: A Cornish Language Coursebook for Schools in the Standard Written Form,* 2nd ed. (Portreath: Agan Tavas, 2010), *Skeul an Tavas: A Cornish Language Coursebook for Adults in the Standard Written Form,* 2nd ed. (Portreath: Agan Tavas, 2010), and *Skeul an Tavas: A Coursebook in Standard Cornish,* 2nd edn. (Westport: Evertype, 2013). The most obvious difference is in the color of the cover (orange, green, and purple respectively). For more detail, see Dave Sayers, "Standardising Cornish: The Politics of a New Minority Language," *Language Problems & Language Planning* 36 (2012): 99–119.

comparative linguistics, being a member of the Celtic language family, which has other living, even flourishing, relatives today (notably Welsh); but it is also not an isolate as a phenomenon of language engineering. The nineteenth-century creation of Modern Hebrew was a stunningly successful variant of the same phenomenon of attempting to undo the isolated status of a non-intrinsic tongue.[72] At the fringes, how about the thousand-or-so *denaskuloj* (native speakers) of Esperanto or, even fringier, the devotees of the Klingon Language Institute in an era when every science-fiction franchise seems to require its own linguistic prop?[73] The relationship to fiction is not accidental; indeed, it is pataphilologically necessary.

What of the (pata)philology of languages used by lifeforms beyond Earth, assuming that such lifeforms exist, that they are intelligent, and that they use (a) language? Is exo-linguistics (pata)philological? Do the practices that we have described here for languages from Old English to Scots and from Anglisc to revived Cornish — narrow in geographical scope, to be sure — apply in the wider universe? These are not questions anyone can answer yet, but once again it is a novel that provides what may be the best thought experiment: Stanisław Lem's *Głos pana* (1968), translated by Michael Kandel as *His Master's Voice* (1983), which goes through the problems with determining what even counts as a language in the absence of any of the usual historical and physical cues. Given the resources currently invested globally in the Search for Extraterrestrial Intelligence (SETI) — peanuts in terms of science funding but handsome from a linguist's point

---

[72] See, e.g., Suzanne Romaine, "Revitalized Languages as Invented Languages," in *From Elvish to Klingon: Exploring Invented Languages*, ed. Michael Adams, 185–225 (Oxford: Oxford University Press, 2011).

[73] Arika Okrent, *In the Land of Invented Languages: Esperanto Rock Stars, Klingon Poets, Loglan Lovers, and the Mad Dreamers Who Tried to Build a Perfect Language* (New York: Spiegel & Grau, 2009); David J. Peterson, *The Art of Language Invention: From Horse-Lords to Dark Elves, the Words behind World-Building* (New York: Penguin, 2015).

of view[74] — the lack of clarity in defining both "language" and "a language" is a colossal shortfall. Pataphilologists to the rescue![75]

---

[74] The annual budget around 2010 was on the order of 2.5 million US dollars, the cost of operating the needed radio telescopes. To put this into context, see the intriguing graphic at http://www.microcosmologist.com/blog/seti-infographic.

[75] We dedicate this paper to our colleague David Bellos, who among other distinctions is the founding director of the Program in Translation and Intercultural Communication at Princeton University. In this capacity he encouraged us to design a new class titled "Imagined Languages" and then sponsored it when we taught it together in 2013 and 2015. We owe much to the students in both iterations of the course, especially Yuval Wigderson, and to David. We are also grateful to the Wissenschaftskolleg zu Berlin, which made a week of concentrated collaboration possible.

Two

"On Epic Naïveté":
Adorno's Allegory of Philology

James I. Porter

"On Epic Naïveté" (1943) is a short but dizzying fragment from Adorno's "Excursus I: Odysseus, or Myth and Enlightenment" that never found its way into the final version of *The Dialectic of Enlightenment*.[1] The fragment, a self-contained essay, is continuous with the larger work's critique of Enlightenment reasoning but is more focused in its approach, in addition to showcasing a hauntingly beautiful reading of epic imagery. In its methodological gambit, the essay resembles a piece of classical philology, though in the way it draws philosophical conclusions based on close readings and on highly focused *Ansatzpunkte* it more closely resembles Erich Auerbach's critical reading of Homer from the year before, "Odysseus' Scar."[2] Perhaps a still closer parallel stylistically

1   Theodor W. Adorno, "Über epische Naïvetät," in *Noten zur Literatur*, ed. Rolf Tiedeman (Frankfurt am Main: Suhrkamp, 1981); Theodor W. Adorno, *Notes to Literature*, 2 vols., ed. Rolf Tiedemann, trans. Shierry Weber Nicholsen (New York: Columbia University Press, 1991–1992), 1:24–29.
2   On this latter, see James I. Porter, "Erich Auerbach and the Judaizing of Philology," *Critical Inquiry* 35 (2008): 115–47.

speaking would be the "parody of the philological method" that Adorno detects in Walter Benjamin's "allegorical" philosophical writing.[3]

Whether Adorno's method has anything in common with pataphilology in the mold of Alfred Jarry's pataphysics is another question. As a disruption of ordinary reading and critical practices that wreaks havoc on conventional linear logic, it most certainly does.[4] But insofar as pataphysics is an ethics of ludic disobedience that borders on nonsense (Jarry called pataphysics "the science of imaginary solutions" — Baudrillard would later add: "to the absence of problems"),[5] it most certainly does not. In Nietzsche's wake, Adorno's philology mimics the objects of its critiques in order to subvert them from within: it is a faithful copy of an unfaithful original, dedicated to exposing problems that are nevertheless very real, politically, culturally, and ideologically. There is nothing blithely indifferent about Adorno's stance, any more than there is about Nietzsche's, even if they both share with Jarry a certain degree of *je-m'en-foutisme* and a rejection of bourgeois values. Perhaps truculence more than insouciance is the common thread that runs through these three models of philology.

That said, "On Epic Naïveté" has a specific signature that is shaped by its object, which as its title indicates has to do with the imputation of naïve simplicity (*Einfalt*) to Homeric poetry,

3 Theodor W. Adorno, "Introduction to Benjamin's *Schriften*" (1955), in *Notes to Literature*, 2:240.
4 See Bök, *'Pataphysics: The Poetics of an Imaginary Science* (Evanston: Northwestern University Press, 2002); and Gurd's introduction to this volume. This disruptiveness is sometimes labeled by Adorno "parataxis," as contrasted with "synthesis" or "hypotaxis" (logical coordination and subordination); it has close affinities with the principle of negative dialectics. See "Parataxis: On Hölderlin's Late Poetry" (1963), in *Notes to Literature*, 2:109–49, esp. 131 and 136. But in the case of Homer, the naïvely paratactic author par excellence, Adorno's project of disruptive insubordination requires an extra layer of complication. See below.
5 Alfred Jarry, *Exploits and Opinions of Doctor Faustroll, Pataphysician: A Neo-Scientific Novel*, trans. Simon Watson Taylor (Boston: Exact, 1996), 22; Jean Baudrillard, *Pataphysique* (Paris: Sens et Tonka, 2002), 41.

one of its hallmark features at least since the dawn of modernity (though not in antiquity).[6] As the essay unfolds, naïveté and simplicity slowly detach themselves from each other and then lose their purchase on Homer altogether. Ultimately, the essay is about the internal antagonism of epic as epic wrestles with its own logic, form, and expression when all three of these elements are pushed "to the edge of madness."[7]

The context, mostly submerged, is supplied by the overarching argument of the book to which the essay belongs conceptually and genetically. There, Adorno discerns in the *Odyssey* "a prescient allegory of the dialectic of enlightenment" that is best illustrated in the travels Odysseus makes through space and time:

> The hero's peregrinations from Troy to Ithaca trace the path of the self through myths, a self […] still in the process of formation as self-consciousness. The primeval world is secularized in the space he measures out […]. Laboriously and revocably, in the image of the journey, historical time has detached itself from space, the irrevocable schema of all mythical time.[8]

Figured as a passage through mythical space, Odysseus's travels perform a rationalization — a distantiation and negation — of pre-reflective space, while in the process they produce a sense of time and history that was never available to myth. In another vocabulary, one that Adorno does not explicitly invoke, the story that Odysseus's wanderings tells is a genealogy, by which we should understand the insertion of the present into the past,

---

6   An important point, and one that Adorno was perfectly capable of knowing. From Plato to Aristotle down through Longinus and beyond, Homeric epic was anything but naïve or simple.

7   Adorno, "On Epic Naïveté," in *Notes to Literature*, 1:27. henceforth, references to the translation will be given in the body of this chapter.

8   Max Horkheimer and Theodor W. Adorno, *Dialectic of Enlightenment: Philosophical Fragments,* trans. Edmund Jephcott, ed. Gunzelin Schmid Noerr (Stanford: Stanford University Press, 2002), 38–39. Henceforth, *DE*.

albeit in disguised form. That is, on Adorno's understanding, which accords with Nietzsche's, genealogy does not trace origins. It problematizes them by exposing the manner in which they are used to construct ideologies in the present.[9] In this way, in producing an untimely disturbance — that is, the sense that philology is constitutively and fatally out of sync with its objects — genealogy lays bare dialectical processes and thought.[10]

Adorno accomplishes this result by insinuating modernity (history) into the Homeric past (myth), which makes Homer's "time" legible in the present as an origin that can be both affirmed and denied. Myth represents the historical starting point for modernity (Adorno calls it for this reason a "bourgeois prehistory," *DE* 46), but one that must be abandoned and disavowed for modernity to begin. And so, although we might wish to call Adorno's method genealogical, it is perhaps better to describe it as dialectical in its logic, allegorical in its readings, and unabashedly anachronistic all the way around. As a result, Homeric epic in Adorno proves to be a slippery thing, less a historical phenomenon than a transhistorical one. It assumes a liquid form — at times seemingly archaic, at times anachronistically projecting itself forward into a future consciousness of itself, at times grasped as if through the backwards-looking lens of a post-Enlightenment awareness.

---

9 See James I. Porter, "Nietzsche's Genealogy as Performative Critique," in *Conceptions of Critique in Modern and Contemporary Philosophy*, eds. Ruth Sonderegger and Karin de Boer (London: Palgrave, 2011), 119–36.

10 See Nietzsche's declaration from 1874 that philology is untimely, in the sense that it works "on time," and "against time, for the benefit of a future time to come" (Friedrich W. Nietzsche, "On the Uses and Disadvantages of History for Life," in *Untimely Meditations*, ed. D. Breazeale, trans. R.J. Hollingdale (Cambridge: Cambridge University Press, 1997), 60; trans. adapted). The declaration cuts two ways. Uncritical philology is helplessly untimely. Critical philology brings out the knowledge of its own untimeliness that uncritical philology either ignores or represses. See further James I. Porter, "Nietzsche's Untimely Antiquity," in *The New Cambridge Companion to Nietzsche*, ed. Thomas Stern (Cambridge: Cambridge University Press, forthcoming).

This same theoretical framework is operative in "On Epic Naïveté," although now the focus shifts from Odysseus to Homer and from the plot of the epic poem to its logical form as poetry, both illustrated once again through the *Odyssey*. And as Adorno adjusts his lens to accommodate a more "micrological gaze,"[11] his method might at first glance appear to pass for a conventional, close philological reading of Homer. It is anything but. There is a perversity to his reading of Homer, which aims to bring out the inner perversities of all classical philology, starting with the radical enjambment of discrepant times that reading ancient texts in the modern day necessarily involves (this is philology's native untimeliness), and from there indexing the ideological sutures that classical philology produces in order to paper over these very discrepancies.

The essay opens with a quotation from the climactic recognition scene between Penelope and Odysseus in the penultimate book of the *Odyssey*:

> And as when the land appears welcome to men who are swimming,
> after Poseidon has smashed their strong-built ship on the open
> water, pounding it with the weight of wind and the heavy seas, [...]
> [...] gladly they set foot on the shore, escaping the evil;
> so welcome was her husband to her as she looked upon him,
> and she could not let him go from the embrace of her white arms (23.233–40).[12]

The passage is carefully chosen. It is built around an elaborate simile that serves as a virtual epitome of the poem: the whole of the *Odyssey* is contained in these few lines.[13] Adorno will use

---

11 Said of Benjamin in Adorno, *Notes to Literature*, 2:241.
12 *The Odyssey of Homer*, trans. Richmond Lattimore (New York: Harper, 1965); quoted by Adorno on p. 24 of his essay.
13 As it happens, the image anticipates a second epitome of the entire poem that occurs when Penelope and Odysseus, reunited in bed, each retells their

this passage to ground a reading of the poem, and then, extrapolating from there, to produce a reading of the epic genre as a whole. Looking closer, we see that a series of contrasts structures the passage: the violently raging sea, the salvific ending, and the competing appeals to the faculties of vision and touch. One sense that is *not* in evidence in the passage, at least explicitly, is that of sound. Yet it is the aural dimension of the imagery, or rather lying behind the imagery and within it, that Adorno singles out for appraisal in his analysis that immediately follows, when he goes on to discover in the simile an immanent dialectical movement that, he will claim, runs through the whole poem, and indeed through all of epic poetry.

If one were one to measure the entire *Odyssey* against these verses, Adorno speculates, what would stand revealed is "the substance [of the epic] appearing in [its] naked form." And that substance, its *Gehalt*, consists in the

> attempt to hearken to [*nachzuhorchen*] the endlessly renewed beating of the sea on the rocky coast, and patiently to reproduce [lit., "to trace," as in a drawing: *nachzuzeichnen*] the way the water floods over the rocks and then streams back from them with a roar, leaving the solid ground glowing with deeper color. This roaring [or "noise"] is the sound of epic discourse [*Solches Rauschen ist der Laut der epischen Rede*], in which what is solid [*das Feste*] and unequivocal comes together with what is ambiguous and flowing, only to part from it immediately again. (24; trans. adapted).

"This roaring is the sound of epic discourse." Adorno's imagery is as complex as Homer's own. What he means to say, on a first approach, is that, in the course of its own action, epic discourse turns, or *would* turn if it could, into a stream of noise, a *Rauschen*, rather than a string of words and meanings. This is

respective personal adventures (23.300–343), as Jonas Grethlein reminds me (personal communication). The image is thus an epitome of an epitome, and thus a highly wrought moment.

its naked substance revealed as the truth of its appearance — the effort on the part of epic to become pure sound, as immediate and overwhelming as the raging sea. To say this is not to say that Adorno, in selecting the verses from book 24 that he does, is blind to the tender and dramatic moment of reconciliation they portray, that he has eyes and ears only for the endless churning of the elements that rage against the return of Odysseus, his ship, and his crew. Hardly. Neither is it to say that, in indulging in the strong visual and especially the tactile pulls of the simile, Adorno has allowed himself to be mesmerized by the senseless yet powerful materiality of epic poetry. These other dimensions of the image and the sensations they evoke will play a role in his commentary on the passage. But in order to see how they do, we first need to attend to what he means by the noise of epic.

By noise Adorno has in mind whatever blocks the transmission of rational discourse from within language. Whenever language discovers its non-rational and non-verbal resources and becomes imagistic, object-oriented, and impossible to translate back into language again, whenever it becomes, in his own words, "stupid" and "dumb," it ceases to communicate, to be "fungible" (offering exchangeable information), and instead becomes mute and opaque, itself object-like. And, as Adorno observes, Homeric epic is peculiarly marked by its relationship to this kind of opacity, which has been the source of its much-vaunted proximity to nature, to the object-world, and to the naïve.

This, at least, is how epic has customarily appeared to the classicizing imagination of the European West, which could characterize the simplicities of epic poetry as either spell-bound by a kind of "primal stupidity" (*Urdummheit*) — so the ethnologist Konrad Theodor Preuss (1904), speaking of the totemic substratum of early religions and myths, and so the classicist Gilbert Murray (1912), who cites Preuss approvingly and labels this terrifying substratum of enchanted nature characteristically Greek (25) — or else as evidence of what Schiller, more delicately, called "naïve," and what Winckelmann before him had bequeathed to later generations under the rubric of "noble simplicity [*edle Einfalt*] and tranquil grandeur."[14]

Adorno partly agrees, but he casts the problem in a different light. Epic poetry *is* fascinated with the objectality of things and with the prospect of approaching and even taming them through a kind of mimeticism. And indeed, "naïveté is the price one pays for" this surrender, however partial it may be, to the fearful attractions and powers of nature contained in myth (25). But there is a catch. For all its noise and opacity, epic can never relinquish its status as language and poetry. It never truly becomes an object; it merely represents itself as approximating *to* the condition of objects. And therein lies the founding contradiction of epic poetry, which cannot escape its own linguistic predicament even as its identity is staked on the attempt to do so. Hence Adorno's qualifications in the passage above: the substance of epic consists "in the attempt to hearken to the endlessly renewed beating of the sea on the rocky coast, and patiently to reproduce the way the water floods over the rocks." But the attempt is doomed to fail: "Because, however, the narrator turns to the world of myth for his material, his enterprise, now impossible, has always been contradictory" (24). And with this, Adorno launches into his dialectical analysis of Homeric naïveté:

> But as long as great epic poetry has existed, this contradiction has informed the narrator's *modus operandi*; it is the element in epic poetry commonly referred to as objectivity or material concreteness [*Gegenständlichkeit*]. In comparison with the enlightened state of consciousness to which narrative discourse belongs, a state characterized by general concepts, this concrete or objective element always seems to be one of stupidity, lack of comprehension, ignorance, a stub-

---

14 Friedrich Schiller, "On Naïve and Sentimental Poetry," in *German Aesthetic and Literary Criticism: Winckelmann, Lessing, Hamann, Herder, Schiller, Goethe*, ed. H.B. Nisbet, 179–232 (Cambridge: Cambridge University Press, 1985 [1795]); Johann Joachim Winckelmann, "Thoughts on the Imitation of the Painting and Sculpture of the Greeks," ibid., 42.

born clinging to the particular when it has already been dissolved into the universal. (25)

This is the ultimate source of the noise of epic poetry — the creaking of language as epic wrestles with its own antinomies. This noise is audible not in individual verses or in their sounds, but in their form and structure, which make meaning possible without having any intrinsic meaning of their own. Adorno means exactly this when he speaks of the "naked substance" of epic poetry. To hear the noise of language is to "receive the substance of poetry not in sensory images that language would suggest but in language itself and in the structures created by it and peculiar to it alone."[15] For "*Rauschen* is not a sound [*Klang*] but a noise [*Geräusch*], more closely akin to language than to sound."[16] Symptomatic of the historical and ideological location of epic, the noisy "sound of epic discourse" bespeaks the essential estrangement of epic from reality: it is the muted and plaintive echo of the "*a priori* impossibility" of epic to be otherwise than it is (27).

Adorno locates this impossibility almost everywhere he looks in epic discourse. For starters, the epic narrator "has always been contradictory from the beginning" in virtue of his self-appointed aim, which was to present a content (a story, a tale, "something worth telling") unlike any ever presented before, "something worth reporting on, something that is not the same as everything else, not exchangeable," be it in an effort to touch some real particular from the historical past ("what has occurred once and only once") or as a way of passing on a token of epic's own incomparable value (24, 25).[17] Telling against this

---

15 Adorno, *Notes to Literature,* 1:68, quoting Theodor Meyer.
16 Ibid., 1:69.
17 If the latter, then Adorno may be thinking of the famous remark from the Odyssey that epic audiences always flock to the latest song (Odyssey 1.351–52) — itself a troubling notion for any view of traditional, oral epic. See Armand D'Angour, *The Greeks and the New: Novelty in Ancient Greek imagination and Experience* (Cambridge: Cambridge University Press, 2011), ch. 8.

ambition is the problem that mythical discourse is a derivative of tradition, the greater sea from which epic emerges and into which it will return once again:

> The amorphous flood of myth is the eternally same [*das Immergleiche*], but the *telos* of narrative is the differentiated [*das Verschiedene*]; and the unrelentingly strict identity in which the epic object [*Gegenstand*] is held firm [*festgehalten wird*] serves to achieve its non-identity, indeed its very difference, with what is simply identical [*mit dem schlecht Identischen*], with unarticulated oneness. (24; trans. adapted)

Simply to name mythical objects is to subject them to the instruments of reason and reflection and to rob them of "the material element [...] that is the extreme opposite of all speculation and fantasy" (27). It is to identify that which ought to resist identification. It is to attempt to grasp hold of the slipping tide of myth.

Adorno is deliberately echoing the language and imagery of the simile with which his essay opens. Only, now we can see that what appears as a simile in Homer is for Adorno an allegory and, what amounts to the same thing, a dialectical image. When Adorno compresses the two halves of the simile into a solitary image, concepts are crystallized, brought to a standstill, and objectified; the substance of the text is made legible in its form; and nature and history trade places, locked in a mutual embrace: nature "becomes the figure of something historical" and "what is historically concrete" becomes an image of nature.[18] All of this is the prime matter of dialectical reflection. The image replays in its static totality the dynamic tension in the simile that stretches between the naïve and the sentimental, between natural danger and sought-for salvation, between flux and fixity. The very form of the simile enacts the conundrum of identity that is wrested from non-identity. Penelope's arms may hold Odysseus firmly in their embrace (*fest hielt*), but they are doomed to release him

---

18 Adorno, "Introduction to Walter Benjamin's *Schriften*," in *Notes to Literature*, 2:226; see also "The Essay as Form," ibid., 1:22.

to another, greater fate once again, back to whence he has come, the world of myth. It is the very intermingling of the visual and the tactile elements of the scene with the meaningful actions they represent that for Adorno constitutes the significance of the noise of epic poetry — its passionate trafficking in "primordial reality" in the throes of language and on the precipice between myth and reason (25).

Epic discourse tries so very hard not to be itself. In trying, it creates its distinctive "noise" and confesses its own limits. Given the nature of *muthos,* the epic poet must yield to the principle of "universal fungibility": unable to say something absolutely unique, the epic narrator has to say something that has an equivalent in what has already been said somewhere else in the tradition. Given the nature of communication, the epic poet has to yield to the same principle, understood now as the principle of communicability: he has to say something that is expressible and repeatable in language. *Muthos,* after all, means "speech." Its objects are meant to be shared. They cannot touch ground with the real of what they present, but can only circle around it, endlessly, and futilely:

> The attempt to emancipate representation from reflective reason is language's attempt, futile from the outset, to recover from the negativity of its intentionality, the conceptual manipulation of objects, by carrying its defining intention to the extreme and allowing what is real to emerge in pure form, undistorted by the violence of classificatory ordering. (27)

Adorno is not outlining the problem, familiar since the discovery of oral theory, that formulaic diction places insuperable strictures on Homeric expressiveness.[19] On the contrary, he is describing an impulse to realism that runs from Homer to Flau-

---

19 See Adam Parry, "The Language of Achilles," *Transactions of the American Philological Association* 87 (1956): 1–7.

bert.²⁰ Aligning these distant relatives brings out a feature of Adorno's portrait of Homer that places Homer on this side of Enlightenment rather than before it. Hence, epic comes to grief not only on the logic of communication, but also on something equally significant, its own temporal logic: "an anachronistic element inheres in all epic poetry: in Homer's archaism of invoking the Muse to help him proclaim events of vast scope" (25; trans. adapted). Adorno labels this feature of epic a "contradiction"; and it is one that "has informed the narrator's *modus operandi* as long as great epic poetry has existed" (25).

At issue is the constitutive logic of epic, which turns on the question — it is really a problem — of how Homer can reconcile his project of producing a distinctive difference out of the "amorphous flood of myth" that originates in the (prehistoric) past. In modern times, the situation of epic has been registered not as a contradiction so much as a tendency towards "objectivity" (*Gegenständlichkeit*), as a "stupid," "stubborn clinging to the particular" (*eines von Dummheit [...] verstockt ans Besondere dort sich Halten*) or to the "object" (*Gegenstand*), as a "rigid fixation" on an object that stares back,²¹ but also as epic "naïveté" (25). Once again, Penelope's clinging to her husband stands in for this kind of object-driven behavior. What she holds in her arms, presuming it to be the particularity that is her husband, has already dissolved into a universality. Odysseus, no longer

---

20 Auerbach's rejection of any impulse to realism in Homer contrasts sharply with Adorno's complication of that impulse in Homer, even if both are taking aim, polemically, at the same contemporary image of Homer.

21 In Voss's translation, Penelope beholds Odysseus' "sight" (the way he "looks") as well as his "gaze" (*Anblick*). Cf. "the intimidating power of the object of the identifying word's stare" (25). Homer's vocabulary for vision, when applied to persons, can encompass this precise range. But Adorno is giving the look an even more material, objective twist, reminiscent of Lacan's anecdote about the sardine can "floating on the surface of the waves" of the sea (though it didn't "see" him, "it was looking at me, all the same") — it materialized a blind spot, a point of opacity, in the field of vision that constitutes the visual field as such (Jacques Lacan, *Seminar XI: The Four Fundamental Concepts of Psychoanalysis*, ed. Alain Miller, trans. Alan Sheridan [Norton: New York, 1981], 95–96).

mythical, is already a mytheme. What does that make *her*? We had better not ask Homer, because he is himself another such mytheme — the product, purveyor, and enabling noble lie of false consciousness all rolled into one. In *Dialectic of Enlightenment,* he is introduced as "the Homeric spirit."[22] For Nietzsche, he was already either a legendary mythical individual or a "concept," or both.[23] The very precision of Homer's language, clinging to the objectively real as it does, is the proof of its contrary. Epic discourse protests the charge of falsehood with a cry that is drowned out only by its own noise.

The question, then, is whether epic hears its own noise, that is, whether epic is or is not naïve — or to what extent it is naïve, be this wittingly or unwittingly. Reading Adorno's intentions here is tricky. The passage from stupid objectivity to anachronism is hardly an obvious move unless one returns to his earlier question about fungibility. The point there had to do with epic's inability to cope elegantly with the logic of particulars and universals. Epic appears to be a hapless victim of its own internal contradictions. But is it? At the end of the same passage about objectivity, Adorno slips in one more remark about myth that I have yet to quote: "The epic poem imitates the spell of myth in order to soften it" (25). Here, epic appears instead to be a *knowing* victim of its own contradictions, and a happy manipulator of its own conditions of possibility at that.

Given the question of how Homer can produce a distinctive difference out of the "amorphous flood of myth," the answer seems to be that he can do so only by gathering up the substance of myth into the form of its concept. This is what is named in the appeal to the Muses, and by extension all figures of myth, who embody anachronism *in their very concreteness.* For the very particular and concrete object that they are "has already been dissolved into the universal," and so too has been

22 Horkheimer and Adorno, *Dialectic of Enlightenment*, 35.
23 See "Homer und die klassische Philologie" ("Homer and Classical Philology") from 1869 in Friedrich Nietzsche, *Kritische Gesammtausgabe: Werke,* ed. Giorgio Colli and Mazzino Montinari (Berlin: De Gruyter, 1967–), 2.1:249–69.

rendered communicable and an object of exchange. Such is the mimeticism of epic, its mimicry of what it is not. Could it be, then, that epic poses as a purveyor of myth and of anachronism in order to achieve its ends, that is, to produce the illusion that it can "achieve its non-identity [...] with what is simply identical, with unarticulated oneness" and, in this way, break free of the past and exercise a measure of control over it, much as Odysseus tries to do in the face of the Sirens? At stake is the mastery of the entire realm of the mythical, which is full of terrifying potential: "In its rigid fixation on its object, which is designed to break the intimidating power of the object of the identifying word's stare, the narrator of the epic account gains control, as it were, of the gesture of fear" (25).[24] It is this transformation of identity (myth) into non-identity (the *telos* of epic narrative) that is the illusion of epic fiction, and that enables us to say today of the epic narrator's enterprise that it "now [seems] impossible" and "has always been contradictory." Epic, so heavily reliant on myth, harbors a deeply "anti-mythological" tendency within (25). Instead of encountering the raw matter of natural objects, epic encounters the objectification of its own internal contradictions: it is self-sensing, but also significantly blind to what it senses.

The illusory change that epic works upon itself, Adorno insists, is a *rational* transformation, effectuated in a passage from *muthos* to *logos* that takes place entirely within *logos*.

> For myth — and the narrator's rational, communicative discourse, with its subsumptive logic that equalizes everything it reports, is preoccupied with myth as the concrete, as some-

---

[24] For a similar critique of the positivist spell exerted by uncritical philology on itself and its objects, see the exchange between Adorno and Benjamin from 1938 in Benjamin, *Selected Writings,* vol. 4, ed. Howard Eiland and Michael W. Jennings (Cambridge: Belknap Press), 99–115 and 200–214. One route to critique is through a "parody of the philological method" (see note 3 above), a tactic that is illustrated in spades in Adorno's later "Notes on Kafka" from 1953 (Theodor W. Adorno, *Prisms,* trans. Samuel and Shierry Weber [Cambridge: Harvard University Press, 1981], 243–71), and in his writings on Homer.

thing distinct from the leveling organization of the conceptual system — this kind of myth itself partakes of the eternal sameness that awoke to self-consciousness in *ratio*. (25; trans. adapted)

That is, the epic narrator participates in *ratio,* the rational processes, just by participating in non-mythic discourse-production, which is to say, by producing itself as an art form that draws upon myth while remaining distinct from it. He participates in the rational processes in the very act of drawing the distinction between myth and epic, and, at a more basic level, simply by drawing a line between his own (would-be) singular product and "the amorphous flood of myth" that is "eternally the same," which is to say, *by producing myth* from within reason. Finally, in the course of epic production, it can be said, but only said, that myth achieves consciousness of itself. This is a Hegelian way of indicating that once the boundary between reason and myth was drawn, myth ceased to exist in a state of formlessness ("noise"): it instantly participated in the logic of reason (*logos*). Consequently, the very idea of a "naïve" epic seems something of a fallacy.

When does the idea of naïve epic originate, then? Evidently, only after some moment of enlightenment, after the dawning of *ratio* and once the distinction between myth and non-myth gets drawn. Adorno purposefully keeps this moment vague:

As an anti-mythological enterprise, epic naïveté emerges from the enlightenment-oriented and positivist effort to adhere [*festzuhalten*] faithfully and without distortion to what once was as it was, and thereby break the spell cast by what has been, by myth in its true sense; hence in restricting itself to what occurred once and only once [*aufs Einmalige*] it retains an aspect that transcends limitation. For what occurred once and only once is not merely a defiant residue opposing the encompassing universality of thought; it is also thought's innermost yearning, the logical form of something real that would no longer be enclosed by social domination and the classificatory thought modeled upon it: the concept reconciled [*versöhnt*] with its object [*mit seiner Sache*]. (25–26)

Even if Adorno pursues this thought with another that sounds precociously modern — "a critique of bourgeois reason dwells within epic naïveté" (26) — one has to wonder just when to date the birth of epic naïveté as well as on what side to place it, ideologically speaking. Not only does naïveté prove to be as plastic as epic's temporal logic on Adorno's account; it also proves to be a potential weapon of critique, but one that is easily misplaced and mishandled. "Homeric simplicity" (*die homerische Einfalt*), identical with Homeric naïveté, appears in different forms and with different values. "It is easy to either ridicule Homeric simplicity […] or deploy it spitefully in opposition to the analytic spirit" (26). In the bourgeois view, this feature of epic appears as the attitude of *Urdummheit* described above: a "lack of comprehension" and a form of "ignorance" that stands in utter contrast with the abstract logic of Enlightenment universal thinking (25).

Yet, from another angle, "Homeric simplicity" turns out to have been "the opposite of simplicity" (26). It is, rather, a self-consciously manufactured gesture produced by post-enlightenment thought so as to create an anachronistic mythical past with which to overcome, or at the very least to express, if not expose, the antinomies of the present:

> The customary eulogizing of the kind of narrative stupidity that emerges only with the dialectic of form has made of that stupidity a restorationist ideology hostile to consciousness, an ideology whose last dregs are currently being sold off in the philosophical anthropologies of our day with their false concreteness. (25; trans. adapted)

Here, Homeric naïveté is merely a bludgeon with which to attack abstract thought; to buy into this story is to accept another myth, that of the falsely concrete product of the modern universal itself. "But," Adorno continues, "epic naïveté is not only a lie intended to keep general reflection at a distance from blind contemplation of the particular. As an anti-mythological enterprise, epic naïveté emerges from the enlightenment-oriented and positivist effort to [...] break the spell cast by [...] myth" (25).

Which brings us back to the question, When does epic naïveté emerge for the first time? Adorno is happy to date its emergence to the origins of epic itself. Epic naïveté is produced willingly by epic as a false appearance of itself out of an internal necessity:

> Through epic naïveté, narrative language, whose attitude toward the past always contains an apologetic element, justifying what has occurred as being worthy of attention, acts as its own corrective. The precision of descriptive language seeks to compensate for the falseness of all discourse. (26)

The irony of this embarrassment is that the very desire to correct what is false reproduces falsity on another level, that of epic simplicity, naïveté, and a mimicry of the mythical past in the epic discursive present. Epic lives off of this false consciousness, and it dwells in it intensively. Its moments of greatest saturation are found whenever the language of words melts before the language of images and the object world replaces the narrative world with an immediacy that narrative could never furnish:

> The impulse that drives Homer to describe a shield as though it were a landscape and to elaborate a metaphor until it becomes an action, until it becomes autonomous and ultimately tears apart the fabric of the narrative — that is the same impulse [*Drang*] that repeatedly drove Goethe, Stifter, and Keller [...] to draw and paint instead of writing, and it may have inspired Flaubert's archaeological studies as well. (26–27; trans. adapted)

This is the "objectivity," or rather "objectality," the *gegenständliches Element*, of epic, as well as its "*a priori* impossibility." Together, both tendencies force epic "to the edge of madness," by which Adorno means unreason (26–27).

One way of making sense of Adorno's sinuous logic in this essay is to recognize that he is not addressing epic in its original historical essence at all but only in its multiforms over time, though most often he is addressing the very idea of epic in its elastic substance rather than the thing itself. For, when we look at Homer,

> "It is ideas, not individuals, that are fighting in combat with one another," writes Nietzsche in a fragmentary note to "Homer's Contest."[25] What becomes visible in the logical disintegration of epic language is the objective transformation of pure representation, detached from meaning, into the allegory of history, parallel to the detachment of metaphor from the course of the literal action. Only by abandoning meaning does epic discourse come to resemble the image, a figure of objective meaning that emerges from the negation of subjectively rational meaning. (29; trans. adapted)

With this appeal to Nietzsche in the closing sentences of "On Epic Naïveté," Adorno seals his reading as an explicit allegory of philology about Homer and the epic form. In this way, he leaves us with the thought that only an allegorical philology, one that parodically explodes the working assumptions of positivist philology (its blind equation of texts with meaning and of both with idealist metaphysics), is capable of deciphering so supple and elusive an object as Homeric epic. In Adorno's hands, Homeric epic has become an allegory of history and of historical consciousness, while the method that is used to grasp epic in

---

25 Friedrich Nietzsche, *Kritische Gesammtausgabe: Werke,* 7:396, 16[9]. The note dates from 1871–72. The posthumously published essay, "Homer's Contest," dates from 1872. Adorno plainly took some trouble to read not only Nietzsche's published and unpublished work, but his early, philological notebooks as well. The full note gives us a better indication as to why: "The contest! And this denial of the individual! It is not historical but rather mythical people [who are depicted]. Even the person only has renown (as in Pindar) if it is cloaked in distant myths. The contest! And [the place of] the aristocratic, birthright, [and] nobility among the Greeks! It is ideas, not individuals, that are fighting in combat with one another."

this way is best described as a counter-philology that allegorizes its own conditions of possibility and those of the philology it opposes.

Nevertheless, the true perversity of Adorno's reading lies in his repeated insistence that he is reading Homer's text, and not just some idea of Homer. The logic is valid, since the allegories that he detects must be lodged deeply in the dialectical processes that produce Homer's poetry: they are, after all, part of its "substance" and visible in its "naked form," which is to say that they become visible whenever that form is laid bare and the substance of the epic is exposed for what it is. Needless to say, by embedding allegory into the substance of epic, Adorno is turning on its head one further tenet of classicism that is easily overlooked today: allegory, from Winckelmann to Hegel, is a product of a later age, that of contemporary modernity, and it runs directly counter to the naiveties of that simpler, earlier age we call classical Greece.[26] Every word of Adorno's essay is meant as an affront to convention, just as every word of his Homer is this too.

For these reasons, Adorno is keen to demonstrate that opacities blot Homer's language everywhere, and not only in his dense imagery. He affects to discover some of these in the distinctive particles of Homeric diction that unhinge the flow of a sentence's logic and that send "syntax and material" into an abyss of "countersense" or "nonsense" (*Widersinn*), for instance the "enigmatic" particle ἦ of *Odyssey* 24.156 (27):

These two [Odysseus and Telemachus],
after compacting their plot of a foul death for the suitors,
made their way to the glorious town; namely [ἦ τοι] Odysseus
came afterwards; Telemachus led the way [...].

---

26 See Johann Joachim Winckelmann, "Thoughts on the Imitation of the Painting and Sculpture of the Greeks," 51–54 ("VII. Allegory") and Hegel's *Lectures on Fine Art*.

The phrase ἦ + τοι, sometimes written as one word (ἤτοι), is an emphatic particle combination that means something like "indeed," "surely," "verily, I tell you." Like so many Greek particles, ἦ τοι is difficult to capture in any language. Adorno follows Voss, who reads: "*nämlich Odysseus / Folgete nach.*" In a note, Adorno quotes the 1910 translation by Rudolf Alexander Schröder, which reads: "*und wahrlich Odysseus…,*" "and truly Odysseus…." Adorno's English translators follow Lattimore: "*In fact Odysseus / came afterwards.*" I have restored Voss' translation above simply to align the English more closely with Adorno's German original. Of these, Schröder's version ("and truly," "verily") is closest to the Greek. Nevertheless, Adorno wants to make the particle say more than it strictly means by pointing, justifiably, to what it strictly does.

He observes that, while ἦ, understood as *nämlich* (viz., "that is to say"), seeks to express the logic either of "explanation or of affirmation," the clause introduced by the particle creates a *non sequitur* with what precedes it. This conclusion is something of an overstatement,[27] but the gist of his argument is clear enough. Indeed, the very problem of how best to render Homer's surd-like particle backs him up:

> In the minimal meaninglessness of this coordinating particle the spirit of logical-intentional narrative language collides with the spirit of wordless representation that the former is preoccupied with, and the logical form of coordination [literally: "sequence," *Fortführung*] itself threatens to banish the idea, which is not coordinated with anything [more literally: "which does not follow on," *der nicht fortführt*] and is really not an idea any more, to the place where the relationship of

27 The second clause does contain a *hysteron proteron* of sorts, and the particle combination ἦ τοι helps to prepare us for the sequence, while a second conjunction, left out of the translation used by Adorno (and by his English translators), helps to soften the apparent reversal: "these two […] made their way; Odysseus <*for his part*> followed, *but* [αὐταρ] Telemachus led the way." Adorno takes the particle ἦ to look back, not forward, but the rupture with what comes before is palpable either way.

syntax and material dissolves and the material affirms its superiority by belying the syntactic form that attempts to encompass it. (27)

In Adorno's eyes, form and content are at variance in Homeric epic. Logic and description are this as well, and so too are language and image, tendentially speaking. For the tendency of all epic, Adorno insists, is to lose itself in the image, to "forget" itself and its own meaning, by "pull[ing] language itself into the image" and then by "abandoning meaning" altogether (28, 29). Language literally stutters, loses its logical trail, and then ceases to signify at all. Nonsense — the obtuse Real — is not what the poetry recovers; it is what it *produces,* or rather strives to produce, out of a sheer contrast with itself. A struggle ensues — not merely a dynamic or a tension, but a literal "enmity" (*Feindschaft*) between images and content and between meaning and action (28). In the place of narrative sequences, epics "are transformed into mere arenas" of their own historical tendencies, as are all works of literature for Adorno, which in the case of Homeric epic reveals an underlying antagonism "between subjectivity and mythology." The very substance of epic is enlisted in this transformation, which no longer falls within the genre of epic because it has risen to the genre of allegory — the allegory of epic naïveté in all of the latter's innermost fragility. Here, the "historical tendency [just described] becomes visible [*sichtbar*] precisely where the pragmatic and linguistic context reveals its inadequacy [*brüchig sich zeigt*]," which is to say, has revealed itself to be "fragile" and "prone to disintegrate" into fragments (29).

This is not to say that the inadequacies of language and image are solved when they are either named or raised to the level of allegory. They are merely reenacted on a more abstract level once more, as Adorno's own patently inadequate metaphors for vision suggest, for how does one *see* an inadequacy? How can we make visible Homer's "blindness"? Adorno's answer is to point us to the place where the antinomies of language, logic, and meaning are concentrated into "a material element" (27). If earlier he located this material element in the noise of epic, in the present context he locates it in a seemingly nonsensical particle, a mere letter or sound, where "what is real" can "emerge in pure form, undistorted by the violence of classificatory ordering." Language becomes — or rather strives to become — a stupid object again, by returning to the condition from which it had never truly emancipated itself, the condition of being a bearer of meaning while being stripped bare of meaning. The question is not whether language can truly achieve this state of pure and senseless materiality — it cannot: it can at most only intimate it — but how such moments are to be understood: what are they symptomatic of? Here, Homer's "blindness" takes on a particular urgency: it expresses the impossibility of the narrator's self-appointed task and his blind, dogged attempt to achieve it nonetheless (27). Such is the "stupidity" of epic.

And so Adorno's argument comes full circle, in its demonstration that as epic pursues the naïveté of the image and dissolves the bonds of logic and language, it brings about, not a condition of pure imagery or materiality, but rather their approximation: "epic discourse comes to resemble the image" by becoming "a figure of objective meaning emerging from the negation of subjectively rational meaning" (20). Here, language achieves, however briefly, a zero-degree of meaning, fantasy, and speculation. But in touching, as it were, the Real of its own language, Homeric epic at the same time gives us a glimpse of a different view of itself. It reveals its historical conditions of possibility, which epic represents performatively in its proper linguistic substance and in its noisy whirring. The paradoxical result is that epic transforms itself into a theater of its own struggles with matter, form, and content. It puts on show, not meaning, but its failure to abandon meaning altogether, and its inability to achieve the noble simplicity that it allegedly sought after. For "no narrative can partake of truth if it has not looked into the abyss into which language plunges when it tries to become name and image." And, Adorno quickly adds, "Homeric prudence is no exception to this" (27).

We were never modern, and epic was never naïve.[28]

---

28 See Bruno Latour, *We Have Never Been Modern,* trans. Catherine Porter (Cambridge: Harvard University Press, 1993). Thanks to Sean Gurd for helpful conversations about this essay.

Three

'Pataphilological Lacan

Sean Braune

"What is 'Pataphysics?" asks the cover of the *Evergreen Review* in 1960.[1] Alfred Jarry defines 'pataphysics this way: "[']Pataphysics is the science of imaginary solutions, which symbolically attributes the properties of objects, described by their virtuality, to their lineaments."[2] The prefix *pata*, a symbiosis of *meta* and *para*, achieves a lettric instance of liminality that "extend(s) as far beyond metaphysics as the latter extends beyond physics."[3] Jarry emphasizes that the neologism *'pataphysique* should be written with an apostrophe at its beginning to avoid punning on the word — puns such as *patte à physique*, which means "the flair of physics."[4] Christian Bök details several other potential puns, such as *épatée physique* ("astounded physics"), *pas ta physique* ("not your physics"), and

---

1 The *Evergreen Review* dedicated a special issue to 'pataphysics in 1960. Jarry's pseudoscience caused such a groundswell of interest in France that the Collège de 'Pataphysique was formed in 1948.
2 Alfred Jarry, *Exploits and Opinions of Doctor Faustroll, Pataphysician: A Neo-Scientific Novel*, translated by Simon Watson Taylor (Boston: Exact, 1996), 22. Original emphasis.
3 Ibid., 21.
4 Ibid., 119.

puns on Jarry's iconic Father Ubu: "Ubu, for example, is a slapstick comedian (*pataud physique*) of unhealthy obesity (*pâteux physique*)," and so on.[5] 'Pataphysics emphasizes wordplay and stylistic invention through a philological aphasia that reveals what is concealed within language; for this reason, it is already so closely linked to etymology and philology that, as James Zetzel asserts, any philology is already 'pataphilology.[6] Zetzel points out that according to Martianus Capella the god Mercury marries a mortal woman named Philology; but he reconfigures this marriage as a love triangle, since Zetzel situates Philology as a twinned being composed of both philology and 'pataphilology or "Mistress Grammar."

This essay will link 'pataphysical linguistic experiments to the punning style so frequently employed by Jacques Lacan in both *Écrits* (1966) and his spoken seminar. Such a collision will suggest that Lacan's approach to the unconscious is 'pataphysical and his approach to language is 'pataphilological. Lacanian psychoanalysis is notable in part because of its varied influences and its links to the avant-garde. Certainly, Heidegger and Freud are often highlighted as sources for Lacan's thinking, but the French avant-garde of the twentieth century is also a tremendously rich resource for Lacan's vision of psychoanalysis: Salvador Dalí, André Breton, Raymond Queneau, François le Lionnais, and many other avant-gardists are both friends of Lacan and influences for his thinking (both Raymond Queneau and François le Lionnais were members of the Collège de 'Pataphysique). Suffice it to say, Dadaism and Surrealism are dominant influences on Lacan's thinking — Dalí's paranoiac-critical method forms the basis of Lacan's theory of paranoia that he develops in his doctoral dissertation (as I will discuss momentarily) — and there is no way to consider his psychoanalytical formulations as distinct from an underlying

5   Christian Bök, *'Pataphysics: The Poetics of an Imaginary Science* (Illinois: Northwestern University Press, 2002), 27.
6   See James E.G. Zetzel, "The Bride of Mercury: Confessions of a 'Pataphilologist," in *World Philology*, eds. Sheldon Pollock, Benjamin Elman, and Ku-ming Kevin Chang (Cambridge: Harvard University Press, 2014), 62.

absurdist tradition. However, even if Lacan is directly linked to a canonical absurdism, then how is he connected to 'pataphysics? Behind surrealism and dadaism lurks 'pataphysics, and even though Lacan does not discuss Jarry in depth, 'pataphysics offers a fruitful approach to apprehending the lucid in the ludic or the surd in the absurd (*ab* means "away" and *surdus* means "indistinct," "harsh-sounding," "deaf," or "out of tune"). The absurd is an intensification of the surd — an intensification of the harsh-sounding. *Surdus* designates a deafness to reason and is, by necessity, signified by an "out-of-tuneness." I claim that this "out-of-tuneness" requires what Lacan calls a "third ear"[7] to find the sound in the din or the din in the sound. This third ear analysis of the soundings of the absurd is important because it will highlight the ontic ground of Lacan's thought and will clarify his overall psychoanalytical project. Such "clarity" will result in a resituating of the barred subject to its anterior iteration as the *'pataphysical subject*.

Sources and Resources

Both Jarry and Lacan share many influences: they were both inspired by the symbolist poetry of Stéphane Mallarmé — Jarry's Dr. Faustroll has an edition of Mallarmé's *Verse and Prose* on his bookshelf[8] — and, furthermore, Jarry attended Mallarmé's funeral.[9] Lacan's interest in language is inspired by both Mallarmé and James Joyce; Lacan famously attended the first reading of *Ulysses* in 1921. However, the piece of writing that Lacan submits to the James Joyce colloquium in 1978 suggests that the self-proclaimed linkage to Joyce may be more of an unconscious desire than an accurate genealogy:

---

7 Jacques Lacan, *Écrits: The First Complete Edition in English*, trans. Bruce Fink, in collaboration with Héloïse Fink and Russell Grigg (New York: Norton, 2006), 394.
8 Jarry, *Exploits and Opinions of Doctor Faustroll, Pataphysician*, 11.
9 Ibid., 124

> Joyce the Symptom to be understood as *Jésus la caille* (Jesus the quail): it's his name. Could people expect anything else omme (of me, though in French it sounds like *emoi*, emotion)?: I name (which in French sounds like *jeune homme*, young man). If that sounds like "young man," that's a consequence I'd say just one thing about. We're men (*sommes hommes*, phonetically "somzoms").
>
> LOM (i.e., *l'homme*=man): in French that says what it means. You only need to write it phonetically: faunetically he's *eaubscéne* (=obscene). Write it "eaub-," with the *eau* as in *beau* (beautiful), to recall that the beautiful is not otherwise.[10]

After this point, Lacan's note becomes both 'pataphilological and untranslatable:

> Hissecroibeau à écrire comme l'hessecabeau sans lequel hihannappat qui soit ding! d'nom dhom. LOM se lomellise à qui mieux mieux. Mouille, lui dit-on, faut le faire; car sans mouiller pas d'hessecabeau.[11]

This moment is akin to an instance of the "melting" of language that occurs in *Finnegans Wake*. If, as Lacan argues, a "letter always arrives at its destination,"[12] then I would suggest that the address of Lacan's letter was not the Joyce colloquium, but the Collège de 'Pataphysique. Lacan is, in his brief letter on Joyce filled with its malleable French, writing to a tradition of French literary composition that predates Joyce. Even though Lacan never explicitly mentions 'pataphysics, he is keenly aware of Jarry's presence in the French literary canon. In *Écrits*, Lacan mentions Jarry at key points. From the "Seminar on 'The Purloined Letter'": "Caught in the act of unduly imputing to me a transgression of the Kantian critique, the subject, who was well-

---

10 Quoted in Elisabeth Roudinesco, *Jacques Lacan*, trans. Barbara Bray (New York: Columbia University Press, 1994), 374. Her original parentheses.
11 Ibid.
12 Lacan, *Écrits*, 30.

meaning in mentioning my text, is not Father Ubu and does not persist."[13] From "The Direction of the Treatment and the Principles of Its Power": "One can perceive here a sort of involuntary humor, which is what makes the example so valuable. It would have delighted Jarry."[14] From "Kant with Sade": "At the risk of some irreverence, let me, in turn, illustrate the flaw in it with a maxim by Father Ubu that I have modified slightly: 'Long live Poland, for if there were no Poland, there would be no Poles.'"[15]

The most telling example of Lacan's appreciation of Jarry's wordplay is when he considers Jarry's use of *merdre* at the opening of *Ubu Roi*:

> I will illustrate it (the split in the subject) in its greatest opacity with the genius that guided Jarry in his find: the condensation of a simple supplementary phoneme in the illustrious interjection "*merdre*." This is the kind of refined triviality we see in slips of the tongue, flights of fancy, and poetry — a single letter was enough to give the most vulgar French exclamation (*merde*: shit) the ejaculatory value, verging on the sublime, of the place it occupies in the epic of Ubu: that of the Word from before the beginning. Imagine what we could do with two letters! For the spelling, *Meirdre,* gematrially offers us everything promising man will ever hear in his history, and *Mairdre* is an anagram of the verb on which "admirable" is based.[16]

David Macey contextualizes Lacan's interest in playful and absurdist etymologies by pointing out that "as Lacan abandons linguistics for *linguisterie,* a note of parody is introduced: Saussure's *langue* becomes *lalangue* as the article is condensed with

---

13 Ibid., 33.
14 Ibid., 509.
15 Ibid., 647. Lacan is adding "Long live Poland" to Jarry's original: "Because if there weren't any Poland, there wouldn't be any Poles!" From Alfred Jarry, *Ubu Roi*, translated by Beverly Keith and G. Legman (New York: Dover, 2003), 73.
16 Lacan, *Écrits*, 553–54.

the noun to produce an onomatopoeic effect and as linguistic scientificity gives way to splutter."[17] Jarry's experimentation with the French language (which can be seen in relation to Mallarmé) anticipates Lacan's future fascination with *linguisterie* and *lalangue*.[18] As registered in his consideration of Jarry's *merdre* neologism, Lacan situates neologistic puns as the material instances acting, in language, as equivalences of a barring or splitting procedure that occurs in subjectivity. The neologism and the 'pataphysical pun symbolize an event of rupture: they each signify the tattooing procedures of the signifier and the lack-in-being that signifies the subject as requiring a suturing object, which can be understood as the originary lost object or the *objet petit a*.

The ancient Greek word for "symbol" — *sumbolon* — designates a token, or one half of a broken piece of pottery or coin that registers an economic relationship between two citizens: each individual held half of the broken token, with one half signifying a payment owing from that holder to the other. The uniqueness of the word *sumbolon* is that it paradoxically refers to a singular concept through reference to two fragmented parts; conceptually, the *sumbolon* exists as a whole, while its material referents (i.e., the tokens) remain fragmented.[19] The etymology of "symbol" speaks to the ways in which every etymology is only ever a part-story or fragment that does not capture a word-in-itself or language-in-itself.

As I have argued elsewhere,[20] an *etym* — my term for the atom of language — is a model of etymological agency in which language adopts a surprisingly vitalist form and Lacan's puns function as etymistic bombs: they are linguistic instances of the rupture of the signifier that reflect the schism that grounds

---

17 David Macey, *Lacan in Contexts* (London: Verso, 1988), 127.
18 *Lalangue* is Lacan's term for the originary space of polysemous potential from which more normative language emerges.
19 See Nicholas Halmi, *The Genealogy of the Romantic Symbol* (Oxford: Oxford University Press, 2007), 103.
20 See Sean Braune, "From Lucretian Atomic Theory to Joycean Etymic Theory," *Journal of Modern Literature* 33, no. 4 (2010): 167–81, at 174–75.

the barred subject. Put differently, at the limits of language the unconscious begins to reveal itself. This framework or schema links Lacanian psychoanalysis with 'pataphysics and points to closely interrelated goals regarding language. However, I am not the first person to argue for a link between 'pataphysics and psychoanalysis: Sylvain-Christian David insists that a connection exists between 'pataphysics and psychoanalysis in his article that associates Jarry and Freud to Gustav Fechner's psychophysics. David writes that "[t]he title of book II of *Faustroll* (where theoretical temptation shows itself strongest), *Elements of 'Pataphysics* echoes the famous *Elements of Psychophysics* of Fechner."[21] David suggests such a linkage, but does not include the work of Lacan. This paper will address this lack.

Paranoia and the Formation of the Subject

Dalí read Lacan's doctoral thesis *Of Paranoiac Psychosis in Its Relationships to Personality* (*De la psychose paranoïaque dans ses rapports avec la personnalité*) in 1933. The thesis left an impression on Dalí, even though he had already used paranoia to formulate his theory of surrealist artistic production called "the paranoiac-critic method," which he initially theorizes in "L'Ane pourri" or "The Rotten Donkey," an article Lacan had read.[22] The two men, both prominent figures of the surrealist movement, shared a similar interest: Dalí linked paranoia to artistic production and Lacan to its foundational relationship for subjectivity.

---

21 "Le titre du livre II du *Faustroll* (où la tentation théorique se montre la plus forte), *Eléments de [']pataphysique* fait écho aux fameux *Eléments de psychophysique* de Fechner." Sylvain-Christian David, "Pataphysique et psychanalyse," *Europe: Revue litteraire mensuelle* 623–24 (1981): 52–61, at 55. My translation.

22 Dalí praises Lacan's thesis in the *Minotaure* article "Interprétation Paranoïaque-critique" (66). From Salvador Dalí, "Interprétation Paranoïaque-critique de l'Image obsédante 'L'Angélus' de Millet," *Minotaure* 1 (1933): 65–67. Also, see Roudinesco, *Jacques Lacan*, 31.

Dalí describes to André Parinaud the importance of Lacan's dissertation: "Lacan threw a scientific light on a phenomenon that is obscure to most of our contemporaries — the expression: paranoia — and gave it its true significance."[23] The emphasis Dalí mentions in terms of "the expression" — that is, the significance of the word "paranoia" — is a point that Lacan returns to in his first contribution to *Minotaure*:

> However, some of these forms of lived experience, called "morbid," present themselves as particularly fertile modes of symbolic expression, which, though irrational in their very foundation of being, are nonetheless provided with an intentionally eminent signification and feature an elevated tension during communication. They (these morbid forms of lived experience) meet in the psychoses, which I have studied particularly, by conserving the originary and etymologically satisfactory label of "paranoia."[24]

Lacan's emphasis on the "etymological satisfaction" of the word "paranoia" hints at the later emphasis he will place on the signifier in terms of the productive powers of the symbolic order and its effects on subject-formation. The very word "paranoia" as that which is *para* or "beside" *nous* or "mind" indicates that the experience of paranoia presents a kind of doubling of consciousness. In other words, paranoia situates the subject as a subject that is apart from itself, observing the other that exists

---

23 Salvador Dalí, *The Unspeakable Confessions of Salvador Dali,* as told to André Parinaud, trans. Harold J. Salemson (New York: William Morrow, 1976), 140.

24 "Or, certaines de ces formes de l'expérience vécue, dite morbide, se présentent comme particulièrement fécondes en modes d'expression symboliques, qui, pour être irrationnels dans leur fondement, n'en sont pas moins pourvus d'une signification intentionelle éminente et d'une communicabilité tensionelle très élevée. Elles se rencontrent dans des psychoses que nous avons étudiées particulièrement, en leur conservant leur étiquette ancienne et étymologiquement satisfaisante de «paranoïa»." Jacques Lacan, "Le Problème du style et la conception psychiatrique des formes paranoïaques de l'expérience," *Minotaure* 1 (1933), 69. My translation.

inside the self and creating absurdist narratives in the frightening absence of knowledge about this other. Two minds exist in the paranoiac relationship, but these minds are closely linked through processes of surveillance instead of identity — a heightened surveillance of the other.

In Lacan's second contribution to *Minotaure,* he focuses on the impact of paranoia in the brutal murders committed by the Papin sisters.[25] Lacan situates his reading of the Papin crime through his earlier case study of Aimée,[26] which grounds his 1932 dissertation:

Affective ambivalence towards the older sister dictates the *auto-punitive* behavior of the "Aimée case." During its course, Aimée deliriously transfers her loving hatred onto several successive individuals, it is by an effort to liberate her from her primary fixation, but this effort is aborted: each of the persecutors is none other than a new image, always a prisoner of narcissism, of this sister whom the patient creates as her ideal.[27]

---

25 On February 2, 1933, Christine and Léa Papin, maids for the Lancelin family, murdered Madame Lancelin and her daughter. Monsieur Lancelin returned home to find his wife and daughter beaten unrecognizably and the two Papin sisters naked in bed together upstairs.

26 On April 10, 1931, Marguerite Pantaine — Lacan later calls her "Aimée" in his dissertation — attempted to murder the actress Huguette Duflos outside the Théâtre Saint-Georges with a kitchen knife. Pantaine attempted to murder Duflos because she felt, in her delusional state, that the actress was persecuting her. Perhaps ironically, the play that Duflos was to star in on the night of the attempted murder was *Tout va bien* or "Everything's Fine" by Henri Jeanson. Lacan began meeting with Pantaine for his dissertation on June 18, 1931.

27 "L'ambivalence affective envers la sœur aînée dirige tout le comportement *auto-punitif* de notre « cas Aimée ». Si au cours de son délire Aimée transfère sur plusieurs têtes successives les accusations de sa haine amoureuse, c'est par un effort de se libérer de sa fixation première, mais cet effort est avorté: chacune des persécutrices n'est vraiment rien d'autre qu'une nouvelle image, toujours toute prisonnière du narcissisme, de cette sœur don't notre malade a fait son ideal." Jacques Lacan, "Motifs du Crime Paranoïaque: Le Crime des Sœurs Papin," *Minotaure* 3–4 (1933): 25–28, at 28. My translation.

The surrealists interpreted the Papin murders through the logic of Dalí's paranoiac-critic method, while the French media tended to consider the murders as exemplary instances of class struggle — the sisters worked as maids for "bourgeoisie" landowners — and the press tended towards a "sentimental Marxism"[28] in response to these murders. This response was so embedded in French media that the American journalist Janet Flanner writes, in her *Paris Journal*, that "it was not a murder but a revolution," or, at the very least, a "minor revolution."[29] This response to the situation delimits the plenitude of the murders to two dominant interpretations that act as apologies for the Papins' choices to murder their employer's wife and daughter: either their behavior is linked to an underlying paranoia or their behavior is the expression of a lived micro-revolution — a harbinger of the "upcoming" Marxist revolution. Both interpretations are severely limited and do not consider the murder victims or the experience of Monsieur Lancelin. Nonetheless, the event itself highlights the sociocultural similarities between Lacan and surrealism; both Lacan and the surrealist movement privileged a "paranoid interpretation" of the Papin crimes.

Like surrealism, Lacan also has ties to dadaism and some aspects of his personality mirror a dadaist impulse. Roudinesco supports this point and pays particular attention to Lacan's third journey to America in 1975: "Summoning up the surrealist and nihilist ways of his youth," she writes, "he challenged the New World with puns, wordplay, and rages."[30] Lacan's puns and aphorisms can be taken many ways: at an absurdist level, in which case his puns can be negated in much the same manner as Chomsky negates them (after seeing Lacan speak at MIT, Chomsky concluded that Lacan was "a madman"[31]), or, at the

28 Jonathan P. Eburne, *Surrealism and the Art of Crime* (Ithaca: Cornell University Press, 2008), 182.
29 Quoted in ibid., 181.
30 Roudinesco, *Jacques Lacan*, 379.
31 From ibid., 379. Chomsky was responding to Lacan's claim that "[w]e think we think with our brains; personally, I think with my feet. That's the only way I really come into contact with anything solid. I do occasionally think

level of a latent meaning that must be discovered through hermeneutical exegesis, which is the approach of Lacanian theorists like Jacques-Alain Miller, Slavoj Žižek, Bruce Fink, Ellie Ragland-Sullivan, and others. Almost as if supporting Chomsky's assessment of his own mental health, Lacan suggests that his provocative lecturing style adopts a pose of psychosis because "[p]sychosis is an attempt at rigor [...] and in this sense I would say I'm a psychotic, for the sole reason that I've always tried to be rigorous."[32] One of the techniques typically deployed by dadaists is to embrace the ludic and "mad" aspects of life and portray this madness through art, but this "madness" is playful — it represents a childlike mischievousness as well — and this trickster quality can be seen in Lacan's decision to publish his psychological articles on paranoia in a surrealist journal and also in the appearance of his name in the table of contents: in the first issue he appears as "Dr. Lacan." Every other contributor's name features both first and last name without a prefix. Whether this was his decision or the decision of the editor (André Breton) is unimportant because its appearance in *Minotaure* reads as absurdist.

This dadaistic tendency presents itself even at the beginning of his career before he was a licensed psychoanalyst: Lacan later conceals Marguerite Pantaine's identity behind the pseudonym "Aimée," but after he publishes his dissertation on her case, Marguerite declines treatment from Lacan because "she found Lacan too attractive and too much of a clown to be trusted."[33] Almost as if agreeing with Pantaine, David Macey points out that "Lacan's style can overlap with a popular ludism."[34] What do these ludic and "clownish" qualities in Lacan's behavior indicate, and where are the ludic and clownish aspects of Lacanian psychoanalysis? The answer to this question can be found at the

    with my forehead, when I bang into something. But I've seen enough electroencephalograms to know there's not the slightest trace of a thought in the brain." Recounted in ibid., 378–79.

32 Quoted in ibid., 376.
33 Quoted in ibid., 51.
34 Macey, *Lacan in Contexts*, 57.

ground of Lacanian psychoanalysis — a ground that is structured by 'pataphysics and 'pataphilology.

'Pataphysical Mathematics, Lacanian Mathemes, and the Planet Borromeo

Lacan's transition from surrealism to mathematical theory can be discovered in his interest in what he calls "mathemes." The mathemes — a pun on Levi-Strauss's mythemes — develop as a syntax or sign system that can apprehend the logic of the unconscious. The mathemes address two problems for Lacan: 1) they allude to a larger pedagogical apparatus that can assist in the training of future analysts, and 2) they depict a unique and idiosyncratic notation that symbolizes the complexity of Lacanian psychoanalysis. When related to 'pataphysics, the mathemes metaphorically connote "exceptions" to normative mathematics and to the functionality of the symptoms of the unconscious. The idea of the "exception" is vital to Jarry's configuration of 'pataphysics because it links to an imaginary dimension that exists alongside our own in an alternate reality called "ethernity." Christian Bök describes "ethernity" as the space "where the reference of a sign does not describe, but conjures, the existence of the real through the ur of simulation."[35] Much like mathematicians who frequently use imaginary "spaces" to articulate mathematical problems — such as Hamiltonian space in quantum mechanics or phase space in chaos theory — Lacan depicts the spatiality and functionality of the unconscious through a topological space that allows him to model and predict the behavior of the symptom, the subject, and the signifier. The Lacanian signifier exists in a space of ethernity — a space of 'pataphysical exceptionality — and the psychoanalytical clinic, for Lacan, is a 'pataphilological laboratory of *lalangue* and mathemes.

The most infamous topological tool in Lacan's 'pataphysical toolkit is the Borromean knot. The Borromean knot resides

---

35 Bök, *'Pataphysics,* 34–35.

in an ethernity of symptomaticity and subjectivity — the site of collision between the conscious and the unconscious — as a topological object that presents and represents the dynamism of subjectivity and the chaotic weaving and interweaving of the real, imaginary, and symbolic orders. This abyssal event horizon — this Borromean black hole that lurks at the center of ethernity — produces what Lacan calls the *sinthome*, which is the exterior, fourth ring that contains the other three rings (of the symbolic, imaginary, and real) and makes them coherent. Lacan's choice of the word *sinthome* adopts an arcane spelling of "symptom," a decision likely adapted from Heidegger who begins to write *Sein* as *Seyn* (its arcane form) in the mid-1930s.

The *sinthome* acts as Lacan's triumphant conclusion to the foundational structure of paranoia or neurosis. If paranoia situates the basis of subjectivity in his early writings from 1932 and 1933, then it is not until the late 1970s that Lacan's privileging of paranoia is clarified: the fourth ring of the *sinthome* maintains the coherency of the other rings by preventing them from floating freely in the wild wastes of ethernity. The *sinthome* speaks through *lalangue*, and this level of linguistic manipulation is essential to understanding the ways in which 'pataphysics and 'pataphilology act as the grounds of Lacan's lettric experimentation. However, the linkage between Lacan's unique appraisal of linguistics and the linguistics practiced by 'pataphysicians is also found in Lacan's idiosyncratic mathematics. Jarry's Dr. Faustroll regularly employs an absurdist mathematics, such as when he calculates the surface of God.[36] For both Lacan and 'pataphysics in general, it is impossible to separate the mathematical from the linguistic.

Lacan's mathemes imply the "edges" or "exceptions" that exist in the subject. They refer to the functionality of the unconscious, a functionality that cannot be proven or adequately located. The pure abstraction of the unconscious registers it as a kind of ethereal or hauntological exception to the material world. Because the unconscious cannot be sited, it is best understood as either a

36 Jarry, *Exploits and Opinions of Doctor Faustroll, Pataphysician*, 111–14.

presence, an absence, an absent-presence, a present-absence, or an absurd space. Why? Because the unconscious is intrinsically noisy, and its noise is disruptive of the normative patterns of the sonic. The unconscious clangs, bangs, and stammers in the background of the conscious, registering either a kind of existential nihilism (because it points to the pure constructivity of the conscious and the complexity of free will), or an absurdity of existence (because of its illogical and irrational manifestations). As a concept, the unconscious exists apart from and outside of any definition of the logical or the rational; it therefore registers an alternative history of narrativity and pattern recognition. To that end, it is a parasite on the head of hegemony — a 'patasite of pure disruption, dislocation, and disorientation.

Jason Glynos and Yannis Stavrakakis point out that Alan Sokal and Jean Bricmont — in their attack on the use of mathematics in "postmodern" French philosophy[37] — find fault with the "manifest irrelevance" of the mathemes.[38] However, Lacan would likely find the "manifest irrelevance" of the mathemes an asset to his version of psychoanalysis. Lacan himself asks: "[H]asn't the role of psychoanalysts so far been to give themselves over to meaningless enterprises?"[39] If this claim is correct — or as "correct" as a 'pataphysical assertion can be — then how can Lacanian concepts be understood in relation to a direct acknowledgement of their intrinsic relationship to an absurdist tradition of French thought? I do not have the space here to explore the absurdist ground(s) of every Lacanian concept, but, to that end, I will focus on one concept above others: the barred subject. However, I will not consider the barred subject directly. In a sense, any direct apprehension of the barred sub-

---

37 See Alan Sokal and Jean Bricmont, *Fashionable Nonsense: Postmodern Intellectuals' Abuse of Science* (New York: Picador, 1998).

38 Quoted in Jason Glynos and Yannis Stavrakakis, "Postures and Impostures: On Lacan's Style and Use of Mathematical Science," *American Imago* 58, no. 3 (2001): 685–706, at 701.

39 Jacques Lacan, *The Seminar of Jacques Lacan: Book III, The Psychoses 1955–1956*, ed. Jacques-Alain Miller, trans. Russell Grigg (New York: Norton, 1997), 50.

ject is prone to failure because its very "presence" is predicated on a foundational lack-in-being, but I will approach this aporetic concept rather obliquely, i.e., not as a phenomenal category, but as an epiphenomenal category. I will consider the barred subject through its mirror image or inverted existence that can be found in ethernity — an imaginary dimension in which the barred subject is 'pataphysical.

The 'Pataphysical Subject

What is the 'pataphysical subject? Sylvain-Christian David claims: "What is being played out from Ubu to Faustroll is none other than a process of method which stages, on the scene of the writing, a *new subject*."[40] David later calls this "new subject" the *sujet de la [']pataphysique* or the "'pataphysical subject," which signifies a subjectivity that exists beyond both physics and metaphysics as a *pata* construction to every other definition of subjectivity. The 'pataphysical subject exists in ethernity as an absurdist incarnation of the barred subject. This 'pataphysical subject is the result of an implicit emphasis of the ludic over the lucid.[41] In 'pataphysics, the signifier is a grapheme of experimental potential and its laboratory is the printed page.

The dyad of barred subject/'pataphysical subject contains a variety of competitions: presence and absence, rationality and irrationality, reality and surreality. As mentioned earlier, 'pataphysics emphasizes the exceptional that is outside of normative rationality and reality. To stress this dynamic, I would emphasize that *metaphysics is to phenomenology what 'pataphysics is to epiphenomenology*. Where phenomenology situates a subject's apprehension — as cognitive and perceptual — of a world of objects, epiphenomenology highlights the phenomena that

---

40 "Ce qui se joue d'Ubu à Faustroll n'est autre chose qu'un procès de méthode, et que la montée, sur la scène de l'écriture, d'un sujet neuf." Sylvain-Christian David, "Pataphysique et psychanalyse," 56. My translation.
41 Ibid.

exist apart from traditional phenomena. In spatial terms, the 'pataphysical gradually transitions beyond the metaphysical. The epiphenomenological is beyond and outside of that which is apprehended by the barred subject; therefore, the epiphenomenological is only perceivable by the 'pataphysical subject. This notion of epiphenomena is not only dimensional but also linguistic, because certain words and textual limit experiences register as exceptional instances of writing or speaking. For example, linguistic epiphenomena manifest, according to psychoanalysis, as representations of the unconscious: parapraxes or slips of the tongue or the schizophrasic in(ter)ventions of psychotic patients indicate a slippage into *lalangue*.

In his survey of 'pataphysics, Christian Bök argues that there are four epistemic phases in the history of the conflict between science (noetics) and poetry (poetics), a conflict that focuses on the ability to speak the "truth":

> the *animatismic* phase, whose truth involves interpreting signs through an act of *exegesis*; the *mechanismic* phase, whose truth involves disquisiting signs through an act of *mathesis*; the *organismic* phase, whose truth involves implementing signs through an act of *anamnesis*; and the *cyborganismic* phase, whose truth involves deregulating signs through an act of *catamnesis*.[42]

Bök clarifies this fantastical teleology when he insists that "the life sciences, for example, have progressed from the *biomagy* of animatism, through the *biotaxy* of mechanism, through the *biology* of organism, to the *bionics* of cyborganism."[43] I would take his argument further and claim that his four phases can also be considered the four phases that organize — or *self*-organize — the development of a 'pataphysical subject. In the following table, I adapt Bök's schema for the purposes of explicating a 'pataphysical subject:

42 Bök, *'Pataphysics*, 17.
43 Ibid.

Epistemic phase of either noetics/poetics or the 'pataphysical subject	The phase's relation to signs	The acts that structure the phase's relation to truth	The progression or genealogy of the phase
animatismic	interprets	exegesis	biomagy
mechanismic	disquisits	mathesis	biotaxy
organismic	implements	anamnesis	biology
cyborganismic	deregulates	catamnesis	bionics

What Bök calls the "animatismic phase" would designate the psychic arrangement of the mythological associations of animatism through the exegetical effects of the sign, once it has withdrawn from a world of practice. In this understanding of the animatismic, there is an essential endowment of certain powers that ground the 'pataphysical subject, an endowment that designates the 'pataphysical subject as being constructed *by* language itself. In the animatismic phase, reality would be rendered as a representation-machine — and a doubled representation-machine in ethernity — that would be given meaning through the direct exegesis of the sign by way of the magical entification of the grapheme and the phoneme. Language would be subject to a process of biomagy during the animatismic phase. As well, the exegesis of the animatismic phase would imply the existence and necessity of an other (as found in Lacan's mirror stage) where the 'pataphysical subject would be made aware of itself to itself by virtue of the fact that there would be a *semblant* acting as an iteration or reflection of itself and to itself. In other words, the 'pataphysical subject would be *double* in and of itself and move beyond the doubling that would be already present, i.e., the doubling that is already (and intrinsically) present in the barred subject.

Bök's "mechanismic phase" would designate a psychic practice of learning that occurs via mathesis, and these learned tasks would permit a more manageable navigation of reality. The mechanismic necessarily builds on the animatismic like layers of snow and complements the biomagical qualities of the animatismic by mechanizing these earlier representational processes. The mechanismic phase points to the origins of technology while the mathetic function relates to an education that properly integrates the 'pataphysical subject in ethernity.

What Bök calls the "organismic phase" would situate the resulting psychic matrix of the subject's habitude and habituation in its ecosystem or environment. During this stage, the 'pataphysical subject would be "constructed" as an effect of parasitic invasion: language would implement itself inside its host — it would suture onto the "walls" of the subject's speech centers — and this siting of the embedded language-parasite would likewise require an anamnestic function (of remembering) to ground its own self-organization.[44] Remembering is essential — as opposed to a form of forgetting — because the subject must, by necessity, *recall* the illusion of its own fantasmatic coherency. The fantasy of the subject's own existence as a holistic totality structures the misrecognition of both the subject as *a* subject (in a reality-construction) and the subject's iterative manifestations in ethernity as a 'pataphysical subject.

Finally, Bök's "cyborganismic phase" would locate the futurity of the 'pataphysical subject, a futurity that occurs at the terminus of the posthuman when the full status of the technological has taken hold. This situation calls for the deregulation of the anthropocentric sign and the emergence of a new cyborg-sign. Psychoanalysis would have little merits in the treatment of the cyborg unconscious, thereby requiring 'pataphysics to take over the work of the clinic. After being repressed for so long, 'pataphysics would be the only applicable discourse that could potentially heal the symptoms of the cyborg unconscious. The catamnestic function of the cyborganismic acts as the historical record of the patient after the onset of illness, which is, in this case, subjectivity itself ("subjectivity" is to be understood here as the result of the various infections created by postmodernism and poststructuralism).

---

44 I explore the idea of a language-parasite and a 'patasite versus a parasite in *Language Parasites: Of Phorontology* (Earth: punctum books, 2017).

Extending this schema from Bök's original context of the shared history of noetics and poetics to the evolution of the 'pataphysical subject, the totality of the above table presents the various generations of specific aspects of this subject: the 'pataphysical subject moves through an animatismic phase of exegetical interpretation; it transitions to the mechanismic phase that disquisits signs through mathesis; it progresses to the organismic phase that implements new signs through anamnesis; and, finally, it finds its apotheosis in the cyborganismic phase that deregulates signs through catamnesis. The transition moves toward the presentation of the illness of the sign, an illness that signals the necessity to transit from reality to complete ethernity.

However, I should point out that each of these "phases" registers as differing perspectives of the same underlying subject position: the contemporary situation of the iterations of subjectivity find themselves mirrored in the absurdity of the 'pataphysical subject. Put differently, living in the contemporary and technologized Western world is patently absurd. As humans limp into the early part of the twenty-first century, we have ignored many of the absurd "truths" (or upcoming problems that register as repressed "truths") of our existence as a species, i.e., we appear to be heading towards an ecological catastrophe that certain powerful factions of Western governments feel compelled to call "a hoax"; access to clean water is a serious concern; having enough arable soil for growing crops to feed a multiplying population is a high-priority problem; fascism appears to be re-emerging in world politics; talk of nuclear re-armament is rearing its head again; race relations and gender relations appear to be halting their forward momentum; the cure for the common cold is nowhere in sight; and there are many other examples of the absurdity of our contemporary situation. I call these examples "absurd" because these problems were not supposed to be concerns in the twenty-first century. *The Jetsons* promised robots and spaceships. Where are my robots and spaceships?

Taking the science fiction of the past hundred years into account, we should now be — as a species — flying into the future with rocket packs and flying cars. Instead, our forward momentum has been halted because of the peristaltic cyclings of human invention and intervention. Humanity progresses in bursts and convulsions as the heaves of technological vomit strike the floor of history. Now, we are stagnating in a stage of dry heaving. 'Pataphysics calls attention to these absurd situations by calling out to activists living in reality and asks them to construct prospective ethernities that can help us escape the seemingly imminent event of the total extinction of the human race. Let us escape on this 'pataphysical spaceship together. This proposal is not a socialist daydream or a fascist's nightmare. We need creative thinking. We need new subjects and new identities that can engage exterior "realities" or "ethernities" in creatively novel and ethical ways.

Floating in Ethernity

'Pataphysics presents the absurdity of existence while psychoanalysis attempts to interpret this same absurdity through the "logic" of the symptom or *sinthome*. Where 'pataphysics reveals the absurd through parody, psychoanalysis reveals the absurd through pathology. Therefore, if the absurd, as a symptom of the ludic, lurks behind the barred subject, then the ludic becomes surprisingly lucid. In this case, the absurd becomes constitutive of a new realism: *if the conscious is phenomenal, then the unconscious is epiphenomenal.* If this situation is true, then it demands a study of the exceptional. This study of the exceptions that result from the theorization of a 'pataphysical subject require a consideration of both the *expected results* (as phenomena) and the *excepted results* (as epiphenomena). Such an understanding of 'pataphysical subjectivity necessitates asking the question of what is *exceptional* in psychoanalysis. The obvious answer to this question would site the symptom as the exception of apparently "healthy" psychic processes. In this schema, the symptom is the exception of *both* the barred subject and the symptom. Obviously, when considering the various transits and transitions between reality and ethernity, a variety of proliferating states and stages emerge — these states and stages present an overall picture of pure complexity because the necessity of epiphenomena is often unconsidered by normative models of physics and rationality. 'Pataphysics rejects the standard models and logic of physics in order to engage in the surrational. In the surrational, the phenomenal has no purchase on the epiphenomenal, which leads to the development of *epiphenomenology* (as opposed to phenomenology), an approach that provides different and bizarre theories for all entities (known and unknown) that exist beyond the narrow confines of the "human."

'Pataphysics coalesces the noetic and the poetic in order to interrogate the meaning that exists in the imaginary *topos* of ethernity. Ethernity exists (or *ek-sists*) beyond and beside (*pata*) traditional "reality." I would go further and argue that the Lacanian real *only* exists in ethernity because, as Lacan maintains, "[t]he real is not of this world."[45] Luke Thurston points out that Lacan's theorization of the Borromean knot encompasses that which is of the world and *also* that which is not of the world.[46] David Macey claims that Lacan's teaching, "with its *dénouement* in an unworldly Real, its interstellar mission to *la planète Borroméean*,"[47] requires contextualization. I would insist that Lacan's mission to the "Planet Borromeo" can only be accomplished in a spaceship that has been built by 'pataphysicians while being accompanied by his fellow spacemen (such as le Lionnais, Queneau, and Dr. Faustroll).

If nothing else, psychoanalysis has demonstrated that certain words can become trapped in the psyche and these trapped signs can produce considerable distress. Suzanne Hommel, one of Lacan's patients in 1974, recounts that she experienced persecution at the hands of Gestapo. In her analysis, Lacan treated her illness as being partly caused by the *word* "Gestapo" (as a

---

45 Quoted in Luke Thurston, "Specious Aristmystic: Joycean Topology," in *Lacan: Topologically Speaking*, eds. Ellie Ragland and Dragan Milovanovic, 314–27 (New York: Other Press, 2004), 315.

46 Ibid., 318.

47 Macey, *Lacan in Contexts*, 320.

plea) and so he reached across to her and caressed her cheek. Lacan heard the phrase *geste à peau* (or "touch the skin") and deployed a gentle and curative gesture. Hommel describes this moment as the turning point of her analysis.[48] This "cure" could only be permitted by Lacan adopting the guise of a 'pataphilologist, which would render him as a pataphilological psychoanalyst. His "aberrant" relationship to language and his willingness to engage in a critical and clinical embrace of the absurdities of existence positions him as one of the foremost 'pataphysicians of French twentieth-century thought.

48 Hommel describes this encounter in Gérard Miller's documentary *Rendez-vous chez Lacan* (2011).

Four

Going Soft on Canidia:
The *Epodes,* an Unappreciated Classic

Paul Allen Miller

ritten during the early years of Augustus's consolidation of power at Rome (the period sometimes, though misleadingly, called the beginning of the empire), many of Horace's *Epodes* display an aggressive combination of sexual, political, and social humor with connections reaching back to the archaic period of Greek poetry. Among the objects of invective in the collection is a certain Canidia, who is attacked in *Epodes* 3, 5, and 17 (she is attacked, also, in *Satires* 1.8, 2.1, and 2.8).[1] In two other *Epodes,* 8 and 12, Horace writes about his own impotence, caused, he says, by the agency of an unnamed old woman (*anus*). I suggest that this *anus* can be associated with Canidia. If that's true, the consequence is that *Epodes* 3, 5, 8, 12, and 17 make a single sequence in which attacks on the putative other are inseparable from confessions of impotence, both sexual and otherwise. Canidia, the ultimate target of Horace's iambic venom,[2] is not the symbol of his poetic power

---

1 David Armstrong, *Horace* (New Haven: Yale University Press, 1989), 60–62.
2 Poems 5 and 17 are among the longest of the collection.

(as Lycambes is for Archilochus and Bupalus for Hipponax) so much as the ironic reflection of his powerlessness — symbolized, here, by his castration.³ The collection ends with Horace's sudden surrender to the superior power of Canidia's *mala carmina* and her declaration that she will not refrain from taking her vengeance lest all her power be held in vain (17.37–41, 74–81). This network of associations, in turn, extends beyond the series to the other poems in the collection, which are linked to it through a variety of textual and thematic echoes as well as through direct juxtaposition.

Using this network of themes as my guide, I argue that Horace uses irony in the *Epodes* both to discipline those he sees as inimical to the emerging political order and to create a sphere of indeterminacy and hence potential freedom (*libertas*), for himself and ultimately for the self writ large. In seeking to discipline others, he follows his iambic predecessors Archilochus and Hipponax (but also Lucilius and Catullus). But he goes beyond them by creating a sphere of indeterminacy or multivalence, delimiting an interior space that makes possible the cultivation of a private ethical self, which is fundamentally different from the iambic personas of his archaic predecessors or from the literary construct of Callimachus's *Iambi*. This is a self that, while intimately connected to its symbolic community through ties of patronage, friendship, and politics, always finds itself at one remove from that community, a self that folds back on itself to create a space of reflection and difference.⁴

Despite being poems about impotence, poems 8 and 12 feature some of the most violent invective of the entire collection.

3   Ellen Oliensis, "Canidia, Canicula, and the Decorum of Horace's Epodes," in *Horace: Odes and Epodes,* ed. Michèle Lowrie, 160–87 (Oxford: Oxford University Press, 2009), 174.

4   Carl Joachim Classen, "Principi et Concetti Morali nelle Satire du Orazio," in *Atti del convegno di Venosa: 8–15 Novembre 1992,* eds. Scevola Mariotti et alii, 111–28 (Venosa: Edizioni Osanna Venosa, 1993), 117; F. Citti, *Studi Oraziani: Tematica e Intertestualità* (Bologna: Pàtron Editore, 2000), 127; R.L.B. McNeill, *Horace: Image, Identity, and Audience* (Baltimore: Johns Hopkins University Press, 2001), 127; Kenneth J. Reckford, *Recognizing Persius* (Princeton: Princeton University Press, 2009), 109–10.

If Horace's invective against Canidia, the only woman to receive such sustained abuse in the *Epodes,* and indeed in the entire Horatian corpus, can be read as an inverted reflection of his own *impotentia,* then, I would contend, every moment of other-directed, disciplinary irony also has the potential to become a moment of self-ironization in which the aim and object of the invective — in its very separateness from the speaking subject — becomes problematized in the moment of its utterance.[5] Such self-ironization, in turn, establishes a necessary distance between the speaker within the poem and the speaker of the poem, forcing us to confront their lack of coincidence.[6]

Moreover, poems 3, 5, 8, 12, and 17 — the Canidia and impotence poems — are interlocked with a series of political poems (1, 7, 9, and 16) as well as with poem 4, a poem featuring the most explicit example of invective irony being reflected back on the speaker himself, since it is an attack on the social climber.[7] That social climber is himself a symptom of the civil discord that forms the object of the more explicitly political poems, even as in certain key respects he recalls Horace himself. The *Epodes,*

5 Cf. Oliensis, "Canidia, Canicula, and the Decorum of Horace's *Epodes,*" 176, 179, 185.
6 Thus, Joel C. Relihan contends that Horatian satire becomes a form of self-parody ("The Confessions of Persius," *Illinois Classical Studies* 14 [1989]: 148-49). See also Maria Plaza, *The Function of Humour in Roman Verse Satire: Laughing and Lying* (Oxford: Oxford University Press, 2006), 169-70, 208. While this facet of Horace's satirical work has become increasing recognized, it has been less discussed concerning the *Epodes.*
7 Armstrong, *Horace,* 63-64. While there continues discussion about the precise nature of the arrangement of the *Epodes* and which of the various schemas identified should take precedence in the reader's mind (and it is possible for there to be more than one), there is general agreement that Horace has taken care with the placement of the individual poems. See R.W. Carruba, *The Epodes of Horace: A Study in Poetic Arrangement* (The Hague: Mouton, 1969); Lindsey Watson, *A Commentary on Horace's Epodes* (Oxford: Oxford University Press, 2003), 15-16, 20-23; David Mankin, "The Epodes: Genre, Themes, and Arrangement," in *A Companion to Horace,* ed. Gregson Davis, 93-104 (Malden: Wiley-Blackwell, 2010), 101-3; Timothy S. Johnson, *Horace's Iambic Criticism: Casting Blame (Iambikē Poiēsis)* (Leiden: Brill, 2012), 20n36, 229. On the close relations between the political poems 1, 7, 9 and 16, see Carruba, *The Epodes of Horace,* 32-38.

then, while for many years the most neglected part of Horace's corpus, show themselves to be poems of great subtlety and complexity. These poems feature some of the poet's most explicit invective and, in the impotence poems, some of his most disturbing sexual imagery. Invective and sexual imagery are both features of the iambic tradition from Archilochus through Catullus. But in Horace's hands that tradition also becomes a complex medium for refined artistry and ironic reflection, without losing its capacity to disturb and discomfit, even as it is adapted to the realities of a new era.[8]

I should define more precisely what I mean by irony, since it is often used in a vague and imprecise manner. Quintilian at 6.2.15 defines it as a form of speech that produces an *intellectum* or "understood meaning" that is at variance (*diversum*) from what it says (*dicit*). Irony is, on this definition, the production of an *intellectum* that does not coincide with the *dictum,* and hence is dependent on the simultaneous presence of at least two distinct levels of meaning: the literal and the ironic. On the pragmatic level, the ironic statement participates in this multiplicity of meanings not simply through the observed fact that multiple possible readings can coexist within a given text, but specifically through a moment of performative self-awareness that signals a conscious act of doubling an initial literal sense with a second, divergent sense. As everyone from Quintilian to de Man recognizes, irony is the *intentional* production of multiple meanings and the ironic speaker must signal that intentionality through a rhetorical wink or nod.[9] Yet this performative moment of self-consciousness, as opposed to either the *dictum* ("utterance") to

---

8   Lindsey Watson, "The *Epodes*: Horace's Archilochus," in *Cambridge Companion to Horace,* ed. Stephen Harrison, 93–104 (Cambridge: Cambridge University Press, 2007), 93; John Henderson, "Horace Talks Rough and Dirty: No Comment (*Epodes* 8 and 12)," in *Horace: Odes and Epodes,* ed. Michèle Lowrie, 401–17 (Oxford: Oxford University Press, 2009), 409; Johnson, *Horace's Iambic Criticism,* 21, 36.

9   Quintilian 8.54; Paul de Man, "The Rhetoric of Temporality," in *Blindness and Insight: Essays in the Rhetoric of Contemporary Criticism,* 2nd rev. ed. (Minneapolis: University of Minnesota Press, 1983), 220–23.

which it is joined or the *intellectum* ("understanding") to which it gives rise, falls outside the signification produced by the statement per se. That moment is not a property of the words themselves. Rather, it is a property of the enunciation, of the act as performed in a given speech or textual context.¹⁰ In any ironic speech act, there is a gap between meaning one and meanings two, three, four, etc., which must be made explicit. The ironist, who says one thing but means another, is ultimately then the master of non-meaning, of literal nonsense, of the gaps between meanings, which must be recognized if the irony is to be perceived.¹¹ Horace is, in this sense, a master ironist, precisely because there is a level at which he makes no sense.¹²

In general terms, we may say that Horace uses irony as an other-directed disciplinary form consonant with a traditional understanding of the function of invective in the ancient world. In this usage, the moment of non-meaning becomes a form of violence, which is deployed against the other. The violence of other-directed irony is not a function of multiple meanings per se, but of the gap between those meanings, of the moment in which we say so and so is not X but really Y.¹³ But in the midst of this use, Horace also creates a zone of non-meaning or aporia that defines a new space of interiority, a gap between the public and private self, between the speaking and spoken subject, between being and seeming. This new space of interiority is ultimately coterminous with what will become the new, ideal form of elite Augustan subjectivity and, as such, comes to serve as a distant ancestor of what modernity understands as the private

10 Michel Foucault, *L'archéologie du savoir* (Paris: Gallimard, 1969), 39–40.
11 Avital Ronell, *Stupidity* (Urbana: University of Illinois Press, 2002), 97–99.
12 Ellen Oliensis, *Horace and the Rhetoric of Authority* (Cambridge: Cambridge University Press, 1998), 17; R.L.B. McNeill, *Horace: Image, Identity, and Audience* (Baltimore: Johns Hopkins University Press, 2001), 50–51; Henderson, "Horace Talks Rough and Dirty," 410.
13 On the violence of satire, iambic, and invective, see Catherine M. Schlegel, *Satire and the Threat of Speech: Horace's Satires Book 1* (Madison: University of Wisconsin Press, 2005), 4, and Catherine Keane, *Figuring Genre in Roman Satire* (Oxford: Oxford University Press, 2006), 49.

sphere.[14] Irony becomes a kind of wall that makes possible the formation of what Pierre Hadot would term, when referring to the Stoic philosophy of the imperial period, the citadel of the self.[15] As the study of words and what they mean, philology has then always been the province of the literal. It relies on semantics, grammar, or a historical reconstruction of the horizon of expectations. Too often, it has posed the problem of meaning in the following terms: "if I had said, x, y, or z, under conditions a, b, or c, I would have meant the following." It has assumed that meaning is straightforward and that if only we had enough of the right kinds of information, we could establish it. Implicit in that assumption is the idea that we are all the same: that the speaking subject is a constant, which is plugged into different historical and linguistic circumstances, and which within those constraints then produces universalizable intelligible meaning.

Irony, consequently, has always proved particularly challenging for philology, because the ironic speaker does not mean what he says. Thus, when confronted with irony, the first impulse of the philologist is always to try to determine what the speaker "really meant," to reduce irony to sincerity and hence literality. I will always remember a conversation with a brilliant scholar who professed to be interested in irony. I asked him about certain famous passages in Ovid's exilic poetry where the poet avows his undying devotion to Augustus. Some read these passages as flattery, others as irony. I posed the question to this highly intelligent and sophisticated young man, "How can you tell the difference?" All these years later, I remember his

[14] Kenneth J. Reckford, *Recognizing Persius* (Princeton: Princeton University Pres), 38; Paul Allen Miller, "Discipline and Punish: Horatian Satire and the Formation of the Self," in *Texts and Violence in the Roman World*, eds. Monica R. Gale and J.H.D. Scourfield, 87–109 (Cambridge: Cambridge University Press, 2018). One of the implicit corollaries of this argument is the paradox that the form of subjectivity that we associate with democracy and human rights only initially became possible under conditions of autocracy.

[15] Pierre Hadot, *La citadelle intérieure: Introduction aux Pensées de Marc Aurèle* (Paris: Fayard, 1992).

response: "It all depends on what Ovid really meant." He was a philologist.

But irony is always in some sense meta-philological, paraphilological, or even 'pataphilological. A 'pataphilogist would read not only literal meaning, but also the nods, winks, and moments of radical non-meaning that occur in the midst of irony's semantic plurivocity. Ironic meaning by definition produces an *intellectum* that is *diversum* from its *dictum*. Irony, in other words, is founded on its own internal difference, its self-division. Any reading that seeks to close that difference is inherently un-ironic, is inherently "untrue." Irony, as Sean Gurd so eloquently put it to me (*per litteras*), "eats its own children." Only a 'pataphilological perspective, at once profoundly philological in its attention to linguistic detail and deliberately perverse in its rejection of all gestures of closure, in its attention to the irreducible materiality of language, in its refusal of all reductions to the ideal and universal, to "meaning," could do justice to irony's cannibalistic instincts. This is the type of reading, I want to argue, that Horace's *Epodes* demands.

• • •

Before examining in more detail the connections between the Canidia poems, the impotence poems, and their collective relations with the more political poems in the *Epodes,* I want to begin by reading *Epode* 3, in many ways the ironic core of the collection. Of the poems in the collection where Canidia appears by name, this one seems the least significant. It is primarily concerned with the poet's gastric distress caused by Maecenas serving a dish heavily laced with garlic. Yet, this seemingly minor poem on an off-color subject is, in fact, of particular importance since it is the only one in which Canidia and Maecenas both appear. Thus, Poem 3, from a structural point of view, represents the nodal point where the political sequence and the Canidia/impotence poems come together.

The poem begins with an exclamation on garlic as an appropriate punishment for parricides. It is, says Horace, a potion more noxious than Socrates' hemlock. The hyperbole is so over the top that it is impossible to take literally. We have all eaten garlic, but few of us have died from it. Literal truth is not a viable option. Enter Canidia.

> What kind of venom rages in my guts? Has viper's blood stewed into these greens deceived me, or has Canidia trafficked in evil feasts?[16]

While there has been much speculation about Canidia's identity from Porphyrion to the present, some of it quite suggestive of the way this sole recurring female character in Horace's *Epodes* and *Satires* might have been received by its initial audience, none of it is conclusive. Canidia has no identity attested outside of the Horatian corpus. Even if we assume her name represents a pseudonym for a real person — a large assumption — that person is never made clear.[17] Canidia is a signifier without a clearly recognized signified, a kind of fantasy object who, on the linguistic level, can receive whatever meaning the poet or reader wishes to attribute to her. She is, in the end, the sum total of the poetic contexts in which she appears. Canidia's initial role in *Epode* 3 is to serve as the object of gratuitous invective. She is the iambic target *par excellence.* There is no reason intrinsic either to the poem itself or to her extra-poetic "reality" why the name *Canidia* should be associated with poison, vipers, or severe gastric distress. Canidia did not serve or prepare the offending dish, nor was she present at the meal. If this poem were read outside the collection, you could substitute almost any name and the poem would be just as effective. If, however, we look at Canidia in the context of the lines coming before and after this passage,

16 *Quid hoc veneni saevit in praecordiis?*
    num viperinus his cruor
  incoctus herbis me fefellit, an malas
    Canidia tractavit dapes? (3.5–8).

17 Even if we accept Porphyrion's identification of Canidia with Gratidia, the sole ancient evidence we have, all we are told is that she was a Neapolitan maker of ointments and a witch, in short, she is Canidia.

as well as the larger collection, a more complex and interesting set of associations appears. In many ways, Canidia functions as the placeholder of the ironic. She is the moment of joining between separate, even opposed, but nonetheless intertwined sets of meanings. It is through her presence that Horace's impotence becomes associated with both his role as an iambic blame poet and with Maecenas as metonym for the larger political world depicted in poems 1, 7, 9, and 16.

Let us try then to describe more precisely the context in which Canidia takes her shape within this poem. If we look just a line above our quoted passage in *Epode* 3, we find the expostulation *o dura messorum ilia!* ("oh the tough guts of reapers!," 3.4). On one level, this phrase simply acknowledges garlic as a peasant food and contrasts Horace's refined (Callimachean) innards with the intestinal fortitude of the typical agricultural laborer. On another, however, it implies that Horace suffers from *mollitia*, the opposite of *duritia*, implying not only refined softness but also effeminacy and even impotence.[18] This association whereby the *dura ilia* ("tough guts" but also "hard loins," — *ilia* can mean both) of the reapers contrasts with the implied *mollia ilia* ("tender guts" or "soft loins") of the poet[19] provides a subtle linkage between the present text and poems 8 and 12, which, as we have already noted above, deal explicitly with sexual impotence, and which, as we will argue below, are to be read in conjunction with the Canidia poems, 3, 5, and 17. Thus, a poem whose primary object appears to be to unleash a torrent of presumably good-humored invective against Maecenas for serving Horace an over-spiced dish, and whose secondary object is to inveigh against Canidia, takes on a self-ironizing edge where Horace becomes an impotent and self-reflective, rather than a violent and other-directed, iambist. This set of associations in turn implicates *Epode* 3 in a much broader field of associations that spreads throughout the collection.

18 Emily Gowers, *The Loaded Table: Representations of Food in Roman Satire* (Oxford: Oxford University Press, 1993), 293.
19 See Catullus 11.20, *ilia rumpens*.

Horace, it turns out, is a softy, an odd pose for the wielder of iambic venom who is normally associated with masculine sexual aggression. Who precisely then is being made fun of here? Maecenas? Canidia? The poet himself? The answer, of course, is "yes." This iambic dart swerves to penetrate its thrower and inflicts no small amount of collateral damage on the way. To the astute reader of the collection, this turn of events will come as no surprise. The poet's *mollitia* was already highlighted in *Epode* 1. There, in a poem that looks forward to Actium, the poet contrasts Maecenas's willingness to undergo any danger for Caesar (1.3-4) with Horace's own nature as *imbellis ac firmus parum* ("unwarlike and none too firm," 1.16). For the reader familiar with the conventions of elegy, such a pose would have nothing surprising about it. *Mollitia* is an occupational hazard for many of Horace's contemporary poets.[20] Nonetheless, the image of softness and refined passivity sorts ill with that of the hypermasculine poet of iambic, often priapic, violence. All the same, it is a recurring pattern within the *Epodes*. In *Epode* 14, Maecenas directly accuses Horace of *mollis inertia*. There, it is for his failure to complete the *Epodes*, but the association echoes the charge of sexual impotence made against the poet just two poems earlier, as well as in *Epode* 8.[21] Now, neither lines 1.16 nor 3.4 deal explicitly with Horace's sexual inadequacy, as we will see in poems 8 and 12, but we need not wait until poem 8 before the topic rears its head (or fails to). At the end of poem 3, the next time Maecenas is mentioned after the opening of poem 1, Horace wishes on his friend and patron sexual failure, although admittedly of a different sort:

---

20 Duncan Kennedy, *The Arts of Love: Five Essays in the Discourse of Roman Love Elegy* (Cambridge: Cambridge University Press, 1993), 31–33; Catherine Edwards, *The Politics of Immorality in Ancient Rome* (Cambridge: Cambridge University Press, 1993), 63–66, 93.

21 See Oliensis, "Canidia, Canicula, and the Decorum of Horace's *Epodes*," 182–83.

> But if ever you will have strongly desired any such thing,
> Maecenas you joker, I pray that the girl will ward off your
> kiss with her hand and will sleep at the very edge of the bed.[22]

Thus, the poet who begins this epode with the image of a criminal who strangles his father using his own *impia manus* concludes it with bad breath and an image of frustrated desire. Maecenas's mouth replaces the paternal *guttur* (3.2) and the courtesan's *manus* with that of the tough-minded criminal (3.1). This ironic doubling both implicitly softens the opening image and places the poet's hand on his symbolic father's throat ("just kidding, of course — *really*"). In the end, though, it is only the tough peasants of the Italic countryside who have hard loins (*dura ilia*) and the ability to use them. Horace's are soft and Maecenas's might as well be. In between, we find Canidia and the question of whether she is in some way responsible for the poet's discomfort: *an malas/ Canidia tractavit dapes* ("or has Canidia trafficked in evil feasts," 3.8)?

At no point, however, does this question represent an actual request for information. It can only be read rhetorically and never truly literally, except to the extent that the literal meaning must be present for the figurative levels — the levels on which the *intellectum* remains *diversum* from the *dictum* — to come into view. The poet's ironic rhetorical question is at once irrelevant to the basic information *Epode* 3 ostensibly seeks to convey ("damn you, Maecenas, and your spicy cuisine") and enfolds that information in a much larger associative field that requires us to reread this seemingly simple poem in an ever expanding set of contexts, since naming Canidia evokes the poems in which we have either already met her (*Satires* 1.8) or will soon (*Epodes* 5 and 17). By the same token, however, it is only the presence of a moment of performative non-meaning, of the ac-

---

22 *at si quid umquam tale concupiveris,*
  iocose Maecenas, precor
manum puella savio opponat tuo
  extrema et in sponda cubet. (3.19–22)

tual difference between these possible meanings, exemplified in the very gratuitous nature of Canidia's naming, that ensures that these various levels of signification are neither collapsed into a single "true meaning" (i.e., Horace really meant X, the rest is just rhetorical window dressing, please ignore the man behind the curtain) or sublimated into some kind of grand synthesis (e.g., the political, the sexual, or the biographical as the master form of all readings).

But in fact, there is another associative chain that further implicates Horace, Maecenas, and Canidia in the same field. Horace develops a lengthy comparison between the person who confected the offending dish and Medea's poisoning of Creusa as well as her subsequent escape on a winged serpent or dragon (*serpente...alite,* 3.14). The appearance of the winged serpent pulls through an earlier reptilian image implicit in the viper's blood. At the same time, the image of the fire consuming Creusa evokes the burning sensation searing the poet's innards, anticipating the next couplet's image of the Dog Star baking Horace's native Apulia (3.15–16). Each of these associative chains creates an alternative *intellectum* that both reinforces the structure of the poem and reveals it as always meaning more than it says. At the same time, the dissonance between the lowly content of the epode — indigestion caused by overly spiced food — and the high-flown mythological exempla creates still another level of metapoetic irony.

When Horace later writes "nor ever did so great a heat/exhalation/warmth/ardor of the stars settle on parched Apulia,"[23] the sharp shift back into an autobiographical register forces the reader to reengage with what he knows about the historical Horace, not as something external to the poem but as an integral part of its structure. *Siderum,* moreover, is poetic plural for the *sidus fervidum* or the Dog Star, in Latin the Canicula,

---

23 nec tantus umquam siderum insedit vapor
    siticulosae Apuliae (3.15–16)

the brightest star in the constellation Canis.²⁴ Thus, *siderum*, by evoking *Can<u>icu</u>la*, echoes phonetically (on the level of the *intellectum* but not the *dictum*) the Horatian neologism *sit<u>icu</u>losae*. Likewise, the <u>*Canis*</u> and the <u>*Canicula*</u> themselves evoke <u>*Canidia*</u>, who is posited as the source of the heat melting the poet's soft innards, but whose scorching fire is on the level of diction transformed into "thirsty Apulia," the poet's parched place of birth. But the key word here is *vapor*. Insofar as one of its commonly accepted meanings is an "exhalation," the burning heat of the Apulian Canis becomes the channel through which Horace's inflamed guts at the beginning of the poem metamorphose into Maecenas's frustrated loins at its end: a noxious vapor rising from within. Moreover, insofar as we know that the dog and the wolf were common figures for the iambist,²⁵ the *vapor* of *Canis/Canidia* becomes a figuration of the voice of the iambist himself, the foul exhalation of parched Apulia.²⁶ Horace's dyspepsia is transformed into Canidia's black magic, her *mala carmina* ("curses," but also "libelous, personal attacks," an ambiguity that parallels the meanings of *epodē*, "incantations" but also "a form of iambus").²⁷ Those *mala carmina*, which we see exhibited in *Epode* 5, are then compared to the burning heat of Medea's poi-

---

24 David Mankin, *Horace: Epodes* (Cambridge: Cambridge University Press, 1995), ad loc; Watson, *A Commentary on Horace's Epodes*, ad loc.

25 Paul Allen Miller, *Lyric Texts and Lyric Consciousness: The Birth of Genre from Archaic Greece to Augustan Rome* (London: Routledge, 1994), 28–29; Renaud Gagné, "A Wolf at the Table: Sympotic Perjury in Archilochus," *Transactions of the American Philological Association* 139, no. 2 (Autumn 2009): 251–74 , at 262–65.

26 On the canine motif, uniting poems 1–7 as well as 12, 15 16, and 17, see Julia Nelson Hawkins, "The Barking Cure: Horace's 'Anatomy of Rage' in *Epodes* 1, 6, and 16," *American Journal of Philology* 135, no. 1 (Spring 2014): 57–85 , at 58, 74n59, 79n74. When added to the Canicular motif in poem 3, the Canis/Canidia becomes central to Horace's portrait of the iambic enterprise. On the Dog Star as associated with Archilochus, disease, female lust, and male impotence — all motifs in the *Epodes* — see Tom Hawkins, "This Is the Death of the Earth: Crisis Narrative in Archilochus and Mnesiepes," *Transactions of the American Philological Association* 139, no. 1 (Spring 2009): 1–20, at 5–9.

27 See Oliensis, "Canidia, Canicula, and the Decorum of Horace's Epodes," 171.

soned gifts, which are in turn identified with the heat of the Dog Star in Apulia or the scorching breath of that other Apulian dog, Horace, who in turn prays that his own searing exhalation becomes the offending *spiritus* of Maecenas himself, from which his *puella* must shield herself with a hand (*manus*) that necessarily recalls the one that crushed the paternal throat (*guttur*) at the opening of the poem. In the end, we no longer have a clearly delineated set of speaking subjects and their respective objects of invective, but a kind of circulating metapoetic irony in which the poet speaks against what he himself appears to embody in his speech, becoming both one with and opposed to Canidia and, through her, identified with Maecenas himself.[28]

• • •

There is no clearer example of this self-ironizing phenomenon than in the immediately following poem, *Epode* 4. On the one hand, this is among the most strongly iambic poems in the collection. It has a clearly delineated target of invective, and it squarely claims the iambic poet's right to exercise his *liberrima indignatio* on behalf of and as the voice of the larger community of right-thinking Romans (4.10; cf. *libera bilis* 11.16). Poem 4 is an exercise in social discipline against a freed slave who has become wealthy and acquired social respectability in the form of a military tribuneship and hence equestrian rank, positions that by custom were not open to freedmen.[29] On the other hand, as almost every commentator has noticed, there are numerous resemblances between the unnamed object of Horace's wrath and the poet himself.[30] In some cases, these resemblances are acknowledged by critics only to be argued away, but the fact that

---

28 Cf. ibid., 162–63, 181–82.
29 Armstrong, *Horace*, 9–13.
30 Cf. Oliensis, *Horace and the Rhetoric of Authority*, 67; Oliensis, "Canidia, Canicula, and the Decorum of Horace's Epodes," 170–71; William Fitzgerald, "Power and Impotence in Horace's Epodes," in *Horace: Odes and Epodes*, ed. Michèle Lowrie, 141–59 (Oxford: Oxford University Press, 2009), 150–51; Johnson, *Horace's Iambic Criticism*, 97–98.

such arguments need to be made unveils the possibility of the identification and hence the impossibility of definitively excluding it from the reader's understanding.[31] Whatever details may be invoked to suggest the illegitimacy of the identification, they remain just that, individual details at variance with a perceived resemblance, a moment in which the understood meaning (*intellectum*) remains at some variance (*diversum*) with the letter of what has been said (*dictum*).

The opening sentence of the poem does two things at once: it establishes *Epode* 4 as the first fully-fledged invective poem of the collection, the true heir to the Archilochian and Hipponactian tradition, and reflects that tradition back against itself and the poet.[32] It opens squarely with a declaration of personal enmity as well as an insult aimed at the social standing of the invective target:

> Discord as great as what has fallen to wolves and lambs obtains for me with you, you who are burned on the side with Spanish ropes and on the shin by the hard shackle.[33]

As I noted in my discussion of *Epode* 3, images of wolves and dogs were associated with the iambic tradition from the very beginning with Archilochus's Lycambes or "Wolf-stepper" and in the earliest traces of the oral tradition in figures like the tricky Dolon in *Iliad* 9 who wears a wolf skin.[34] The wolf is the symbol

---

31 D.R. Shackelton Bailey, *Profile of Horace* (Cambridge: Harvard University Press, 1982), 4. Mankin goes so far as to argue without proof that the object of the invective in this poem is not simply a freed slave like Horace's father but a criminal, yet the resemblance is still too close for comfort, and he then feels compelled to go on to argue that the speaker is not Horace (Mankin, *Horace: Epodes,* ad loc).

32 Johnson, *Horace's Iambic Criticism,* 99.

33 *Lupis et agnis quanta sortito obtigit,*
   tecum mihi discordia est,
Hibericis peruste funibus latus
   et crura dura compede. (4.1–4)

34 Alberto Cavarzere, ed., *Orazio: Il libro degli Epodi* (Venezia: Marsilio,1992), 140; Miller, *Lyric Texts and Lyric Consciousness,* 28–36; Gagné, "A Wolf at

of iambic aggression and the dog his domesticated cousin, the image of a possible taming of that aggression as a tool for social discipline. But the dog still bites and sometimes nips his master (on dogs and wolves, see *Epodes* 2.60, 6.1–10, 7.11–12, 12.26). Nonetheless, a question immediately arises as we read these lines: who is the wolf and who is the sheep? The animal imagery indicates a clear distinction between victim and aggressor, yet the human drama is more confused. Horace appears at best to be a wolf in sheep's clothing. If the object of Horace's attack is cast as the wolf, then the poet is clearly a sheep that bites back. But if Horace is the wolf, then we are forced to imagine the object of the attack as the hapless victim of the iambist's predatory aggressions.[35] The term *discordia* is particularly loaded in this context. It bears with it the concept of civil conflict and, depending on the date of either the writing or the reading of the poem, it evokes the ongoing or recently concluded civil wars against Antony at Actium, Sextus Pompeius off Sicily, or Brutus,[36] Cassius, and Horace himself at Philippi.[37] This wolf and this sheep, then, in all the instability of their relative positions — just who *is* preying on whom? — are emblematic of the ongoing social conflict and Horace's ironic reflections on it. In civil conflict, each side claims to have been victimized by the other. One side's aggression is always a justified retaliation for the wrong done by the other. The memories can be very long. This is the history in which the iambist seeks to intervene: an endless retaliatory cycle of sheep and wolves, predators and prey, political actors who are constantly shifting positions and ultimately consuming their own. And this is why irony is such a potent rhetori-

the Table," 262–65.
35 Cf. 2.60.
36 On the three passages in which Horace recounts his role as military tribune in Brutus and Cassius's army, see Italo Lana, "Le Guerre civili et la pace nella poesia di Orazio," in *Atti del convegno di Venosa: 8–15 Novembre 1992*, eds. Scevola Mariotti et alii, 59–74 (Venosa: Edizioni Osanna Venosa, 1993), 60.
37 Mankin, *Horace: Epodes*, ad loc; Watson, *A Commentary on Horace's Epodes*, ad loc; J. Hellegouarc'h, *Le vocabulaire latin des relations et des partis politiques sous la république*, 2nd edn. (Paris: Les Belles Lettres, 1972), 134, 538.

cal tool in this situation, for it is not self-evident who are the wolves and who the sheep, nor is it the case that all the wolves are really sheep and vice versa and that hence there is no difference between them. The reality is complex: iambists and their objects are always both wolves and sheep, and yet the difference between them never quite collapses. The victims are in fact *always* and *necessarily* the original aggressors and therefore must be attacked mercilessly, even as they truly remain victims. In the memorable words of Clint Eastwood's character, William Munny, in the film *Unforgiven* (1992), when the young would-be gunslinger asks him if the man he just gunned down had it coming, "We all have it coming, kid." The opening statement of *Epode* 4 expresses both a literal meaning (its *dictum*) and the precise opposite of that meaning (its *intellectum*), but it also insists on maintaining the difference between those meanings as well as their potential commutability.

Similarly, in poem 7, immediately before the first of the impotence poems, Horace denounces the recent history of political warfare and the possibility of its continuation into the future, writing:

> Where are you criminals rushing off to? Or why are swords that had been put away now fitted to your right hand? [...] *Not even wolves or lions* act this way, never savage except against the different. [...] That's the way it is: harsh fates goad the Romans and the crime of fratricide, since the sacred blood of innocent Remus flowed on the ground for his descendants.[38]

38 *Quo quo scelesti ruitis? Aut cur dexteris*
    aptantur enses conditi?
  [...]
  neque hic lupis *mos nec fuit* leonibus,
    numquam nisi in dispar feris.
  [...]
  sic est: acerba fata Romanos agunt
    scelusque fraternae necis,
  ut immerentis fluxit in terram Remi
    sacer nepotibus cruor. (7.1–2, 11–12, 17–20)

There are wolves, there are sheep, and then there are humans: the lone kind to prey upon their own. This poem posits a third position between generic victim and aggressor, producing a kind of meta-irony that does not deny the previous opposition between wolves and sheep, iambists and objects, but resituates them on that third level of commutability. Were Caesar's assassins, who made Horace the son of a freedman a military tribune, wolves or sheep, victims or aggressors? Or were they just blind actors in a larger historical drama that they were powerless (*impotens*) to change: the heirs to Rome's original sin, the spilled blood of Remus?

In such a context, what is the heir to Archilochus, the foe of Lycambes ("the wolf dancer"), to do? Who is he and where does he stand? The speaking subject of the *Epodes* is himself surrounded by an ironic *cordon sanitaire*. As ever new levels of meaning unfold, it becomes impossible to say who he *really* is, what he *really* means, to be able to label and to categorize all his possible meanings, to empty him of *all* interiority, to render him a mere function of a describable social, political, personal, or sexual position. Each new *dictum* produces a variety of *intellecta,* meanings that are at once intentional (they are products of a performative structure that partakes of the Real) and resistant to reduction (they cannot be synthesized into a single coherent meaning that can be separated from the performative structure that makes them possible).

Returning however to *Epode* 4, the abstract notion of *discordia* in the poem's opening couplet is given more concrete form in the next two lines' images of bondage and enslavement. The forcible deprivation of freedom as both cause and consequence of civil conflict is a recurring theme throughout the epodes. The social wars, Spartacus's uprising, Sextus Pompeius's recruitment of slaves to man his navy, and Octavian's propaganda against Antony, Cleopatra, and their supposedly unfree oriental hordes are all specifically cited in poems 9 and 16.[39] These two poems

---

39 Cf. 9.9–16; 16.5; Adolph Kiessling and Richard Heinze, *Q. Horatius Flaccus: Satiren* (Zurich: Weidmann, 1999), 501; Watson, "The *Epodes*" 97.

round out the series of political epodes that began with poem 1 on Maecenas as the willing companion of Octavian, as he prepares to sail for Actium, and continued with poem 7's vision of Roman civil conflict (*discordia*) being the result of *acerba fata* and Romulus's murder of Remus. These political poems (1, 7, 9, and 16) are then intercalated with the series of Canidia and impotence poems (5, 8, 12, and 17). They find their point of intersection in poem 3, where the vile, parching vapor of Apulia serves to join Horace, Canidia, and Maecenas into a singular comic knot, which is then given a distinctly iambic point with poem 4's opening image of sheep and wolves, before poem 5 repeats almost word for word *Epode* 3's evocation of Medea's burning gifts for Creusa in the final tirade of a boy about to be sacrificed to satisfy Canidia's lust.

• • •

Poem 5, in many ways, serves as a masculinist fantasy genealogy of the origin of iambic. In it, the combination of Canidia's sexual insatiability and disgusting physical appearance lead first to literal violence, when she and Sagana capture and bury an innocent boy to the chin. Their physical assault and grotesque torture leads to a violent verbal riposte on the part of the boy, who offers his own iambic tirade in response to Canidia's *mala carmina*. Here again, the narrative of iambic violence traces its origin to a prior moment of the aggression, and it is generically appropriate that the boy is transformed into an iambic poet by the enormity of Canidia's crimes. The surest sign of that poetic transformation is the boy's own use of intertextuality, when he cites almost word for word passages from poem 3, the very passages in which Horace, Canidia, and Maecenas begin to share certain traits and imagistic associations, becoming the *dicta* of certain common *intellecta*.[40] Poems 3, 4, and 5 thus serve both as the nodal point between the political and the Canidia/impotence poems, and

---

40 The boy also knows his Archilochus. See Johnson, *Horace's Iambic Criticism*, 103.

as the place in which the poet's iambic irony bends back most clearly to include himself. As such, these poems should take on a particular importance for any attempt to understand the *Epodes* as a whole. Returning once more to the beginning of poem 4, we should lastly note that the image of "burning" caused by the ropes and shackle (*peruste*) on the body of Horace's iambic victim provides a further imagistic link between this poem and its predecessor. That linkage, unsurprisingly, is ironic in that it produces multiple and even opposed *intellecta* from the same *dicta*. In poem 3, we saw the fire that roiled the poet's tender guts transformed into the product of Canidia's witchcraft. It then became the dog's breath of the Canicula, which parched Horace's native *siticulosa Apulia*, before finally being metamorphosed into the breath of Maecenas himself, a foul vapor that will cause his *puella* to beat a hasty retreat. In this fashion, the poet's *mollitia*, of which he complains in his invocation of the *dura ilia* of the reapers, and which in poem 1 renders him *imbellis*, is transformed over the course of poem 3 into the source of Maecenas's own sexual frustration or *impotentia*.[41] Thus, the fire of Horatian halitosis, which is also the iambic breath of the dog, becomes the inflammation that rubs raw the slave turned military tribune of *Epode* 4, branding him with the sign of social transgression, the cause and the consequence of *discordia*. The fire of Horatian *liberrima indignatio* in poem 4 becomes at once a force of rage turned against the other, whose very existence threatens the emerging Augustan settlement, and an impenetrable wall between the poet and the social world, a wall that obscures his position in the moment he appears to reveal it.

For Horace himself is born of a freedman (*natus libertino patre*), as he memorably repeats throughout *Satire* 1.6. Likewise, he too was raised to the position of military tribune and hence to equestrian status by the very Brutus whose assassination of *Divus Caesar* produced the most recent round of *discordia*, a

---

41 Ellen Oliensis, "Erotics and Gender," in *Cambridge Companion to Horace*, ed. Stephen Harrison, 221–34 (Cambridge: Cambridge University Press, 2007), 226.

round which will only finally play itself out at Actium, whose Liburnian galleys are evoked in the opening lines of *Epode* 1, lines which also call to mind Callimachus's *Ibis*.[42] Horace is the fiery voice, the barking dog, the wolf whose anger gives voice to the outrage of the community, *and* the soft poet, the unwarlike sophisticate, the object of Canidia's wrath and disappointed lust (more on this lust in a moment). He is the son of doubtful origins, raised to the rank of military tribune in a time of social discord, as well as the poet who decries that discord and with it the spilled blood of the innocent grandchildren of Remus. The fire that burns the skin and sides of the social climber in *Epode* 4 is both a fire that has burned Horace himself and the flame his iambic persona embodies.

Within this complex ironic constellation, Canidia becomes more than just a quasi-archetypical witch figure and poisoner who serves as a stock object of the invective poet's wrath. She is also the vehicle through which the poet's power as a bestower of blame, as an iambist, is reflected back on itself. Asking in *Epode* 3 whether Canidia has "trafficked in foul feasts" is not only ironic in the sense that it equates the dish proffered by Maecenas with a meal prepared by someone whom we learn in *Epode* 5 is a sexually frustrated and murderous practitioner of black magic. It also implicates the poet himself in a larger pattern of sexual frustration and inability to perform. Thus, in poem 5, Canidia is burying a young man up to the neck and starving him to death, so she can extract his liver and make a philter that will cause her wandering lover to return:

> O Varus, not by means of the usual potions, O face about to shed many tears, will you run back to me. Your mind will come back called not by Marsian voices. I will prepare a more powerful cup. I will pour on your disgust a greater cup, and the sun will not set beneath the sea, above the outstretched

---

42 Carrubba, *The Epodes of Horace*, 56–59; Ellen Oliensis, *Horace and the Rhetoric of Authority* (Cambridge: Cambridge University Press, 1998), 66; Johnson, *Horace's Iambic Criticism*, 100.

earth, before you burn for my love with black flames, like bituminous pitch.[43]

The dark flames of lust roused by Canidia's magic, of course, recall the flames of Medea's magic exercised in vengeance against Creusa, flames which were evoked earlier in this poem (5.61–64) and in poem 3 as well. At the same time, Canidia's need to overcome her erstwhile lover's disgust looks forward to poems 8 and 12, where the poet cites the woman's repulsiveness as the reason he is unable to rise to the occasion. And while the clear points of resemblance between Canidia, whose lover has fled, and the hag, who provokes impotent disgust in our poet, have been noted before,[44] it will repay our effort to look more closely at these poems in conclusion.

• • •

We need not prove the absolute identity of the frustrated hag with Canidia—an impossibility in any case, since Canidia is not named in poems 8 and 12. We need only demonstrate the possibility, indeed the invitation, to make that identification. That invitation comes in the opening lines of poem 8. There, Horace describes a grotesque old woman who provokes disgust in him, much as Canidia, the *obscena anus* whom the innocent lad, turned voice of iambic rage, curses in 5.98.[45] Having dared to ask why Flaccus is flaccid, the woman in *Epode* 8 is anato-

---

43 *Non usitatis, Vare, potionibus,*
    o multa fleturum caput,
ad me recurres, nec vocata mens tua
    Marsis redibit vocibus:
maius parabo, maius infundam tibi
    fastidienti poculum,
priusque caelum sidet inferius mari,
    tellure porrecta super,
quam non amore sic meo flagres uti
    bitumen atris ignibus. (5.73–82)
44 Armstrong, *Horace*, 60–63.
45 Who had of course also excited disgust in her former lover, Varus.

mized in grotesque detail: generic old age, wrinkles, a gaping asshole, drooping breasts, a noticeable paunch, and swollen ankles. There is an almost erotic luxuriance in this blazon of revulsion, leading up to the final command that if she wishes the poet to come to attention, she will have to work on him with her mouth (*ore allaborandum est tibi,* 8.20). With no other woman of similar description in the corpus, and with poem 8 coming shortly after poem 5 (the longest poem in the collection), it would be difficult for the suggestion of their identity not to come to mind. Yet, the resemblance with Canidia goes beyond generic disgust with an aging female body. In line 3 of poem 8, there is a direct verbal recollection. There, Canidia's "black and blue tooth" (*dens lividus*) of 5.47 is recalled in the image of the *dens ater* or single "black tooth" of our archetypical hag. That tooth in turn recalls both the black flames of Varus's rekindled lust ("black flames" [*atris ignibus*]) and the *dens ater* of traditional iambic vengeance cited at the end of poem 6, where the poet asks, if someone should attack him "with a black tooth" (*atro dente*), should he weep like an unavenged boy (*puer*)?[46] The boy in need of vengeance, of course, can call to mind none other than the *puer* of 5.82, who fell prey to Canidia's own *dens lividus*. This same "iambic" tooth in turn is associated in *Satires* 2.1 with both the fierce bite of the wolf (*dente lupus,* 2.1.52) and the carping of Horace's detractors ("envy [...] will hurt its tooth trying to strike against the solid with the weak"[47]). Many years later, Horace would present his genealogy of satire and invective in *Epistles* 2.1, and he would refer to the "bloody tooth" of uncontrolled invective verse as what would eventually necessitate a law against *mala carmina* and a return to the care for speaking well (2.1.148–55). Thus, we have a complex multivalent web of associations surrounding the black-toothed hag of *Epode* 8. She both provokes Horace's momentary impotence or *mollitia* and actualizes a potential softness within him, the presence of which

---

46 6.15–16; cf. Nelson Hawkins, "The Barking Cure," 78.
47 *invidia* [...] *fragili quaerens illidere dentem*
    offendet solido (2.1.77–78)

was acknowledged from the very first poem. At the same time, her black tooth is directly associated with Archilochus and Hipponax, who are specifically cited at 6.13–14, immediately before the black tooth of abuse cited above. She is, then, simultaneously the cause of the poet's impotence, the object of his abuse, and his iambic doppelgänger. The same black tooth of abuse, which also recalls the *dens lividus* of Canidia, is in turn commanded in poem 8 to call Horace's flaccid phallus back to life. But, as we have seen, that very tooth is identified throughout the Horatian corpus with the iambic poet in his most archetypical incarnations as the biting mouth of the wolf, the barking mouth of the dog, and the voice of both protection and disgust. One way or the other, it seems, we all get badmouthed in the end.[48] The burning, garlic, dog breath of *Epode* 3 is just the beginning. That same unclean, iambic mouth, described and commandeered in poem 8, talks back in poem 12. There, the lady in question responds to Horace's blazon by retailing the poet's sexual shortcomings, launching her own iambic attack on the soft poet: "you were less limp for Inachia than for me/ you were up for Inachia three times in one night, for me it's always one/ *soft* job."[49] As Watson cautiously observes,

> It is possible that, in her gracelessness, old age, grotesque ugliness, and obscenity of word and deed, we are meant to see in the *vetula* an analogue of Iambe (Baubo), the eponymous deity of iambic, who encompassed all these attributes.[50]

This view that the hag who is Horace's nemesis in poems 8 and 12 is also his generic double, which is consonant with both the structure of poem 3 and the image of the savage tooth of iambic

---

48 On poems 8 and 12 as directly derived from Archilochus and Hipponax, see Watson, *A Commentary on Horace's Epodes*, 8, 40. On dogs, bites, and iambic, see also Nelson Hawkins, "The Barking Cure," 63–70.

49 *Inachia langues minus ac me;*
Inachiam ter notce potes, mihi semper ad unum
    mollis *opus* (12.14–16)

50 Watson, *A Commentary on Horace's Epodes*, 83.

abuse, is further reinforced by Mankin's suggestions concerning the import of Canidia's name and the significance of her activities. Her name seems to point to two associations, with "the dog" (*canis*) (but also the *Canicula*) and the furiously "dogged" genre of iambus (cf. *Ep.* 6), and with "old-age" (*canities*) and the decrepit impotence not only of the poet but of Rome as it collapses into ruin (*Ep.* 16.1–12) under the weight of its ancient curse (*Ep.* 7.17–20).[51] This same image is recalled in appropriately inverted form at the end of poem 12, when Canidia/Baubo/the hag exclaims, "Oh how unhappy I am whom you flee as the lamb flees fierce wolves and she goats flee lions!"[52] The image of the wolf and his somewhat domesticated confrère, the dog, has been part of the iambic genre from its earliest manifestations, but this passage specifically recalls the opening lines of poem 4, where the relation between wolf and lamb is peculiarly overdetermined: who is the aggressor and who the victim? Who the attacker and who the attacked? Iambic poison is always a response to aggression, and hence the roles depend in their very nature on a potential reversibility. At the end of poem 12, the iambic poet not only becomes the object of attack (i.e., the wolf becomes the lamb), but so too does the masculinist poet in his passive impotence become the she goat, the penetrated prey, a role he assumes as iambist, *as* poetic ironist. Ellie Oliensis has succinctly summed up the case:

> Invective originates as a compensation for impotence. But impotence remains a part of the story. What distinguishes the *Epodes* is precisely the failure to erase the origin of invective in impotence. The failure is luridly obvious in *Epodes* 8 and 12.[53]

---

[51] Mankin, "The Epodes," 100; cf. Oliensis, "Canidia, Canicula, and the Decorum of Horace's *Epodes*," 163, 167.

[52] *o ego non felix, quam tu fugis ut pavet acris*
   agna lupos capreaeque leones! (12.25–26)

[53] Oliensis, "Canidia, Canicula, and the Decorum of Horace's *Epodes*," 175.

Iambic violence becomes the sign of weakness in an age of instability. Canidia becomes the double and the antagonist of Horace: simultaneously the iambic subject and object. She is the evil twin of the iambic dog, like the social climber of *Epode* 4.[54] And so, it is only appropriate that she be given the last word in the collection. Rather than ending with the triumph of the iambic poet over his adversaries, with the death of Bupalus and Lycambes, the *Epodes* ends with a cry of triumph by Canidia, the poet's ostensible object of iambic aggression and persistent doppelganger:

> I will be a rider carried on the shoulders of my enemies and the land will yield to my insolence. Or shall I, who can make waxen images come alive, as you yourself know from your spying, and tear down the moon from the pole with my chants, who can bring back to life the cremated dead and mix the cups of desire, weep that my art is of no avail against you?[55]

The Horace of the *Epodes* is thus not the triumphant enforcer of a masculinist or aristocratic social discipline. Nor is he the herald of a new Augustan settlement after Actium's end, though clearly all of these elements are in play. He is not given — or, more accurately, does not give himself — the last word. Rather, Horace as we see him in *Epode* 3, in the Canidia poems, in the political and in the impotence poems, is both the subject

---

54 Alessandro Barchiesi, "Final Difficulties in an Iambic Poet's Career: *Epode* 17," trans. Maya Jessica Alapin, in *Horace: Odes and Epodes*, ed. Michèle Lowrie (Oxford: Oxford University Press, 2009), 241; cf. Oliensis, "Canidia, Canicula, and the Decorum of Horace's *Epodes*," 72–73.

55 *Vectabor umeris tunc ego inimicis eques,*
meaeque terra cedet insolentiae.
an quae movere cereas imagines,
ut ipse nosti curiousus, et polo
deripere lunam vocibus possim meis,
possim crematos excitare mortuous
desiderique temperare pocula,
plorem artis in te nil agentis exitus. (17.74–80).

and object of iambic invective, the perpetrator and the victim of sexual aggression, the voice of social norms and of their enforcement as well as the embodiment of their breach. The ironic voice of Horace's *Epodes* leads us less to the adoption of any one definite point of view, a doctrine or explicit ideology, than to the creation of the subjective space from which the personal, the political, the sexual, and the aesthetic contradictions of the emerging Augustan settlement can be both sharply interrogated and immediately experienced.

And this unending interrogation is the 'pataphilogical gesture *par excellence,* a simultaneous gesturing toward the possibility of communication and its ultimate refusal. Horace does not give us his views in the *Epodes*. He does not advocate for a position or a program, even as we may well recognize the elements of communication within the *Epodes*. We may even identify within this text the semantic undergirding of an ideological program, but the moment we try to establish what that program would be in its finite actuality, then we must engage in a drastic reduction of this rich and ironic text. We must drag the *intellectum* back into conformity with the *dictum*. We must reduce the materiality of language to an idealized and universal "meaning," which can only ultimately be a reflection of ourselves, and which thus must necessarily be "untrue" to the text and untrue to the most basic philological impulse, an impulse that can only be satisfied, I would contend, by its beyond (*meta*) and its besides (*para*).

Five

The Paraphilologist as 'Pataphysician

Erik Gunderson

This volume is predicated on the notion that 'pataphysics constitutes the avant-garde destiny of a doomed conservative metaphysics. A conservative metaphysics fetishizes "the rule of the rule." 'Pataphysics relishes in such a phrase only the logic-cleaving of a sideways-splitting pun: "how many inches in a ruler, my liege?" And, as a lover of puns, 'pataphysics is just getting started precisely where one had been asked to end. When wearing his or her outlandish grammatical hat, the 'pataphysicist become 'pataphilologist — or is it the other way around, I forget — oversees the emancipation of *logos* in a parallel revolutionary moment. This revolt upends the dour hegemony of generalities in the name of a mass uprising of laughing particularities.

The consonance of *physis* and *logos* was always a key metaphysical gambit in the west. Shifts in the one domain affect the other because the two are different aspects of the same underlying unity. The "natural reasonableness" of the world, its contents, and human conventions alike has long been "axiomatic." And many have set themselves up as guardians of this obviousness, guardians who will never acknowledge that there might be anything ill-fitted about the world.

I wish to explore the philological word-lover who positions himself to the side of the being-and-meaning pair. Such a process begs any number of questions about wheres and hows. And yet, keeping a zealous watch over his thesaurus, the word-lover would never think himself to be begging for anything. Nevertheless, this figure has in fact arrogated for himself a curious and impossible *ou*-topia that has been designated as a *eu*-topia. And he can only live there to the extent that he refuses to acknowledge the pun, a pun that a good 'pataphilologist would explicate by beginning, "Ewww. Well, no…" For myself, I would designate this nowhere-man as the paraphilologist, the grey, double- and stern-faced straight-man to the colorful and comic 'pataphilologist. But even a grey clown is nevertheless a full-fledged clown and duly distinguished matriculant from clown college: it would be wrong not to fête him as well in the course of our celebration of 'pataphilology.

A sketch: The paraphilologist keeps a solicitous watch. The aims are conservative. The results anything but. He cries trebly (in a two-fold sense) as he notes that sheep, apples, and tears are running down his cheeks all at once: "ὦ μῆλα, μῆλα, μῆλα!" The fruits of all labors to shore up the side-and-head-splitting facts of language tumble lamentably to the ground, and thereafter germinate seeds from which grow novelties that are unwanted by the gardener himself.

(Derrida's) Plato's Pharmacy seems like the place to begin and, likely, end. One can offer a miniature history by way of supplement to his tale of the philosophy of supplanting. Chapter One: The Attic philosopher as (aberrant) guardian of truth gives way to the aberrancy of philology as a bastard discipline that substitutes itself for legitimate philosophical guardianship. Chapter Two: Then, and worse still, the Romans arrive and imperiously arrogate for themselves the role of guardians of the (ill-gotten) gains of both philosophy and philology. These new parasitical paraphilologists know that they do not even have the words for the words that give the truth to all of the things: "The poverty of the Latin language," they say whilst lolling amidst the spoils of the world.

Those other chapters of a (para-)history of erudition will need to be "taken as read" even if it is not quite the case that they have all already been written. I wish to linger in the here and now of "late antiquity" as an exemplary moment in the long history of the failure of the philological example to establish authoritative genera. *Pars* fails to hook up to *totum*. Instead one sees the reproduction of aberrancy amidst the narrative of normativity. It's a farce: all of the parts want to play one and the same role, but the ill-signed forgery that is the sign system itself has given quite different parts to all of these parts. Cabbageheads have mistaken themselves for the kingly-minded.

The Latin Grammarians write up their artfully artless *Artes* several hundred years into the language game: *noch einmal* a voice rings out defining for us what a *vox* is. Moreover, they know that we know that it's all been said before. But has it? Amidst the authoritative citations, bald declarations, and general stagecraft of Settled Questions a reader might well note discord instead of concord, texts that do not quite agree with their peers and antecedents, texts, indeed, that do not even agree with themselves.[1] Meanwhile the professor drones on and on so as to narcotize the student from noting the exciting possibility of linguistic failure and slippage. But not every student has always been so inattentive. And that's where we will end, with a gesture to the fecundity of the failure of the stuffy to stuff others with

---

[1] See José Carracedo Fraga, "Un capítulo sobre barbarismus y soloecismus en el códice CA 2° 10 de Erfurt," *Euphrosyne: Revista de filologia classica* 41 (2013): 245–58, for a detailed walk-through of the way a seventh-century grammatical text gets composed out of various antecedent sources. Many of those predecessors were themselves composed according to a similar logic. See Maria Laetitia Coletti, "Il barbarismus e il soloecismus nei commentatori altomedievali di Donato alla luce della tradizione grammaticale greco-latina," *Orpheus* 4 (1983): 67–92, on the heterogeneity (at the expense of rationality) of the adoption of arguments about barbarism and solecism in the middle ages. A similar process can easily be retrojected back into the late antique and classical periods. This model can explain the panoply of convergent but also subtly divergent arguments one reads when going through the *Grammatici Latini* (H. Keil, Grammatici Latini [Leipzig: Teubner, 1857–1880], henceforth *GL*). If you read one, you feel like you have read them all, but, then again, you have not in fact read them all.

all their stuffing: their words do indeed get taken up by their own students, but they are taken up not as truths but instead as amusing truisms, as mobile signifiers that can be whirled in now this direction and now that. The potential for ironic misreception will be the only eternal verity that we will be able to discern in here. The professor's words are always also mere words that can take one down any number of paths. They can and will be detour(n)ed again and again. Even, of course, as these same stolid nostrums of the magisterial would themselves need (errant) repeating, if only to inspire still further quixotic students in their questing.[2]

• • •

Vox vocis. What did I just say? Did you hear the beginning of a grammatical paradigm: *vox vocis voci vocem voce*?[3] That is, does one hear the word *vox* and at once feel the overwhelming urge to "decline" and so to analogize this *ox* by yoking it with some other that one might thereupon plow the field of language to spread a life-giving layer of dung over it? But if *vox vocis* is taken as a phrase, it is difficult to translate, and the one who uttered it stands guilty of the vice of amphibolia.[4] For *vox* means both the voice and that which is uttered by the voice. In fact,

2   See D.S. Colman, "Confessio grammatici," *Greece and Rome* 7, no. 1 (1960): 72–81, for a praise of folly: "I am proud to be a modern *grammaticus*; it does the youth of today good."
3   See Priscian, *Institutiones* 7.44 (= *GL* 2.323–24) to learn how to decline words that end in *ox, ox, ux, ux, yx, aex, aux, alx, anx, unx, arx, ac, ec,* and *ut*. Some of the beans were already spilled in 3.32 and 5.38, though [*GL* 2.106 and *GL* 2.166]. Priscian was active at the end of the fifth and the beginning of the sixth centuries CE. He taught at Constantinople. He is also the author of a panegyric to Anastasius. He was one of the leading scholars of his day.
4   Donatus, *Ars Grammatica* 3.3 (= *GL* 4.395): "Amphibolia est ambiguitas dictionis, quae fit aut per casum accusativum, ut siquis dicat 'audio secutorem retiarium superasse'; aut per commune verbum [...] fit et per homonyma, ut siquis aciem dicat et non addat oculorum aut exercitus aut ferri. fit praeterea pluribus modis, quos percensere omnes, ne nimis longum sit, non oportet." Donatus was active at Rome in the middle of the fourth century CE. He was one of the leading scholars of his day.

vox also means any sound whatsoever. And as a phrase *vox vocis* can signify, *inter alia*, "the sound of one's voice," "talk about a word," or "the word for speech." Of course, a good stylist would avoid the collocation to begin with. But this artless gaffe allows a phrase to emerge that exposes problems circulating among the grammarians and their *artes*. At the foundation of the "art" of grammar stands a confusion about the status of language. In fact, this very confusion constitutes the sand upon which the castle of erudition will be built. Where to begin? With the voice? Perhaps, but what do we mean by *vox*? Thankfully, the grammarians are happy to define their terms for us. Unfortunately, they are all too happy to do so, and one is left with a surfeit of information.[5] The knowledge comes pre-packaged as *rationes*, but one casts about in vain for reasonable ways to sift it.[6] Priscian and Diomedes begin their discussion of the *vox* by reporting the philosophers' definition of it. Which philosophers? Exactly how did they justify their position? Why this definition and not some other? The answers to such questions are less clear: philosophy is hauled onto the stage only long enough to have its authority conjured. We will not explore its methods and insights or, for that matter, even its basic bibliography. Priscian adumbrates a distinction between vox as "stricken air" and *vox*

5   See John Henderson, *The Medieval World of Isidore of Seville: Truth from Words* (Cambridge: Cambridge University Press, 2007), 28 on Isidore's "conveyor-belt of constantly unfolding explication."
6   Reynolds and Wilson may well talk about "decline," the "dreary" and the "potted" relative to this era (L.D. Reynolds and N.G. Wilson, *Scribes and Scholars: A Guide to the Transmission of Greek and Latin Literature*, 3rd edn. [Oxford: Oxford University Press, 1991], 29), but the uncritical accumulation of *rationes* is already several scholarly generations old by the time we get to Gellius in the second century CE. There is little reason to think that the worst one sees in late antiquity is somehow peculiar to late antiquity itself. See Anonymous, *Nox Philologiae: Aulus Gellius and the Fantasy of the Roman Library*, ed. Erik Gunderson (Madison: University of Wisconsin Press, 2009), 114–15 on thoroughly encrusted rationes in Gellius. And, as Henderson notes, users of reference works like these are always addressed as if they were already advanced users, never readers who are really and truly themselves beginning at the beginning. See Henderson, *The Medieval World of Isidore of Seville*, 31.

as "air that strikes the ear."[7] Diomedes flags the idea as Stoic and gives roughly the same distinction.[8] Neither really does much with this information beyond brandishing it.[9] And one may well wonder how many philosophers either man has read and how closely: many seeming pieces of knowledge in this world are more indices of a kind of know-how that relates to repeating the already-said within the domain of a specific and narrow professional discourse.[10] In short, many other discussions by many other *grammatici* begin in this fashion.[11] After a brief philosophical flourish we get into the grammatical trenches. Let us try to follow along with Priscian for a while as he attempts to lead us. Priscian encourages us to think of *vox* as being that *aer tenuissimum ictum* he spoke of: this definition is taken from the essence of the thing, not some accident that befalls it. But even if *vox* is substantively *aer*, this same air has had one of four destinies bestowed upon it by that fateful beating/blowing. *Vocis autem differentiae sunt quattuor: articulata, inarticulata, literata, illiterata.* Each of these qualifying terms will be defined presently. *Articulata est quae coartata, hoc est copulata cum aliquo sensu*

---

7   Priscian, *Institutiones* 1.1 (= *GL* 2.5).
8   Diomedes, *Ars Grammatica* 2 (= *GL* 1.420). Diomedes seems to have composed his work in the late fourth or early fifth centuries CE.
9   On the doctrine itself, see the index entries for ἀήρ and φωνή in Von Arnim's *Stoicorum Vererum Fragmenta*.
10 Robert A. Kaster, *Guardians of Language: The Grammarian and Society in Late Antiquity* (Berkeley: University of California Press, 1988), 12. The product of the schools had no synthetic appreciation of history, philosophy, or even language, just a familiarity with certain approved individual items from various categories.
11 Servius, *Commentarius in artem Donati* (*GL* 4.405): "plerique artem scribentes a litterarum tractatu inchoaverunt, plerique a voce, plerique a defintione artis grammaticae. sed omnes videntur errasse [...]." One might well be intrigued by so many different heteronomously errant majorities: *plerique... plerique... plerique...* One wonders what Servius would say about Diomedes who starts his *second* book on grammar by offering to tell us *quid sit grammatica* and thereupon launching into a discussion of *vox*. Only at the opening of Book 2 do we learn how to categorize whatever it was that was happening in Book 1. Servius was active at Rome in the last part of the fourth and early part of the fifth centuries CE.

*mentis eius qui loquitur profertur.*¹² "Articulation" entails "coupling": mind-and-voice.¹³ The air is not "mere" air, it is instead air that has been signed-and-sealed with the thought-and-will of the speaking subject.¹⁴ It travels from the psychic-and-physical interior of the speaker and makes its way into the ear of the auditor.¹⁵ The yoking of words to thoughts is hardly something unique to the grammarians: one of the key senses of the word *sensus* is "a thought expressed in words, a sentence."¹⁶ But here we are forging a collection of bonds that will be set down as the foundations for an authoritative technology of language. And, significantly, though indeed forged and fabricated, these as-if rational foundations have been cloaked in the abstract and

12 *GL* 2.5.
13 *Articulo* in this sense is a wide-spread "technical" metaphor: see Lucretius, Apuleius, Gellius, Cledonius, and Isidore. "To divide distinctly" is obviously what Apuleius has in mind when he talks about the ability of a parrot to mimic human speech *(eis lingua latior quam ceteris auibus; eo facilius uerba hominis articulant patentiore plectro et palato.* Apuleius, *Florida* 13). By adding coupling to the notion of quasi-mechanical articulation in a passage like Apuleius's the *grammatici* can shift from the merely qualitative to the interior and the intentional.
14 See Jacques Derrida, *Limited Inc.* (Evanston: Northwestern University Press, 1988) on this sort of thing.
15 The philosopher's version of this can be found in Ammonius, *In Aristotelis librum de interpretatione commentarius,* 24: "νῦν γὰρ ὁ λόγος ἡμῖν οὐ περὶ τῆς τυχούσης φωνῆς, ἀλλὰ περὶ τῆς σημαινούσης τὰ πράγματα διὰ μέσων τῶν νοημάτων κατά τινα συνθήκην καὶ ὁμολογίαν αὐτῆς τε σημαίνεσθαι διὰ γραμμάτων δυναμένης." Compare Diocles Magnes apud Diogenes Laertius 7.55–56 (= Diogenes Babylonius frr. §17ff in Hans Friedrich von Arnim, ed., *Stoicorum Veterum Fragmenta* [Stuttgart: Teubner, 1964], henceforth *SVF*): ἔστι δὲ φωνὴ ἀὴρ πεπληγμένος ἢ τὸ ἴδιον αἰσθητὸν ἀκοῆς, ὥς φησι Διογένης ὁ Βαβυλώνιος ἐν τῇ περὶ τῆς φωνῆς τέχνῃ. Since Ammonius will shortly discuss Aristophanes' *Frogs* and their κοάξ, there is likely some attenuated kinship between Ammonius's discussion and Priscian's. But Priscian's closest relative is something like the *Commentaria In Dionysii Thracis Artem Grammaticam, Scholia Marciana,* 310, which gives his same material in Greek: "Τῶν φωνῶν αἱ μέν εἰσιν ἐγγράμματοι καὶ ἔναρθροι, αἱ δὲ ἀγράμματοι καὶ ἄναρθροι, αἱ δὲ ἐγγράμματοι καὶ ἄναρθροι, αἱ δὲ ἀγράμματοι καὶ ἔναρθροι." And we will soon hear of the Frogs there as well: "αἱ δὲ ἐγγράμματοι καὶ ἄναρθροι, αἱ γραφόμεναι μὲν μηδὲν δὲ σημαίνουσαι, ὡς τὸ βρεκεκεκὲξ κοάξ καὶ πάλιν τὸ φλαττόθρατ."
16 Lewis and Short's *Latin Dictionary*: s.v., *sensus* B.2.b.

eternal idiom of science. The terms are all defined as being thus, and so there is no argument that leads us up to this position.[17] A matrix of possibilities is being constructed: *articulata, inarticulata, literata, illiterata*. Inarticulata is a word that seems to exist only for a moment such as this: the *not-articulata*.[18] One notes a minor hyperbaton: *mentis* has been held off to end its sentence: "mind" is what we are emphasizing here. *Vox*-without-*mens*: it is not really "speech," just "sound" that is specifically failing to be speech. There are words for mere sound, and this is not one of them, or, to the extent that this is such a word, it becomes such a word only when seen from a very specific and specifically linguistic angle. "Defective relative to its valorized twin": this same structure characterizes the relationship between the other two possible qualities of *vox*, the *literata* as against the *illiterata*.

> The lettered [*literata*] is the one that can be written down, the unlettered cannot be written. Therefore one finds certain articulated *voces* that can be written and understood as, for example, "*I sing of arms and a man*." Others cannot be written but are understood nevertheless, as is the case with men's hisses and groans. These are *voces* and they attest to the thought [*sensum*] of the person who produces them, but writing them is not possible. There are others which even though they can be written are nevertheless called non-articulated since they signify nothing, words like *coax* and *cra*. But there are others that are non-articulated and non-transcribable [*illiteratae*]: they can be neither written nor understood. Examples are clattering, lowing, and the like.[19]

[17] Compare foundational mathematical axioms such as "if a = b, then b = a." Unless you want to do set theory, this is where your discussion of arithmetic, algebra, and calculus will begin.

[18] "inarticulata est contraria, quae a nullo affectu proficiscitur mentis." Priscian, *Institutiones* 1.1 (=GL 2.5)

[19] "literata est quae scribi potest, illiterata quae scribi non potest. inveniuntur igitur quaedam voces articulatae quae possunt scribi et intellegi ut: Arma virumque cano, quaedam quae non possunt scribi, intelleguntur tamen ut sibili hominum et gemitus: hae enim voces, quamvis sensum aliquem significent proferentis eas, scribi tamen non possunt. aliae autem sunt quae

The "inarticulate" choice is itself a "literate" one: Aristophanes' *Frogs* sing Βρεκεκεκὲξ κοὰξ κοάξ.²⁰ But even that non-signifying signifier was itself turned into an object of knowledge/power/grammar within the play: τὸ κοάξ was a meaninglessness given meaning by way of the definitive supplement of the definite article.²¹ So too the "empty" quality of the terms chosen by the grammarians is not "fully empty" given that there are high-status and highly literate precedents for these terms. Each is brought on to mean precisely "the meaningless." And so, there is a meaning here. Κοάξ is always coaxed into becoming τὸ κοάξ. Zero is a number, too, and it "counts for something" even as it is itself nothing. Hisses and groans cannot be captured in writing even if one has no trouble writing either the word "hisses" or the word "groans." These *voces* are perfectly intelligible and perhaps also "scriptable," provided that one is willing to accept that the inscription is itself somewhat imperfect and ill fits the precise sound to a recognized, legitimate word.

In the middle one finds the exemplary example of an "articulate voice", an "articulated utterance." It is a speech-act that is also a writing-act, namely the singing of arms and a man. Priscian does not adduce the simple, neutral case of a "literacy" which need only mean "can-be-put-into-letters." Instead he evokes the loftiest imaginable example of *litterae*-as-literature: these are the opening words of the most famous Latin poem, the poem that serves as the constant point of reference for the

---

quamvis scribantur tamen inarticulatae dicuntur, cum nihil significent ut 'coax', 'cra'. Aliae vero sunt inarticulatae et illiteratae quae nec scribi possunt nec intellegi, ut crepitus, mugitus et similia." Priscian, *Institutiones* 1.1 (= *GL* 2.5–6).

20 The orthodox Stoic choice would be Chrysippus's and Diogenes' βλίτυρι, as can be seen in the notes below.

21 See Aristophanes, *Frogs* 266 and 268: ἕως ἄν ὑμῶν ἐπικρατήσω τῷ κοάξ (266).Ἔμελλον ἄρα παύσειν ποθ' ὑμᾶς τοῦ κοάξ (268). "That κοάξ of yours: I know what it's all about. I'll get it under control and put a stop to it." See also Sean Gurd, *Dissonance: Auditory Aesthetics in Ancient Greece* (New York: Fordham University Press, 2016), 55–56, for the meaning in/as music that can be found in these "empty" words that are fully a part of a choral song.

teaching of a grammarian. Understanding Vergil is the task par excellence of the *grammaticus* whose schoolhouse teaches Latin as Vergil's Latin.

Sound is always already tending towards speech. And speech is always "literate" speech in the fullest sense of the word, the speech of the speaker who has gone through training in a specific variety of literary study. The articulate voice is both intelligible and destined-for-writing. Sound in general becomes speech in particular and speech is always also inhabited by a manifold version of The Letter.[22] For it is not just the case that valorized speech can be transcribed with the mechanical service of letters, but the speech that is signed, sealed, and delivered by the soul of the speaker hits the ear of the listener enmeshed in a web of literate literature. One can read-and-hear the (Derridean) trace of literature in every human voice, said the grammarian who parroted the other grammarian who parroted still another, Pretty

---

22 Diogenes Laertius's report about Diogenes Magnes continues: "Λέξις δέ ἐστι κατὰ τοὺς Στωϊκούς, ὥς φησιν ὁ Διογένης, φωνὴ ἐγγράμματος, οἷον 'ἡμέρα'. λόγος δέ ἐστι φωνὴ σημαντικὴ ἀπὸ διανοίας ἐκπεμπομένη" (7.56). Speech-as-*lexis* is always be-lettered, and speech-as-reason-as-argument-as-*logos* always gives a sign-of-interiority. The two differ in that *lexis* can be bereft of signification, but logos always signifies: "λόγος ἀεὶ σημαντικός ἐστι, λέξις δὲ καὶ ἀσήμαντος, ὡς ἡ 'βλίτυρι', λόγος δὲ οὐδαμῶς." See also Ammonius's list of meaningless words: "τῶν φωνῶν αἱ μέν εἰσιν ἄσημοι οἷον κνὰξ βλίτυρι σκινδαψός" (Ammonius, *in Porphyrii isagogen sive quinque voces*, 59). Ammonius repeats the list several times. Similarly see Asclepius, *In Aristotelis metaphysicorum libros A–Z commentaria*, 252.28: "ὁ γὰρ εἰρηκὼς βλίτυρι οὐδὲν εἴρηκεν." βλίτυρι and σκινδαψός are preserved among the fragments of Chrysippus as well (fragment 149 in SVF 2). Meanwhile, if you wait long enough, someone will declare that these non-words are in fact words and that they in fact do have meanings. See the *Corpus paroemiographorum Graecorum* 1.56: "Βλίτυρι καὶ σκινδαψός· ταῦτα παραπληρώματα λόγων, εἰσὶ δὲ καὶ παροιμιώδη. Ἰόβας δὲ τὸν σκινδαψὸν ὄργανον λέγει μουσικόν, τὸ δὲ βλίτυρι χορδῆς μίμημα." And the *Etymologicum Magnum* offers roughly the same account. See also Aelius Herodianus's word list: "Τὰ ἀπὸ τῆς βλι συλλαβῆς ἀρχόμενα διὰ τοῦ ι γράφεται· οἷον· βλίτον, εἶδος λαχάνου· βλίνος, ἰχθύς· βλίτυρι, ζῶον· βλιμάζω, τὸ ἀποστάζω μέλιτος· καὶ τὰ λοιπά" (*Partitiones* 6.6). If it can be written, it really is fated to signify despite even the διανοία of a man like Chrysippus.

Poly-Pittacus with his *patentiore plectro et palato*. After defining *vox* Priscian transitions to the *litera*.

> The letter is the smallest element of composite speech [*vocis*], that is, of the voice that subsists by means of the arrangement of letters.[23]

After noting what he means by *minima,* Priscian writes a second, supplementary definition: "We can define it thus: the letter is an individual *vox* that is capable of being written down."[24] Letters are the atoms of speech: all utterances (that can be written) are made up of letters (whose essential function is the writing up of utterances).[25] The over-defining of the letter in terms of the voice emerges as a function of this circularity: letters are already speech; speech is already a letter. Each inevitably points to the other and defines itself by means of its partner. And this partnership is not just something that joins (external) sign to (internal) presence, a yoking of λέξις and λόγος. This same unconvincing melange also allows for reading-and-writing to be inserted into the destiny of the lettered voice and voice of the letter. Priscian's argument continues/jumps:

> *Litera* is so named as if from *legitera* because it offers a path-for-reading [*iter* + *legere*] or from erasures [*lituris*], as some would have it, because men of old generally used to write on wax tablets.[26]

The etymological fantasy hurls itself into the discussion: the truth of words is that they bear their own truth within them-

---

23 "Litera est pars minima vocis compositae, hoc est quae constat compositione literarum." Priscian, *Institutiones* (*GL* 2.6).
24 "possumus et sic definire: litera est vox quae scribi potest individua." Ibid.
25 The atom of speech: τῆς δὲ λέξεως στοιχεῖά ἐστι τὰ εἰκοσιτέσσαρα γράμματα (Diogenes Magnes, fr. 20 *SVF*).
26 "dicitur autem litera vel quasi legitera, quod legendi iter praebeat vel a lituris, ut quibusdam placet, quod plerumque in ceratis tabulis antiqui scribere solebant." Priscian, *Institutiones* (*GL* 2.6).

selves, a truth that is legible — because the road to meaning was meant to be travelled — just around the phonetic bend.[27] Your deaf ear can hear-the-voice inside the voice-of-letters just as clearly as your vacant, staring eye can see that the letter is really an erasure. Provided you are willing to assume your own conclusions this all works out quite nicely. Priscian hands us on a platter sight-and-sound, silence-and-speech, here-and-there, writing-and-present-absence. Thanks! The voice is always inhabited by letters, but letters are not some incidental aspect of the voice, they are all part of the destination/destiny of voice: books that capture arms, men, and songs at the end of an errant itinerary.[28] There is no such thing as rational/cultured speech "before the letter."[29] Either it is the true-story/etymology of the word, or, as some would have it, a letter is a sound-sign that points to a thought-sign that is not so much showing the way

---

[27] While much of the discussion here centers around late and less prestigious authors, this truth-of-words thought extends all the way back to the classical Greek philosophers. See David Sedley, "Etymology as *techne* in Plato's *Cratylus*," in *Etymologia: Studies in Ancient Etymology: Proceedings of the Cambridge Conference on Ancient Etymology, 25–27 September 2000*, ed. Christos Nifadopoulos, 21–32 (Münster: Nodus Publikationen, 2003) on etymology in Plato's *Cratylus*. For a thorough meditation on power/knowledge and etymology "out here" at the edge of late antiquity, see Henderson, *The Medieval World of Isidore of Seville*.

[28] Fellow travelers met along the road: [Sergius], *De Arte Grammatica*: "Littera dicta est quasi legitera, eo quod legentibus iter praestet. ea est vocis articulatae pars minima. vox autem dicitur articulata quae scribi potest, confusa quae scribi non potest" (*GL* 7.538). Servius, *Commentarius in Artem Donati*: "Litteras Latinas constat Carmentem invenisse, matrem Euandri. quae ideo dictae sunt litterae, quod legentibus iter praebeant, vel quod in legendo iterentur, quasi legiterae" (*GL* 4.421). If you trace the path back far enough, you will discover that Roman letters are older than Rome itself. See also Isidore, *Etymologiae* 1.3.3.

[29] Note as well that, for his scholiasts, "Homer writes" and he writes "books": he is not a bard within an oral culture. See, for example, Eustathius, *Commentarii ad Homeri Iliadem* 1.7: "ὅθεν ἐκεῖνο μὲν τὸ βιβλίον ἀπὸ ἑνὸς προσώπου τοῦ Ὀδυσσέως ὠνόμασεν ὑποδηλῶν τὸ ὀλίγον τῆς τοῦ γράφειν ὕλης." Compare the scholia to the *Iliad* that explain why Homer starts writing his epic just where he does: the earlier battles were inconsequential, "περὶ ὧν ἀναγκαῖον αὐτῷ γράφειν οὐκ ἦν, μὴ παρούσης ὕλης τῷ λόγῳ" (1.1b.6).

as it is a muddled way of talking about muddling: the letter in this case is an effaced word for effacement, *litura*. The name of the defenders of such an interpretation of the word for means-of-interpretation is fittingly blotted out from this text. Priscian continues to weave his web of intersecting heterogeneities into a single would-be coherent cloth: one can and will correlate the material, psychic, heard, seen, and understood. "They (juridically) designated them as letters by means of the word for 'atoms' after their likeness to the fundamental particles of the cosmos."[30] Letters are "like" atoms. Their combination forms an as-if body that compounds a literal/letteral voice (*literalem vocem*). But it is more than mere likeness and this body-of-voice is by no means merely some "as-if" entity: the air really has been struck and that sound is a physical phenomenon. Priscian even attempts to map vocal qualities onto space-time so as to insist upon the materiality of *vox literalis*. A dance of the *quasi* ensues: comparisons emerge but they arise as images that are not supposed to be mere images. Sometimes the image turns into the thing itself. At others, it is not a metaphorical stand-in but rather a legitimate/leg-iter-mate representative of the underlying substance. "Therefore the *litera* is the mark of the atom and as it were a certain image of the 'literate' voice, one which is known from the quality and quantity of the shape of its lines."[31] The letter is the mark of the atom is the image of the voice. The letter is the im-

30 "Literas autem etiam elementorum vocabulo nuncupaverunt ad similitudinem mundi elementorum." Priscian, *Institutiones* (*GL* 2.6). The translation is odd. But so is the Latin. *Nuncupare aliquem nomine* should mean "to call someone by a name." But the "they" comes out of nowhere in this sentence unless "they" = "the *antiqui*" from the previous sentence who did not in fact name letters after atoms, at least they did not in so far as what we read there is concerned: letters were either "roads-to-reading" or (ancient) "erasures." The point being made in this sentence is that "some scholars say that letters are like 'atoms of speech,'" but the actual Latin makes it sound like *litera* is itself somehow etymologically connected to "atom" and that there was a formal proclamation to that effect. *Nuncupare* is often legal, and it is certainly not mild or neutral.

31 "Litera igitur est nota elementi et velut imago quaedam vocis literatae, quae cognoscitur ex qualitate et quantitate figurae linearum." Priscian, *Institutiones* (*GL* 2.6).

age of the lettered voice. This whole presentation fits awkwardly with issues that arise later for anyone in Priscian's line of business, issues that in fact occupy much of the bulk of an *Ars*: what about the semi-scandal of a letter like *K* which need not exist? Indeed, *K*, *Q*, and *C* may well seem to form a redundant triplet.[32] Meanwhile there are sounds that are not always represented by a letter.[33] *H* has an unusual status: its properties are only letter-like.[34] Further, there is the whole question of accent, a phenomenon which does not have a written component.[35] A letter's essence: "image of the voice." The accidents that attach themselves to this oh-so-material essence-as-simulacrum: (mere) name, (incidental) shape, and (real, material) force.[36] The last turns out not to be an accident at all but rather something that governs the other two terms and is itself profoundly connected to *vox*. Living speech as performed (*pronuntiatio*) will unveil the truth of the letter/voice/voice-as-lettered/letter-as-voice.

• • •

We have been following along with Priscian as he maps out the space-and-place of living speech and of word/voice as the image of presence. As we traverse our own road-to-reading/*legiter*, we will begin to take a number of detours and side roads in order to get a more complex appreciation of the territory over which

32 Priscian 1.14 (= *GL* 2.12): "k enim et q, quamvis figura et nomine videantur aliquam habere differentiam, cum c tamen eandem tam in sono vocum quam in metro potestatem continent. et k quidem penitus supervacua est." *Supervacua* also appears in Scaurus's work on orthography: "k quidam supervacuam esse litteram iudicaverunt, quoniam vice illius fungi satis c posset" (*GL* 7.14). See also Servius's commentary on Donatus (*GL* 4.422)

33 Hence, as Priscian reports, Varro sees the Chaldeans as the first authors of letters because, he says, their alphabet has a one-to-one mapping of letters and sounds (1.7 [= *GL* 2.8]). Any drift away from this happy state is evidence of decay and/or secondariness.

34 Priscian 1.16 (= *GL* 2.12–14) says that some deny that it should be considered among the letters.

35 Priscian 1.6 (= *GL* 2.7): "Accidit igitur literae nomen, figura, potestas."

36 Priscian 1.8 (= *GL* 2.9): "potestas autem ipsa pronuntiatio, propter quam et figurae et nomina facta sunt."

grammatical knowledge extends itself. There are a number of different approaches to getting a grammar started, and the very variety is indicative of a somewhat confused intellectual substructure that supports the whole enterprise. Nevertheless, the varied efforts all labor in parallel directions even if they start from different particular elements and move through their material at varied rates. Speech is meaning. Meanings are intentions.[37] Deep down words are "true," and grammar helps us to suture true images to true things. Of course, the number of stand-ins tends to multiply and the quantity of substances to slip away. And so: The word is the image of the thing-thought. The letter is the image of the voice-spoken. The *vox* is word-and-voice. It is substance and spirit(-as-air) and spirit(-as-soul). All of this has to be pinned down and put in its place if the enterprise is to begin and to have legitimacy. And yet what emerges is instead an as-if legitimacy, an image of knowledge rather than knowledge itself.

"Locution" [*loqui*] is derived from "location" [*locus*]. This is because one who speaks initially utters terms and speaks words before he knows how to say things in their proper place [*suo loco*]. Chrysippus denies that this person speaks [*loqui*] but calls this as-if-speaking [*ut loqui*]. And as the image of a man [*imago hominis* (cf. *imago vocis literatae* above)] is not a man, just so the words used by ravens, crows, and children starting to use language are not actually words since they are not speaking [*non loquantur*]. And so that man speaks [*loquitur*] who knowingly places each word in its own

---

37 Servius's commentary makes intentions one of the agenda items. And we can wonder if, like the number of books in a work, *intentio* is itself akin to an objective fact for someone like Servius. "In exponendis auctoribus haec consideranda sunt: poetae vita, titulus operis, qualitas carminis, scribentis intentio, numerus librorum, ordo librorum, explanatio" (comm. in *Aen.* I *praef.*) For a practical example, see 1.pr.70: "intentio Vergilii haec est, Homerum imitari et Augustum laudare a parentibus." Compare the commentary on 1.286: "et omnis poetae intentio, ut in qualitate carminis diximus, ad laudem tendit Augusti."

> proper place [*suo loco*] and locution [*prolocutum*] is a case of bringing forth what one has within one's breast [*animus*] by means of speaking [*loquendo*].[38]

The account of language is suffused with a conflated set of ideas about "propriety": proper places, proper persons, and things properly used. The discussion is almost never about language in general or some sort of neutral account of the empirical. Indeed, the domains of *usus* and *consuetudo* are filled with ugly necessities and not valorized terms. Instead this is the good Latin of good people: an elite sociology is mapped onto a quasi-scientific description of language.[39] To the extent that grammar is chiefly invested in the reproduction of the cultural relations of production, one is unsurprised at the tendency of discussions to degenerate into word lists and various catalogs of knowledge as know-how rather than rigorous scientific appraisals. Accordingly, the generic category of *usus* which was initially scorned as "mere use" returns in the form of reams of citations of "proper (elite) use." Professors — a collection of sociological also-rans — keep a tally of the bold strokes made on the field of play by their betters and transmit the scorecard on to the next generation as a (crushing) burden of tradition.[40] In short, Latin is already a "dead language" for these men even as they are fetishizing the living voice on the first pages of their works. These are lepidopterists who may praise winged words, but the only

---

38 "loqui ab loco dictum, quod qui primo dicitur iam fari[t] vocabula et reliqua verba dicit ante quam suo quisque loco ea dicere potest. hunc C<h>rysippus negat loqui, sed ut loqui: quare ut imago hominis non sit homo, sic in corvis, cornicibus, pueris primitus incipientibus fari verba non esse verba, quod non loqu[eb]antur. igitur is loquitur, qui suo loco quodque verbum sciens ponit, et †istum prolocutum, quom in animo quod habuit extulit loquendo." Varro, *De lingua Latina* 6.56.

39 Kaster, *Guardians of Language*, 14: "Whatever its other shortcomings, the grammarian's school did one thing superbly, providing the language and mores through which a social and political elite recognized its members."

40 Ibid., 7: The grammarian is "the man whose function set him amid many vital spheres of activity most often was without a place at the center of any of them."

legitimate specimens are the ones firmly affixed in their position by the stylus rammed through them.

It is in this context that I would like to explore a couple of tendentious etymologies and then to move on to barbarism and solecism. Grammarians teach a bounty of falsehoods. Contrived etymologies are thick on the ground. The errancy of their interpretations is less interesting than the poetic spark that motivates it. This particular poesy is generally quite retrograde and might well be seen as exactly the sort of thing designed to preclude the much freer play of the imagination that one associates with the poetry of the poets.

For the etymologist, instead of enjoying untrammeled liberty, language needs to have a necessary relationship to the world. And the professors are quite happy to dig out of words a meaning they knew had to be there all along. Isidore has good news: there is a one-church/Catholic truth to language.[41] But his position — as well as that of the other crypto- and not-so-crypto-Christian *grammatici* — is less an imposition upon the original material than it is a bringing out of a "truth of the truth of words," namely that the Word is always ready to be impressed into the service of (some) One that is (rhetorically) positioned as The One.[42] *Artes grammaticae* can even begin with an etymology of *ars* itself. What is the truth of *ars*/an *ars*? Servius's commentary on the *Ars* of Donatus starts with just such a commentary on the word *ars* itself:

> *Ars* is so named owing to *aretē* — that is it is derived from (manly) excellence [*virtus*] — which is the name Greeks give to the knowledge of each individual topic. Or it is most assuredly called *ars* because it encompasses everything in tight [*artīs*] precepts, that is in narrow and brief ones.[43]

---

41 See Henderson, *The Medieval World of Isidore of Seville*, 24.

42 Kaster, *Guardians of Language* flags the many grammatici who were likely Christians. But their texts do not announce such on every page, quite the contrary, in fact.

43 "ars dicta est vel ἀπὸ τῆς ἀρετῆς, id est a virtute, quam Graeci unius cuiusque rei scientiam vocant; vel certe ideo ars dicitur quod artis praeceptis

Either A, which is not especially convincing, or B, which is even less convincing.[44] Balking at such loosey-goosey arguments would be a disaster: everything is ship-shape says the man, even as the shapes shift before your very eyes: *vel... vel...* But not some other *vel,* of course. Isisore gives Servius's argument but in a different order:

> *Ars* is so named because it consists of tight [*artis*] precepts and rules. Others say that the word is drawn from the Greeks, ἀπὸ τῆς ἀρετῆς, that is, from "manly excellence" [*virtus*], the name they gave to knowledge.[45]

cuncta concludat, id est angustis et brevibus." Servius, *Commentarius in artem Donati* (GL 4.405).

44 The pedigree for this particular argument perhaps includes a trace of the noble blood of Homeric scholarship wherein a valiant effort is made to etymologize the word "hero": "ἡρώων· δεῖ γινώσκειν ὅτι ἥρωες ἐκλήθησαν ἀπὸ τῆς ἀρετῆς ἢ ἀπὸ τοῦ ἀέρος, ὥς φησιν Ἡσίοδος ἐν Ἔργοις καὶ Ἡμέραις" (Ephimerimi Homerici, *Iliad* 1.5.1; compare *Etymologicum Gudianum* (ζείδωροσ-ὤμαι), Alphabetic entry eta, 249 and Eustathius, *Commentarii ad Homeri Iliadem*, 1:29.) Missing from the argument of Donatus, however, is the rather obvious fact that τέχνη is the word that is routinely found in the titles of Greek "technical" works. The Latin translation of Τέχνη ῥητορική is *Ars rhetorica*. More to the point, a Greek would call his *Ars Grammatica* a Τέχνη γραμματική. See, for example, the opening words of Dositheus's *Ars grammatica*: "ἔστιν γνῶσις διωρθωμένης ὁμιλίας ἐν τῷ λέγειν καὶ ἐν τῷ γράφειν ποιημάτων τε καὶ ἀναγνώσεως ἔμπειρος διδασκαλία." See Massimo Gioseffi, "A Very Long Engagement: Some Remarks About the Relationship Between Marginalia and Commentaries in the Virgilian Tradition." *Trends in Classics* 6, no. 1 (2014): 176–91 for some preliminary notes on how to deal with "as others would have it" within authors like our grammatici: how much comes from the reading of distilled, excerpted and highly derivative works and how much from an engagement with longer, continuous pieces? And what degree of freedom do our authors show relative to antecedents such as these? One can compare the remarks of Robert A. Kaster, "Servius and Idonei Auctores," *American Journal of Philology* 99 (1978):181–82.

45 "ars vero dicta est quod artis praeceptis regulisque consistat. Alii dicunt a Graecis hoc tractum esse vocabulum ἀπὸ τῆς ἀρετῆς, id est a virtute, quam scientiam vocaverunt." Isidore 1.1.2. Isidore's text is identical to Servius, *Commentarius in Artem Donati,* 405, l. 2. Isidore was the archbishop of Seville and he died in 636 CE. See also Pompeius's *Commentum artis Donati* (GL 5.95) for the same etymology. Pompeius seems to have been an African and to have been active in the fifth or sixth centuries CE. Note also that

There is an "internal consistency" to such arguments that is provided by the "tight" binding of words like *ars* and *artus* to one another within an imaginary plane of signification that is perfectly indifferent to any failure of an actual etymological (in our sense) affiliation: manliness is scientific; science is manly; Latin art is really Greek excellence... All of this "makes sense" and is "sense-making" because it leverages a pre-existing universe of symbolic associations in order to generate a "voice of reason" that then speaks an arbitrary truth of words which has been posited as an essential truth of words. Meanwhile language in general constricts into a domain fully territorialized by elite speech. This elitism is both political and cultural. Nor should there be any real gap between aesthetic domination and socio-economic domination. The exemplary examples are all canonical, for, of course, we are working in the rule/ruler factory. Says Probus:

> The *articulata vox* is the one that can be captured by letters: for example/put in your head the following injunctions, "Write, Cicero"; "Read, Vergil"; and other such items.[46]

The structure of the lesson is itself part of the lesson. To say that a *vox* is something that can be transcribed requires only a citation of line one of the *Aeneid* if you are Priscian. Those words can be turned into those letters. But here the exemplary word is a command: "Get to work, Cicero. Go to it, Vergil." And the

---

Servius will sneak the *ars* = *virtus* equation into his commentary on the *Aeneid*: "reddidit arte: id est virtute, ἀπὸ τῆς ἀρετῆς." This is a gloss on *Aeneid* 5.704–5, a place where one feels no special need to translate *ars* with anything that lies very far from the English term "art": "tum senior Nautes, unum Tritonia Pallas | quem docuit multaque insignem reddidit arte." Of course, now that one knows that *virtus* is an equivalent for *ars,* why not imagine swapping it in for every instance of *ars*? Something quasi-sensible will always emerge in the wake of the substitution.

46 "(vox) articulata est qua homines locuntur et litteris comprehendi postest, ut puta scribe Cicero, Vergili lege et cetera talia" Probus, *Instituta artium* (*GL* 4.47). Probus was active in the fourth century CE. He was perhaps an African who (perhaps) migrated to Rome to teach.

work these men are asked to do converges with the work that the professors and the students engage in as consumers of these cultural producers: read-and-write. Professor Probus gets after that shiftless Chickpea and that none-too-chaste Vergil: "Write that we might read." And while *ut puta* is more or less dead as an imperative and means little more than "for example,"[47] one might as well revitalize it just a bit and think of it more as "Imagine a situation like…." The imperative thing is to get into your head the imperative to fuse voice, reading, writing and then to set them into a relationship with the spirit or soul (*animus*) (if we are allowed to pull a key word from other passages in other authors into this one).

The hortatory mode of instruction is no mere boosterism. Instead the injunctions are convergent with legal education if not just plain old legislation. If laws (*leges*) have legislators (*latores*) in Livy and Quintilian, so does grammar itself in Probus. "The letter is the atom of *vox*…."[48] After going through some familiar arguments about letters, Probus then transitions to the "problem" of the gender one is to assign to the names of the letters. The letter is the atom of the word, but even these atoms seem to be burdened with the as-if metaphysical question of (grammatical) gender. This question is "assuredly" (*sane*) a settled question, and one settled by legislative fiat:

> Assuredly the legislators of the art of grammar [*artis latores*] and Varro in particular have all decided and commanded that the name of each individual letter is neuter in gender and to be declined accordingly.[49]

---

47 The collocation is extremely common in Justinian and is used to illustrate a general legal situation by means of a pertinent specific situation to which it might be applied. And Probus himself will spread it liberally across this same page.

48 Probus, *Instituta artium* (*GL* 4.48).

49 "sane nomen unius cuiusque litterae omnes artis latores, praecipueque Varro, neutro genere appellari iudicaverunt et aptote declinari iusserunt." Ibid.

Varro and others passed the Art-law that says that it's *hoc a* and not *hic a* or *haec a*. The use of *latores* is something of a throwaway moment, but it is nevertheless a revelatory one as it provides one of the proper domains within which to think about "the art," how it works, and where it comes from. And this genealogy is not especially close to the sort of neutral, empirical work that is demanded by modern linguistic science.

• • •

As I have been arguing, an analysis of ancient philology at the atomic level exposes that this same level is governed by what one might call quantum effects: strategic superimpositions and structuring uncertainties govern the account of the foundations of language. And these same effects can be observed once we have fully embarked upon the erudite road to reading. Various tics can be observed throughout our teachers' presentations. And one need little more than to ask grammar to offer a grammatical account of itself in order to precipitate a crisis. And this is the sort of thing we will see Lucian and Petronius in fact did.

One of the chief justifications for submitting oneself to a grammatical education is not something like an ability to read Vergil better and to love him all the more. Instead the teachers emphasize that good grammar helps you to avoid linguistic failures. And these same failures are always also class failures. Education teaches the ruling rules, how to recognize and to deploy them, how to submit oneself to them, how to insist that others submit as well. Accordingly, one of the first items to be discussed after the mechanical issue of letters is proper spelling.[50] In fact there is not so much a word for proper spelling as there is a word for improper spelling: barbarism. Avoid it.[51]

50 Next order of business: what we should do, er, what we should not do... See Servius, *Commentarius in Artem Donati*: "Decurso octo partium tractatu incipit iam transire ad illud, quod docet nos, vel quem ad modum possumus vitare vitia vel habere virtutes" (*GL* 4.443).
51 Quintilian conjures it away early on: "Prima barbarismi ac soloecismi foeditas absit" (*Institutio* 1.5.5). But no sooner has he dispelled these specters

Two complications arise at once: first, teacher himself has been barbarizing, and, second, Vergil is chock-full of barbarisms.[52] Let us look at the latter issue first. The examples of barbarism and other transgressions will regularly be drawn from the *Aeneid*.[53] Diomedes says that we cannot make it two lines into the *Aeneid* without confronting the poem's coarse barbarity: *Italiam fato profugus* has a long initial *i*, even though the vowel should be short.[54] Obviously my own argument is itself somewhat tendentious. Nobody is saying that Vergil's Latin is bad. Quite the contrary, in fact. But bad Latin prose is consistently illustrated by means of appeals to good Latin verse: "If a poet does it, it is *metaplasmus*. If you do it, it is *barbarismus*."[55]

Naturally, one suspects that any old poet is not allowed to make any old change: poetic licenses are not handed out willy-nilly. And yet once you have such a license, it is really more like a blank check: either all irregularities in a good poet are part of his genius and to be explained as such, or they are to be dismissed

> than they return in the very next words: "sed quia interim excusantur haec uitia aut consuetudine aut auctoritate aut uetustate aut denique uicinitate uirtutum […]."

52 The word "barbarism" is itself a quasi-barbarism? One can accept it to the extent that neologisms are admissible. See Gellius, *Noctes Atticae* 13.6.4: "Itaque id uocabulum, quod dicitur uulgo 'barbarismus', qui ante diui Augusti aetatem pure atque integre locuti sunt, an dixerint, nondum equidem inueni."

53 For a less tendentious take on the manner in which our teachers have to warn their students that some Vergilian uses are deviations from *proprietas* and not to be understood as "proper Latin" itself, see Robert Maltby, "The Role of Etymologies in Servius and Donatus," in *Etymologia: Studies in Ancient Etymology: Proceedings of the Cambridge Conference on Ancient Etymology, 25–27 September 2000*, ed. Christos Nifadopoulos, 103–18 (Münster: Nodus Publikationen, 2003), 108–9.

54 Diomedes, *Ars grammatica* (*GL* 1.452). This is a canonical example: compare Quintilian, *Institutio* 1.5.18 and Servius, *Commentarius in Artem Donati* (*GL* 4.444).

55 Donatus, *Ars grammatica*: "est una pars orationis vitiosa in communi sermone. in poemate metaplasmus, itemque in nostra loquella barbarismus" (*GL* 4.392). Servius on Donatus: "si autem in poemate, metaplasmus vocatur" (*GL* 4.444). Diomedes, *Ars grammatica*: "ceterum apud poetas barbarismus metaplasmus dicitur" (*GL* 1.455).

as uninteresting examples of places where "the meter made him do it." Or maybe the transgression was a harmless bit of pleasure-seeking in the name of beauty (*decoris causa*).⁵⁶ On second viewing, the vice might well be a virtue, provided, of course, that the right sort of sinner has sinned in the right sort of way and is said to have done so by the right sort of reader.

The fetish for the good and the bad leaves these readers relatively numb to any number of hermeneutic possibilities. Nevertheless, even as they are fostering a strong, clear sense of right and wrong uses, the grammarians produce a jarring double acoustic experience. In good verse, we hear an echo of something bad, and every time we say *Italiam* "the right way," we hear ourselves also not speaking it "beautifully." And every time we read Vergil, our ears are inundated by an endless array of transgressions against propriety.

Adding or subtracting letters is one of the prominent species of the class of barbarisms. And, of course, the phenomenon needs to be illustrated. The *grammatici* are happy to oblige. Quintilian cautions against deriving examples of transgressions from the poets. He says that it is easy enough to invent misspellings and mispronunciations without vaunting a perverse brand of erudition by digging up problematic verses.⁵⁷ And yet the boastful learnedness of *iactatio eruditionis* constitutes a key

---

56 Donatus, *Ars grammatica*: "metaplasmus est transformatio quaedam recti soluti sermonis in alteram speciem metri ornatusve causa" (*GL* 4.395). Rectitude (*recti*) makes way for either meter or adornment. Compare Charisius, *Institutio grammatica*: "metaplasmus est dictio aliter quam debuit figurata metri aut decoris causa" (*GL* 1.277). Obligations (*debuit*) are suspended: meter-or-beauty takes precedence. Charisius was active at Rome in the late fourth century CE.
57 Quintilian, *Institio Oratoria* 1.5.10–11: "tertium est illud uitium barbarismi, cuius exempla uulgo sunt plurima, sibi etiam quisque fingere potest, ut uerbo cui libebit adiciat litteram syllabamue uel detrahat aut aliam pro alia aut eandem alio quam rectum est loco ponat. sed quidam fere in iactationem eruditionis sumere illa ex poetis solent, et auctores quos praelegunt criminantur." But Quintilian himself will draw from Vergil in just a few sections when he notes the scansion of *Italiam* at *Aeneid* 1.2.

element of the knowledge performance of the grammarians. The learned mask projects this self-satisfied voice most eagerly.

If we linger with the idea of masks, and stages, and theatricality, we can describe the *ars grammatica* as an art of staging oneself as a professor. For example, the incoherent description of *vox* on offer need not be read as a failure of argument or reason. That puts things in the wrong register. Instead the specious story of *vox* is part of a performance of the would-be coherence of the professor's own *vox*. Furthermore, as a would-be coherent performance of authoritative knowledge the various *Artes* perform a mastery of *Artes grammaticae*. They are about mastering this character and performing him on this stage. It is not really clear that an *Ars* is really about Latin in general (as it was really spoken) or even about the Latin of a given era or genre. One notes then that several of the *Grammatici Latini* write commentaries on Donatus's commentary. Scholarship is more a matter of a mastery of the secondary literature and its idioms than it is something that is predicated on a devotion to the primary texts.[58]

Again, the argument about barbarism is completely hollow: "If a poet does it, then it is not a barbarism." The Latin of the poets obeys its own rules, say the people who teach "the rules." And yet a good many of these same rules seem to be made up on the spot as a means of explaining what one sees in the poets.[59] The explanations tend towards the tautological: even though

---

58 See Roger Wright, "Even Priscian Nods," in *Latin vulgaire, latin tardif VI: actes du VIᵉ Colloque international sur le latin vulgaire et tardif, Helsinki, 29 août–2 septembre,* ed. Heikki Solin, 577–88 (Hildesheim: Olms, 2003), 577 on the way that *grammatici* tend to read only *grammatici,* even when common sense might give them some pause about certain issues.

59 The closed-off quality of the "barbarism" debate can be seen in the fact that the examples of failures tend to themselves be centuries old and drawn from other authors' notes on the topic. Pompeius's use of the actual (mis-)spoken Latin of his day sets him apart. See Luigi Munzi, "Per il testo dei grammatici latini," *Bollettino dei classici, a cura del Comitato per la preparazione dell' Edizione nazionale dei Classici greci e latini* 21 (2000): 103–14 , at 104–5 on *GL* 5.285–49.

this is wrong, it is right because this is poetry.[60] Indeed, an educated, backwards-looking fantasy of "authorial intention" determines whether or not a variation from the norm is a poeticism or a lapse.[61]

Meanwhile, as fans of good spelling may well have noticed by this point, the professors' Latin is itself full of variants, or, as they would put it, barbarisms. Some of our authors have been writing about *literae*, others about *litterae*. There is li(t)terally a failure to agree about first principles, and we find disorder at the atomic level.[62] Even as the *grammatici* obsess over pure Latin and aver that there is such a thing, and that it can and, indeed, must be taught, their concrete practice reveals that they are promulgating a fantasy of Latin. And the clear-eyed will notice any number of superfluities, remainders, and omissions in the course of their account of an immaculate Latinity.[63] This is a dream of Latin that subsists with the keenest "reality" only as a concrete character trait of the proffessoriat. This Latin inhabits only the brainpans of a certain species of highly influential cul-

---

60 Or maybe it is wrong. Homer nods, say Amphipolites and Chrysippus. See *Scholia in Homeri Iliadem* A 129: "Ζωΐλος δὲ ὁ Ἀμφιπολίτης καὶ Χρύσιππος ὁ Στωϊκὸς σολοικίζειν οἴονται τὸν ποιητὴν ἀντὶ ἑνικοῦ πληθυντικῷ χρησάμενον ῥήματι."

61 Pliny says as much. See Servius, *Commentarius in artem Donatum*: "Quaesitum est apud Plinium Secundum quid interesset inter figuras et vitia. nam cum figurae ad ornatum adhibeantur, vitia vitentur, eadem autem inveniantur exempla tam in figuris quam in vitiis, debet aliqua esse discretio. quidquid ergo scientes facimus novitatis cupidi, quod tamen idoneorum auctorum firmatur exemplis, figura dicitur. quidquid autem ignorantes ponimus vitium putatur" (*GL* 4.447).

62 Lewis and Short's *Latin Dictionary*: "*littĕra* (less correctly *lītĕra*), ae, f. *lino*, q. v." Why "less correctly" and not "barbarously"? It seems that critics have grown soft over the centuries.

63 See Daniel C. Andersson, "Did Diomedes Know Latin? A Problem with His *De optativis*," *Hermes* 139 (2011): 110–11 on how it is that Diomedes comes to utterly botch a description of the use of the subjunctive with *priusquam* and *antequam*: "What appears to have happened is that the authority of Vergil within the teaching environment that Diomedes knew so well has warped the descriptive function of Charisius' grammar and that he has constructed an ad hoc explanation to deal with an apparent difficulty in Vergil's text."

tural gatekeepers. It was never obviously on anyone's tongue either "back then" or, especially, in the benighted "here and now."

Latin is conservative speech is "pure speech": "Latinity is that which preserves pure speech, a speech free from every failing. There are two possible failings in speech that cause it to be less than Latin, the solecism and the barbarism."[64] Barbarity produces less-than-Latinity. The least linguistic variation is tantamount to an unnatural act. The schoolmasters trot out Pliny on pure Latin and (dangerously) supplement the citation with an asseveration that Pliny's Latin was itself pure while he was speaking of purity:

> Look how Pliny puts it, how well and irreproachably he speaks. What is barbarism? That what is not spoken naturally [*per naturam*]. What is solecism? That which is ill spoken artfully [*per artem*].[65]

The proper individual word is as natural as the atoms of the universe. Bad phrases represent bad art in every possible dimension: they break both with nature and with the appreciation of language that *artes grammaticae* have. And, in all likelihood, these bad phrases make their transgressions in the name of their own perverse, ignorant, and oxymoronic species of artless art. The secondary senses of the vocabulary in such passages

---

64 "Latinitas est, quae sermonem purum conservat, ab omni vitio remotum. vitia in sermone, quo minus is Latinus sit, duo possunt esse: soloecismus et barbarismus." See [Cicero], *Rhetorica ad Herennium* 4.17.

65 "Et vide quem ad modum expressit Plinius, quam bene et integre dicit. quid est barbarismus? quod non dicitur per naturam. quid est soloecismus? quod male per artem dicitur." Pompeius, *Commentum artis Donati* (*GL* 5.283). The passage continues with definitions of solecism and barbarism. Then it concludes: "We will clearly explain how we can avoid such in our *Ars Grammatica* [haec qua ratione vitare possumus, in arte grammatica dilucide dicemus]." Compare Servius's Pliny: "Pliny says that a barbarism is a single word whose force is unnatural. The name barbarism comes from the fact that barbarians speak in a warped manner, as if one were to say 'Rume' instead of 'Rome' [*Plinius autem dicit barbarismum esse sermonem unum, in quo vis sua est contra naturam. barbarismus autem dicitur eo quod barbari prave locuntur, ut siqui dicat Rumam pro Roma*]." See *GL* 4.444.

tell a tale of legitimate conservative hegemony fighting valiantly against degenerate outsiders, the alien, and the déclassé. And yet the very people who repeat this lesson century after century are themselves often usurpers. They may well be successful occupants of privileged positions, but theirs is more a rhetoric of legitimacy than some sort of substance thereof. Hermit crabs flail their claws menacingly as they lecture about the making of the shell that they wear on their back, an act of fabrication of which they have only second-hand knowledge, if any.

This calcified, formal posture of philological rigor says: "Every letter matters, no least detail is too small." Meanwhile variant spellings swirl about us, and they do so less as a simple function of stupidity and error than as an element of a self-blinding knowledge that cannot let language live. Living speech and the dead letter have to be fused together if this sort of by-the-book Latinity is to be promulgated. And so, the *Artes* get written up century after century, more likely to cite one another and familiar bundles of citations than to read verses with fresh eyes.

It all suits them to a missing-*t*, this *literatus* insistence upon the rule-bound nature of Latin. And their erudition runneth over. The bluff and bravado of the institution as a whole is swaddled in the rhetoric of stuffy asseveration. "In poetry this is metaplasmus, but the same thing is a barbarism in everyday speech."[66] And yet how does one spell the word for "everyday speech"? Is it *loquella* or *loquela*? That's an easy one, just open up Flavius Caper's *De Orthographia*: "*narro* and *narratio* are spelled with two *r*'s, *querela* and *loquela* with one *l*."[67] One and only one *l*. If Catullus, Lucretius, and Ovid use two, then that must have been a metaplasmus, right?[68] That's the rule we have seen before: poetry means wrong-but-right means metaplasmus.

---

66 Donatus, *Ars grammatica*: "in poemate metaplasmus, itemque in nostra loquella barbarismus" (*GL* 4.392).

67 Caper, *Orthographia*: "narro narratio per duo r, querela loquela per unum l" (*GL* 7.96).

68 Catullus, *Carmina* 55.20: "verbosa gaudet Venus loquella". Lucretius is kind enough to even be talking about linguistic variation in one of the places where he uses the word. See Lucretius, *De rerum natura* 5.71: "quove modo

And sure enough it looks like we might be seeing it again. Varro's *De Lingua Latina* has only one *l*. And Servius's commentary on *Aeneid* 4.360 specifically says that the doubling is what poets do.[69] It would be easy enough to close the book on this one were it not the case that our very same Servius had used *loquellis* in his own prosy voice when commenting on *Aeneid* 1.595.[70] A proper count should be the work of an instant. A glance could sort the byproducts of coprolallia from the products of a golden tongue. But this is not really about counting in the end. Instead, the field of play circles around a different statement, namely "we all know that there is a right number of consonants." "Know" and "right" are the important terms, the real words that we really care about. The actual number of consonants can and will vary. As with the heterogeneity of *litera/littera,* one cannot but marvel at a failure of the word masters to agree about the spelling of the word for word. And, further, the failure of agreement within the professional discourse is itself quietly effaced even as one volubly denounces the ignorant masses for their failure to adhere to the norm (whatever that norm might be).

As an illustration of barbarity that is not barbarity because it is really licensed poetic metalepsis we are pointed to an example with which we must certainly be familiar: *relliquias Danaum.* Donatus tells that barbarism can result from the addition of a letter or a syllable: "cf. *relliquias Danaum.*"[71] The phrase in question is used three times in the *Aeneid* and occurs at 1.30, 1.598, and 3.87. Donatus is probably thinking of the first of these given

genus humanum variante loquella." Ovid is even talking about literal barbarism. See *Tristia* 5.2.68: "Graecaque quod Getico victa loquela sono est".

69 "QVERELLIS: 'l' litteram metri causa addidit: nam 'querela' dicitur, quia 'querulus' facit: hoc modo et 'loquela', 'suadela'." Servius, *In Vergilii Aeneidos Libros* 4.360.

70 "sane coram quidam adverbium putant, quia non subsequitur casus, quidam praepositionem loquellis, non casibus servientem." Servius, *In Vergilii Aeneidos Libros* 1.595.

71 Donatus, *Ars grammatica*: "per adiectionem litterae fiunt barbarismi, sicut 'relliquias Danaum', cum reliquias per unum l dicere debeamus; syllabae, ut 'nos abiisse rati' pro abisse; temporis, ut 'Italiam fato profugus;, cum Italiam correpta prima littera dicere debeamus [...]" (*GL* 4.392).

that there is a bias towards early lines in his examples. Nevertheless, one will be hard pressed to find any remainder of the phrase *relliquias Danaum* in a printed text of Vergil.[72] And that is because, outside of a passage like this, one does not spell the word that way. Indeed, the spelling is tough to find in Servius's commentary on Vergil. When he glosses these lines, Servius tells us about items like *Danaum* and is silent about the spelling of *reliquiae*. And yet Servius's commentary on Donatus faithfully transcribes an example that he himself does not follow.[73] It looks like we are seeing in Donatus some sort of retrojection into the text of Vergil of a later way of saying/syllabifying a word. And then this non-Vergilian Latin is made into an element of an erudite gloss on something that "seems off but is really spot on because, see, it's in Vergil."

When we step back and take stock of this soundscape, it's all starting to feel like we are overhearing some sort of bizarre inside joke: won't spell letter right; slurring the word for words; leftover letters in the word for leftovers. And, to cap it all off, many of them are unable to spell the name of their favorite poet properly: it's Vergil, not Virgil, you idiots. His friend Horace called him that, and so should we.[74] And yet this misspelling has a canonical status. It starts early and persists well beyond the classical era. In fact, Virgil becomes the standard way of writing the name. If one cares about spelling and abhors barbarity as per the eight thick volumes of the *Grammatici Latini,* then one

72 Vat.lat.3225 is a fourth-century manuscript of Vergil. At XVIv (i.e. at 1.598) one reads *reliquias*. But a small extra l has been written in above the word. But which version is the "mistake," the first or the second? It depends on where you went to school and when and with whom, I suppose. In the next line *exaustis* was written and then double corrected to read instead *exhaustos*. And the latter is what one prints today: change the case; add an *h*.
73 Servius, *Commentarius in Artem Donati*: "[barbarismus] fit quinque rebus, littera syllaba accentu tempore adspiratione. haec omnia aut adiciuntur aut detrahuntur. adicitur littera, ut 'relliquias Danaum', syllaba, ut induperator pro eo quod est imperator: tempore, ut 'Italiam fato profugus', cum Italiam priore correpta syllaba dicere debeamus" (*GL* 4.444).
74 See, for example, Horace, *Sermones* 1.10.44–45: "molle atque facetum | Vergilio adnuerunt gaudentes rure Camenae."

can only shudder to heft the *Oxford Classical Dictionary* whose second edition has an entry only under "Virgil." Seek for something that starts "Ver..." and you will find only "Vergiliomastix." A poet is being beaten. But who? And why? Presumably he barbarized when he thought he was being metaplastic.

The entry to "Virgil" — whoever he might be — begins: "The spelling with an 'i' is traditional; contemporary inscriptions give the name Vergilius. It was corrupted by the fourth or fifth centuries, and so passed into all vernaculars."[75] Virgil is what highly exquisite barbarians of all centuries call the poet they fetishize and most adore. The very ages that are starting to have trouble spelling his name are the same ones in which *artes grammaticae* are exploding, these books full of voice-and-letter stuff. Amidst all that talk about writing and writing about talk there ensues a becoming-right of the wrong, an institutionalized acculturation of barbarism that is so powerful and so well-placed that the noble savages of Oxford cannot bring themselves to call Vergil by his own name: the post-classical vernacular takes precedence over the classicism of the *Classical Dictionary*.

• • •

I have been bringing out the most dire potentialities folded within the discourse of the *grammatici*, and I will continue to do so for a bit longer. Obviously, they can and would train sensitive, open-minded readers of literature, but an emphasis on that sort of end is hard to note amid page after page of talk about right vs. wrong and catalogues of approved uses.[76]

---

75 The *Oxford Classical Dictionary* (2nd ed.), s.v. "Virgil" [*sic*].

76 Dionysius Thrax begins his *Ars Grammatica* with a much more expansive definition of the project: "γραμματική ἐστιν ἐμπειρία τῶν παρὰ ποιηταῖς τε καὶ συγγραφεῦσιν ὡς ἐπὶ τὸ πολὺ λεγομένων." And even if many of the chief members of the practice have a certain stiffness to them, he does not phrase things in the most dire possible way. Moreover, he privileges interpretation as the noblest of the elements. See 1.1.5: "Μέρη δὲ αὐτῆς ἐστιν ἕξ· πρῶτον ἀνάγνωσις ἐντριβὴς κατὰ προσῳδίαν, δεύτερον ἐξήγησις κατὰ τοὺς ἐνυπάρχοντας ποιητικοὺς τρόπους, τρίτον γλωσσῶν τε καὶ ἱστοριῶν πρόχειρος ἀπόδοσις, τέταρτον ἐτυμολογίας εὕρεσις, πέμπτον ἀναλογίας

Education takes on the air of class indoctrination. The "guardians of knowledge" take on a gatekeeper function: their role is to produce a natural-*cum*-artificial yoke between good language and good people.[77] Students become heirs to a cultural legacy which they have earned by dint of the fact that they have submitted themselves to their teacher's lessons. Or, more accurately, by dint of the fact that their already successful fathers have sent them to the school of submission.

Even if *amphibolia* is a vice, double-meanings hover over every term and multiple ends are served simultaneously.[78] The technical discussion is always also about something more than mere technicalities. A self-referential air wafts over the discussion. Examples are frequently not mere examples. Do you want to know about the comparative and superlative degrees? The words chosen to illustrate the phenomenon are *doctus, doctior,* and *doctissimus*.[79] Do you want to know what an abstract noun is? *Pietas* will do as an example, a word that defines both Aeneas and, *sotto voce,* commentators (on commentators) on the *Aeneid* who piously invent, er, I mean, transmit to their students, the *scribentis intentio.*

Proprie is a word often deployed when drawing legitimate scholarly distinctions. But scholarly distinction cannot be segregated from social distinction. Legitimacy is the proper possession of the educated. See, for example Servius:

> In the case of every part of speech there ought to be definitions that separate them from the others and that indicate

---

ἐκλογισμός, ἕκτον κρίσις ποιημάτων, ὃ δὴ κάλλιστόν ἐστι πάντων τῶν ἐν τῇ τέχνῃ." As someone who was active in the second century BCE, Dionysius is a much earlier writer than most of the people we have been talking about.

77 This is Kaster's thesis. See the opening chapter of Kaster, *Guardians of Language.*
78 Quintilian, *Institutio oratoria* 9.4.32: "Amphiboliam quoque fieri uitiosa locatione uerborum nemo est qui nesciat."
79 Servius, *Commentarius in artem Donati* (GL 4.406).

some specific individual property [*proprietas*] of that part that they define.[80]

Definition, boundary setting, propriety. That sounds good. But notice that this remark by Servius is offered as a commentary on the following statement by Donatus: "A noun is a part of speech that has a case and indicates a (material) body or an (abstract) thing in a manner that is either particular or general."[81] Servius's sequel uses the same terms but differently, and it steers the point towards a different end. Donatus's self-appointed heir appropriates *propie* and drops *communiter*. Servius's point is more narrow and technical than I let on, but he has nevertheless strategically shifted the terms of the discussion. Donatus wanted to talk about proper nouns as distinguished from "common nouns." His examples were Tiber and Rome as against river and city.[82] In Servius, it is exclusively an exclusionary Rome that we will inhabit: to hell with other cities and any community of common nouns. Karthago and its accursed *K* should be deleted. Remember as well that *k* is not a "proper *vox*" since it mimics *c* and *qu* and is accordingly "common." Instead let us speak only of purity/propriety, and let us do so in the midst of an incredibly hybrid text composed during an era of radical cultural change.[83]

80 "in omnibus partibus orationis definitiones ita esse debent, ut et segregent ab aliis partibus et ipsius partis quam definiunt aliquam proprietatem dicant." Servius, *Commentarius in artem Donati* (*GL* 4.406).
81 "nomen est pars orationis cum casu corpus aut rem proprie communiterve significans." Servius, *Commentarius in artem Donati* (GL 4.406).
82 Cledonius uses the same argument in his *Ars* (*GL* 5.10). Cledonius seems to have been active in the second half of the fifth century CE. He was a grammarian and a senator who lived in Constantinople.
83 In this period, we are undergoing the decisive shift from a pagan culture of Rome to a Christian one: the number of reasons there is not going to be a next Cicero compounds itself century by century, starting with the 1st century CE. Nevertheless, the syllabus still consists of "the classics." See L. D. Reynolds and N.G. Wilson, *Scribes and Scholars: A Guide to the Transmission of Greek and Latin Literature*, 3rd edn. (Oxford: Oxford University Press, 1991), 34–35. And yet, unlike Quintilian who will cite both Vergil and Cicero on every single page, the *grammatici* are in fact much more interested in Vergil than in Cicero, and, accordingly, "Augustan verse" and not

The contrived, baroque rhetoric of the letter that serves as the preface to Diomedes' *Ars* is just the sort of thing that some rhetoric teachers could pick to pieces for its swollen style. And yet we are not allowed to laugh, at least not yet. Please see below for who chuckles, when, where, and how. Instead this tumescent rhetoric that opens up the volume is a vindication of education in general and it hammers us with a Latin no uneducated man would ever produce as it describes the Latin only education can yield.[84] Overwrought metaphors about metalworking are indicative of a neurotic and hyperbolic effort to show-and-do-and-tell, a rhetoric where these modes have all become fused as we listen to this *vox* about *vox* about *vox* echo in our ears ideas parroted from others.

Diomedes begins thus: "The Art of undiluted Latin, the teacher of pure eloquence: the grandeur of human cleverness has polished it, a thing forged by learned blows of a scholarly hammer making educated strikes."[85] The overstuffed prose is hard to parse at first glance, and this is exactly the sort of failing that teachers teach one to avoid. And yet Diomedes doubtless "intends" for us to take this sentence about shine and polish as

---

"Republican Latin" tends to sound like "(classical) Latin" for them. On the weight and pattern of citations, see Paolo De Paolis, "Cicerone nei grammatici tardoantichi e altomedievali," *Ciceroniana* 11 (2000): 37–67. And, finally, note that a strong rhetoric-vs-poetry antithesis is not operative. Quintilian uses Vergil to teach us Cicero. And Donatus reads Vergil via a rhetorical filter and assigns the *Aeneid* to the *genus laudativum* and so forth. See Luigi Pirovano, "Deformare e deformatio nel lessico di Tiberio Claudio Donato," in *E io sarò tua guida: raccolta di saggi su Virgilio e gli studi Virgiliani*, ed. Massimo Gioseffi, 217–38 (Cambridge: Cambridge University Press, 2000). For a fuller account of rhetoric and poetry's symbiosis, see Irene Peirano, *Persuasion, Rhetoric, and Roman Poetry* (Cambridge: Cambridge University Press, forthcoming).

84 As Kaster, *Guardians of Language,* 38, insists, illiteracy is far and away the norm. Any attainment sets one apart. Being an imperfect student of Cicero's Latin is assuredly not the most salient issue in a world where virtually nobody can claim to be an accomplished one.

85 "Artem merae Latinitatis puraeque eloquentiae magistram sub incude litteraria dociliter procudendo formatam humanae sollertiae claritas expolivit." Diomedes, *Ars grammatica* (*GL* 1.299).

something that is itself shiny and polished. *Claritas* is abstract and empty but it radiates a warm sociological glow: *clarus* is a word that is used to designate a very specific sort of man, after all. For an up-and-comer schoolmaster clever clarity and cleverness as *claritudo* will do just fine as a surface sense with some not-so-hidden depths to it.[86]

This sentence beats us over the head with its ideas about education and hammers home its thought about hammers. Literary study teaches the teachable its learned learnings learnedly. *Dociliter* is doing a lot of work. The fact that Diomedes seems unaware of or indifferent to the sorts of things that Cicero, Seneca, and Quintilian say about style shows us that this is a book about "today" and "today's Latin" even as it is stuffed full of backwards-looking passages and precepts.[87] The Book of Good Latin™ is replacing books that are filled with good Latin. The textbook has an immanent force that is only incidentally connected with the sort of projects embedded in the Latin that it quotes.

For example, when Diomedes used the phrase *meatus aurium* our own erudite ears shudder at the sort of collocation that would be a problem for older writers. *Aures* should not be a genitive modifier of a concrete noun unless there is a good reason to do such a thing. An abstract noun is what one will see governing *aurium: voluptas aurium, sensus aurium, mensura aurium, causa aurium.... Meatus* takes something like "moon," "sky," or "stars" as its typical object: very few passages will not fall into that pattern. At a minimum, a Vergil — or is it Virgil? — professor will have Vergil, *Aeneid* 6.849 to hand, a verse which contains the phrase *caelique meatus. Meatus pectoris* is a late and bold extension. See [Quintilian], *Declamationes Maiores* 8.18. Accordingly, *meatus aurium* reads like the pushing of an already forced us-

---

86 See Kaster, *Guardians of Language,* 57–62, on the precarious claims to membership in high society of the *grammatici*.

87 See Kaster, "Servius and Idonei Auctores," on the conjuring of approved classes of author who are ranked by time-as-merit: *antiqui, neoterici, idonei.* More recent writers are admitted to discussions only provisionally and when they support an "older" consensus and can be slotted into some sort of "establishment" position.

age. Well, that's how it reads if the Latin one is familiar with is the "pure Latin" of Cicero and not the "pure Latin" of Diomedes the Latin teacher whose life and Latin are to be placed centuries later despite the rhetoric of "timelessness" in which his work is couched. Of course, it should be remembered that Quintilian's Ciceronean Latin is a retrograde-but-contemporary construct that can and should be distinguished from Cicero's Latin. And, similarly, Cicero's Latin was itself an invention that was decried as a modernist, hybrid monstrosity back in the day. "Good Latin" names/has named/will name a gambit wherein one pretends that there is such a thing as Good Latin, even as it is never a thing in its own right.[88]

Diomedes' prologue closes with an injunction to remember. Memory and nostalgia save us from horror. Those who remember what their teachers taught them will be OK in the end. What remains is the task of cultivating-and-recultivating an atomized Field of Latinity, of committing remainders like *relliquiae*-with-two-*l*'s to our memory and therewith triumphing:

> For the rest, one should rehearse one's individual lessons and so fix them fast in the memory. Otherwise one's efforts would fade over time, and effort is the thing that principally allows us to be recognized as being superior to the ignorant. With the monstrosity/non-normativity of their rustic and uncultivated speech the ignorant wound, no, they utterly warp, the well-regulated/normative integrity of speech. They bring darkness upon its polished light, a light brought forth by means of art in the same measure as they themselves differ from beasts.[89]

---

88 See Michel Banniard, "Le latin classique existe-t-il?," in *Latin vulgaire, latin tardif IX: Actes du IXᵉ Colloque international sur le latin vulgaire et tardif, Lyon, 2-6 septembre 2009*, eds. Frédérique Biville, Marie-Karine Lhommé, and Daniel Vallat, 57–78 (Lyon: Maison de l'orient et de la Méditerranée, 2012) for a critique of the concept of "classical Latin."

89 "superest ut singula recolendo memoriae tenaci mandentur, ne frustra cum tempore evanescat labor, quo tanto maxime rudibus praestare cognoscimur, qui rusticitatis enormitate incultique sermonis ordine sauciant, immo de-

This learned praise of learning is written in a terrible-but-educated Latin that poses as terribly educated Latin. Diomedes does a fine job, though, of hitting his key terms: book-labor distinguishes us from rustic labor. But there is an overlap despite the fundamental divide that sets the abstract over and against the concrete: both parties cultivate. It is just that one cultivation is sublime and the other gross. Rules are emphasized. We see both *enormitas* and *normata*. Mangled Latin reminds us of mangled bodies. "Abnormal" Latin is bad Latin, is rustic Latin, is "unenlightened" Latin. Indeed, bad Latin darkens, and, conversely, the Latin imparted by *artes* brings light.

One might feel a bit anxious even before the catastophic ending: throughout this sentence the praise of purity is suffused with mixed metaphors. But then, in the place of a crescendo, risible bluster. After complaining about the bad order of bad Latin, Diomedes tacks on a lame extra limb whose lack of coordination is glaring. The *tanto… quanto…* that bridges the two members of the sentence is forced and unbalanced: *tanto cognosimur… quanto ipsi videantur.* Huh? Oh, right: the uneducated are halfway between beasts and the educated. Weak verbs and a pile of intervening material means that the pointed finale falls short. The sympathetic reader has to do the work that Diomedes' own Latin fails to do. And the work that Diomedes has failed to do well is, scandalously, the work of praising reading-as-work.

If we are going to get ourselves in a high Sallustian dudgeon, then a sensible idea is that "by so much as" education brings light, "by that much" does want of education consign one to darkness. But the sentiment we read here is unmeasured and monstrous (*enormis*). Diomedes instead mixes two ideas together and then leaves one branch out. He wants to say both something about "educated is to uneducated" as "rustic is to animal" and to correlate illumination from the *ars grammatica* with the darkness of boorish speech. Diomedes' sentiment is clear enough, but the

> formant examussim, normatam orationis integritatem politumque lumen eius infuscant ex arte prolatum, quanto ipsi a pecudibus differe videantur."
> Diomedes, *Ars grammatica* (*GL* 1.299).

Latin itself is flailing and utterly deformed (*examussim*) exactly at the moment when it has invested its all in the idea of the well-tempered linguistic distinction that education imparts.[90]

Though grammatically viable, Diomedes has very nearly solecized in his abuse of the ignorant. Consider his definition of a solecism (as well as its forced Latin):

> A solecism is [something which] disorders speech in contravention of the logic of Roman tongue and it is a failure in the weaving together of the parts of speech made in contravention of the rule of the grammatical art. That is, it is a joining together of words that does not converge with the logic of the language.[91]

While solecism is typically discussed as a matter of syntactical failures like "I are stupid," there is nevertheless a connection between badly woven parts of speech and badly woven clauses. And I would like to push that connection for at least a moment.[92]

One can also see here yet another brush with failure. Though he will teach us to eschew tautology, there is a quasi-tautological idea in Diomedes' argument. Specifically, the *ratio sermonis* and the *regula artis grammaticae* are virtually one and the same: the logic of speech itself blurs with the rules of the art of analyzing speech. In fact, Diomedes' prose stutters here as he decides whether or not to make them identical: *id est...* To paraphrase his sentiment: "The *ratio* is the *regula,* that is, the *regula* is the *ratio.*" The *ratio* of Diomedes' own *sermo* hinges on this ability to allow for a free movement between academic description and

---

90 Many of Diomedes' key terms recur in the discussion of *Latinitas,* that is "good Latin." See *GL* 1.449.

91 "soloecismus est contra rationem Romani sermonis disturbans orationem et vitium in contextu partium orationis contra regulam artis grammaticae factum, id est non conveniens rationi sermonis iunctura verborum." Diomedes, *Ars grammatica* (*GL* 1.453).

92 See Julia Burghini and Beatriz Carina Meynet, "Casos equívocos entre barbarismos y solecismos: *scala, scopa, quadriga* en Quintiliano, Donato, Diomedes, Pompeyo y Consencio," *Argos* 35 (2012): 40–59, at 47–49: Diomedes' discussion is itself more expansive than that of his predecessors.

academic prescription. "That is," grammar teaching "is" organically connected to language's internal logic. At least that is what Diomedes needs us to understand.

Fine, we all flatter ourselves with such notions about the metaphysics of our epistemology. And yet, symptomatically, Diomedes' very next item is a (familiar) pair of utterly unconvincing etymologies for the word solecism itself. Either it comes from λόγου σώου αἰκισμός or it is coined off of the bad linguistic habits of some people named the Soloi whose gaffes were so numerous as to give a name to the thing. And then Diomedes tells us that there are 14 ways one can solecize. Well, some say there are 15.... The argument/λόγος makes sense only from moment to moment. Anyone who wants the sort of *ratio* or λόγος that a philosopher attempts to provide will be pained at the αἰκισμός inflicted upon the rules of reasoning. Of course, the "rules of reasoning" are not quite the same thing as the "rules of speech": the latter obey a secret logic that allows the *iunctura* of ill-yoked arguments and heterogeneous species of argumentation. But there's nothing to worry about because the rules of speech and the rules of grammar teachers are somehow — but don't ask just how… — connected to one another.

• • •

The *grammaticus* is a paraphilologist who attaches himself to language as its guardian. But the attachment has a parasitical and moribund structure. The doctor may well be the disease rather than the cure. Nevertheless he, like any good parasite, feasts away while language itself is left in a somewhat precarious state. Even if the fruits of the grammarian's labors are not necessarily useless, one has to note that the *grammatici* are seldom setting out to do productive new research. Most of their time is spent repeating the old bibliography and disputing narrow questions like whether there are 14 or 15 species of a certain class of error and what names to give to them. Interesting things happen, but these moments arise more in the gaps and cracks than they do within the terms of the surface of the text. These textbooks are supposed to be dry as dust. A pursuit of technical mastery within a static field squeezes out a self-critical analysis of just what it is they are doing and how it might be refined or improved more generally.

See, for example, Diomedes' pointedly toothless definition of comedy: "Comedy is a compassing of private, civic station that entails no risk to life. The Greeks define it thus: κωμῳδία ἐστιν ἰδιωτικῶν πραγμάτων ἀκίνδυνος περιοχή."[93] Despite any curiosity that this statement might arouse in certain directions, we are not going to learn more about the terms "private" or "harmless."[94] Instead we are told that this bit of Latin is really just Greek (even if that is not quite true). And within that Greek which is not quite the same as the Latin, the item of interest is κωμ-, a stem that is explained via an appeal to the word κῶμαι.[95]

Learning to read the *grammatici* critically entails figuring out how to excavate something from a translation of a commentary on a commentary despite several textual generations' worth of insistence that there is nothing more to see here than that which the professor says there is to see. Just listen to the master's *vox* and don't think too hard. And yet the professor is churning up a host of issues that seem to emerge "unintentionally" despite the insistence upon the importance of intentionality. However, no sooner does the desire to ask a follow-up question burble forth

---

93 Diomedes, *Ars grammatica* (GL 1.488).
94 For example, one might wonder as to why the Greek ἀκίνδυνος has been over-translated in the Latin. The source material is using a potentially strong word in a mild sense: ἀκίνδυνος literally means "free from danger," but in a context like this it has the force of "harmless." Meanwhile the Latin translation lurches towards "without risk to life" when one instead expects to read, at the furthest limits of a strong Roman-minded version of ἀκίνδυνος, something that means "without bringing risk to another's civil or legal standing." And to indicate "standing" one should either write *status* or *vitae status* and not just *vita*. Such philological exercises ought to be discouraged: they might lead us to doubt the professor's grasp of his material.
95 At best only the faintest echoes of Aristotle's definition in *Poetics* 1449a32 can be found. Instead Diomedes' argument is engaged with something like the *Commentaria In Dionysii Thracis Artem Grammaticam*: "Κωμῳδία ἐστιν ἡ ἐν μέσῳ λαοῦ κατηγορία ἤγουν δημοσίευσις· εἴρηται δὲ παρὰ τὸ κώμη καὶ τὸ ᾠδή, [...]" (172).

than the discussion has flowed off in a different direction with a completely different emphasis.

But not everyone was quite so unwilling to do something more and something new in the wake of sitting though their lessons. The grammarians' paradigms may well constrain, but they also enable. Lucian's *Lis Consonantium* arises as a free play of the imagination from the barren soil prepared by the grammarians. If the *grammaticus* trains you for the *rhetor* who trains you for the courts, then Lucian short-circuits the institutional hierarchy. The least elements perform the most exalted role: the *voces*-as-letters are literally given voices. Though a light piece, Lucian's oration delivered by Sigma against Tau before a court of Vowels makes literal the sociology that subtends the technical discourse of proper spelling. Change over time turns into howls of outrage: "Time for changes." Sigma establishes his good character. He emphasizes his reluctance to use and abuse the court system. In so doing, Sigma inevitably generates a witticism surrounding the multiple possible senses of an idiom like ἡσυχίαν ἀγαγόντα, "keeping quiet."[96] Meanwhile σύνταξις will mean both social order and grammatical order.[97] This comic conflation forms the core of the piece. And Sigma is keen to point out that verbal-*cum*-social chaos is running rampant: Lambda and Rho have been quarreling for some time. The same is true of Gamma and Kappa. Sigma's own *narratio* tells the story of Tau's constant and shameless encroachments upon Sigma's property: a host of objects that should be spelled with σ now have a τ in them instead. And the crowning outrage is that the word for speech itself has been depraved: "Will we allow γλῶττα to supplant γλῶσσα?!?"[98]

---

96 We can tell there is a joke afoot because the two times words formed on ἡσυχ- are used in this speech both occur in the same paragraph. See Lucian, *Lis consonantium* 2.

97 See ibid. 3: "οὐχ ὁρῶ τίνα τρόπον αἱ συντάξεις τὰ νόμιμα, ἐφ' οἷς ἐτάχθη τὰ κατ' ἀρχάς, ἕξουσιν."

98 Ibid. 11: "οὐ γὰρ ἐπιτρέπει γε αὐτοὺς κατ' εὐθὺ φέρεσθαι ταῖς γλώσσαις· μᾶλλον δέ, ὦ δικασταί, μεταξὺ γάρ με πάλιν τὰ τῶν ἀνθρώπων πράγματα ἀνέμνησε περὶ τῆς γλώσσης, καὶ ταύτης με τὸ μέρος ἀπήλασε καὶ γλῶτταν ποιεῖ τὴν γλῶσσαν. ὦ γλώσσης ἀληθῶς νόσημα Ταῦ."

Sigma evokes the trope of the lawgiver so commonly found in forensic oratory. If we go back to the invention of letters we will see that there is a fundamental order and hierarchy that must be preserved. The story of who invented and organized the alphabet is given with multiple variants: either Cadmus or Palamedes or Simonides.[99] This argument faithfully captures the constant over-determination of origins within the *Artes grammaticae*. Similarly, Sigma demands that Tau be crucified by Tauing him since that would suit him to a T: the cross for the cross-shaped letter.

Lucian's games only work if everyone has been to school. The audience for the piece can only be schoolboys past and present who find themselves all too ready to smirk at what really goes on in the lecture hall. Moreover, the things one learns in more advanced classes or hears in actual speeches become fodder for another set of laughs. It's all rather trite, isn't it? Nevertheless, Lucian himself is hardly a linguistic relativist. His Greek is an erudite Attic, an idiom which can only be acquired after great efforts, if one happens to be born at a distance of hundreds of kilometers and hundreds of years from the Athenian Miracle. For example, the *Adversus indoctum* argues in favor of exactly the sort of technical linguistic skill that is imparted by the *grammatici*: a man who buys many books is not the same thing as a man who knows how to read them, and the piece unfolds at the expense of the former and to the credit of the latter. Lucian shows that there is no need to either passively absorb philological knowledge or to repudiate it outright. Instead literary 'pataphilology offers the most erudite commentary of all.

And this 'pataphilology opens up new passages for the signifier by composing dramatic dialogues of the bookish.[100] Lucian's *True History* is able to fly off into outer space precisely because

---

99 See ibid. 5.
100 Consider as well Terentianus Maurus's versification of grammar lessons. Rather than use erudition to read Vergil one can make erudition itself into a sort of (humble-but-not-entirely-humble) epic. His verse prologue is full of elaborate self-positioning when it comes to the sort of *labor* and *ingenium* that is capable of producing what will come in the body of the work.

it plays with the absurdity of a certain species of erudition.[101] Meanwhile our own philology becomes anxious in the face of *The Solecist*. Is it by Lucian, or isn't it? Are the errors part of the joke? Intentions and authorship, authenticity and merit: the endless academic game transmits itself across the ages.

But it is easy to oversell the uses to which this sort of 'pataphilological response to grammatical paraphilology has been put. The humor is often principally concerned with maintaining social control and privilege even more effectively. There is a smirking return to terms like barbarism and solecism that can and should give us pause. The joke is often that, despite an ostensible preoccupation with rightness, the representative of learning is either a fake representative or a failed representative. Meanwhile, by not so subtle implication, the author and reader are positioned as genuine representatives.

Mocking bad Greek or bad Latin is frequently a sociopolitically reductive move. Catullus's abuse of Arrius's *chommoda* and *hinsidiae* instead of *commoda* and *insidiae* scolds a linguistic outsider who has become a bit too much of a political insider. When in Rome you absolutely must speak as the smart-set Romans do.[102] Suetonius's account of the works of Claudius is hardly glowing. "Not bad" is the best he will say of some of it. But the story of Claudius's addition to the alphabet is framed so as to make the emperor look like a self-important, second-rate scholar.[103] Martial plays the spelling game to make fun of a Cinnamus and to put him in his non-place. If a Cinnamus is

---

[101] Compare the *Battle of Frogs and Mice*, a Homeric epic in mousy miniature that emerges around the time that scholars are first really digging into Homer. It is both a derivative work and a novel one, as the poem itself notes in its third line: "ἦν νέον ἐν δέλτοισιν." These are new verses for modern book technology, not old sung lays.

[102] See Catullus, *Carmina* 84. Rough words are allowed into the smooth and polished book only to be singled out as an affront to those whose ears like things *lenis* and *levis*.

[103] Suetonius, *Claudius* 41.3: "nouas etiam commentus est litteras tres ac numero ueterum quasi maxime necessarias addidit; de quarum ratione cum priuatus adhuc uolumen edidisset, mox princeps non difficulter optinuit ut in usu quoque promiscuo essent."

allowed to appropriate a grand name like Cinna, then let us go all in with our barbarisms and call a (noble) Furius a thief (*fur*) instead.¹⁰⁴ The extra twist of the joke here is that this madman (*furiosus*) has indeed been thieving, and he was mad enough to think that he could get away with it. But Martial the *grammaticus* caught the barbarism and so saved the sociolinguistic day. Everyone knows that proper nouns, especially aristocratic ones, should never be expected to suffer the vicissitudes of barbarous assaults of either the semiotic or the phonetic stamp.

Against the largely reductive and conservative deployment of "the right" as against "the wrong," more productive paths are traced out by the Latin novelists. Petronius's book of scoundrels shows the worldliness of learning. The antihero pretends to be a scholar. The actual scholars are spongers. The *nouveaux riches* despise learning but also acknowledge the sort of cultural capital it represents. Names are constantly changing. False labels are affixed to everything. Poetry is endlessly mis-cited. The embedded epic in hexameters is thoroughly discredited by an internal audience of even worse (prose) offenders. Conte's thesis that this book is really some sort of praise of conservative literary tastes is hard to sustain in the face of a Bakhtinian riot.¹⁰⁵

Meanwhile in *Metamorphoses*, Apuleius's Lucius is teased for being a *scholasticus* by Photis. And the set-up to the narrator's asinine transformation circulates around a clever, educated youth who is not nearly so clever as he thinks he is. The self-staging of the narrator prior to his transformation presupposes a gentlemanly world of erudition and the station that goes with it, and yet Lucius is not taken seriously by others even before he becomes the unwitting star of the Festival of Laughter. The fact that the book has a quasi-hieroglyphic structure, complete, of course, with Isis and Egyptian priests, shows a sort of internal limit to voice-as-letter-as-book and the confidence of the savvy

---

104 *Epigrammata*, 6.17: "Cinnam, Cinname, te iubes vocari. | Non est hic, rogo, Cinna, barbarismus? | Tu si Furius ante dictus esses, | Fur ista ratione dicereris."

105 See Gian Biagio Conte, *The Hidden Author: An Interpretation of Petronius' Satyricon* (Berkeley: University of California Press, 1996).

schoolboy who is sure that he knows how to read and to understand what is written.[106]

A whistle-stop tour of Greek and Roman literature will only do these texts a variety of injustices. The main point is to appreciate the manner in which both the spirit and the letter of grammatical education suffuses the literary and cultural landscape. An education in spirits (in multiple senses) and letters (in multiple senses) plants a variety of seeds from which many other texts can germinate. And this efflorescence has an ironic quality given that so much time is spent by the schoolmen scorning the idea of change and insisting upon a rigid normativity.

It is easy enough to dismiss the *grammatici* as marginal figures. They are not politically or culturally central. Their material constitutes the stuff of early education. The texts we have are "late" even if the practice itself is centuries old.[107] Their texts are multiply derivative, usually of one another. Even the intellectual core of the enterprise is on loan from the linguistic theories of the philosophers. And many of our "native informants" insist upon several of these same critiques. For example, Quintilian certainly does not aspire to train the next generation of *grammatici*. Quintilian is training the next Cicero (in an age when there cannot be a next Cicero).

But it is precisely this marginality and derivativeness that enables one to see something important about the underpinnings of literate society more generally. If we take the *faux*-high road we can try to out-*grammaticus* the *grammatici* and note the uneven, shoddy workmanship executed by second-rate thinkers. There are risks along this alternate reading itinerary (*legitera*

---

[106] See Werner Riess, *Paideia at Play: Learning and Wit in Apuleius* (Groningen: Barkhuis, 2008) for a whole volume's worth of investigations of these aspects of Apuleius's corpus.

[107] The basic template of ancient education stretches all the way back to classical Athens, but the advent of the grammaticus in particular is a bit trickier to pin down. They emerge in the first century BCE, it would seem. See Alan D. Booth, "The Appearance of the 'Schola Grammatici,'" *Hermes* 106 (1978): 117–25. Nevertheless, who does what and how we feel about the people who do that (and not this) are questions that are constantly re-adjudicated over the course of the social history of education.

altera). For example, if we assume that Chrysippus succeeded in establishing a philosophy of language (because he was a Greek philosopher, and philosophers are wise and therefore right) where Priscian failed (because he was a Latin *grammaticus* and *grammatici* are shallow and therefore wrong), we merely reveal our own passion for the syllogisms of authority.

Instead we should note the desire in many quarters to establish a "metaphysics of presence" by means of a metaphysics of phonetic writing. In short, much of what Derrida says in *Of Grammatology* can be quickly adopted to a reading of these stories of the phonetic alphabet. The *grammatici* present incomplete, cursory, contradictory accounts of the relationship between writing and speech and soul.[108] In fact, these accounts are not just incomplete, they are also at the same time over-complete as well. One is offered multiple incompatible explanations without comment or cues for adjudication. If the more rigorous and scrupulous realm of philosophy will do a tidier job of positing unity within the heterogeneity of the sign, that does not mean that the philosophers got it right, only that they are craftier craftsmen of *logoi* about *logoi*. And we should not let our own longing for a unity of speech and reason — that is, our own desire that we ourselves say and mean always and only what the *ego* of our ego-speech says it says and means to mean — seduce us into a belief that that sort of present-to-itself voice-of-reason that can and should be written-and-read is an established fact instead of a metaphysical fantasy.[109]

The *grammatici* offer the perfect site to watch *différance* at work. They not only show that a deconstruction of *logos* is possible, but they further reveal the potential fecundity of a deconstructive relationship to the sign even as, of course, the *gram-*

---

[108] See Jacques Derrida, *Of Grammatology*, trans. Gayatri Chakravorty Spivak (Baltimore: Johns Hopkins University Press, 1976), 3–12, for the initial adumbration of the problem.

[109] See ibid., 20, on conscience as the hearing of the voice of the transcendental signified.

matici are doing their best to prevent any such radical projects.[110] The failure to offer a satisfying account of the sign at the opening of the *Artes* is a repeated, ritualistic gesture that pays obeisance to a desire for a closure that will ground the practice of grammar as a would-be science. What these *faux*-satisfactory accounts reveal instead is that the being of speech is indeed "derivative with regard to difference."[111]

Each of the grammatical projects above ends up telling a double story as it attempts to shore up precious singularity. Each positions itself as a legitimate heir to earlier efforts while also resembling a parodic distortion of them. Nevertheless, this "degeneration" can also be a liberation. And various adventurous then-contemporary literary projects can be seen tapping into the conjoined wisdom and folly of the erudition of the hour. Learning and literature were long associated in antiquity as a noble, stable pair. But this scandalous slide in the form and contents of learning opens up productive gaps. And therein one can find the wherewithal for various free-spirited exercises that launch language into the "beyond of the beyond" and give rise to a generative 'pata-discourse inspired by the stagnant academic para-discourse.[112]

---

110 Jacques Derrida, "Structure, Sign, and Play in the Discourse of the Human Sciences," in *Writing and Difference,* trans. Alan Bass, 278–93 (Chicago: University of Chicago Press, 1978), 279: "Nevertheless, the center also closes off the play which it opens up and makes possible. As center, it is the point at which the substitution of contents, element, or terms is no longer possible."

111 See Derrida, *Of Grammatology,* 23.

112 My overall conclusion converges with the position of Raymond Starr, "The Flexibility of Literary Meaning and the Role of the Reader in Roman Antiquity," *Latomus* 60 (2001): 433–45, but with a key difference. Starr sees the internal diversity of the tradition ("some say… others say…") as something that liberates readers and gives them a role. I believe that *ultimately* this is true, but that scholarly mastery often baldly declares "the right" version outright. Meanwhile major avenues of exploration are never opened up, and only narrow, technical questions are allowed. *Auctoritas* plays a key role here, and none of these modes is especially liberating in and of itself: one is free only to follow one's master and so to become him. Compare ibid., 441: "The commentator often models the reader's task." I am most interested in

The *Artes'* "authoritative contents" arise in the wake of and by means of an endless negotiation of the "problem" of differing/deferring folded into the would-be objective object of study, namely the ephemeral voice, and the way that both spirit and letter mediate it simultaneously. A contemporary deconstruction of the *Artes* might seek to inhabit them and subvert them from within. That is all well and good, but one needs to note as well the productive quality of their internal incoherence within the ancient context.

In the schoolhouse, the non-simplicity of the problem of the sign and the need to appeal to not just *ratio* but also *auctoritas* and *usus* enables this branch of knowledge to swiftly become an instrument of social power. A specific contemporary configuration of proper authority, good use, and right reason swoops in to save the day by reaffirming the order of the day. Similarly, it is entirely possible within the ancient world to smirk condescendingly at the insipid *grammatici* and then to follow up by engaging in their same game of cultural hegemony, only "better" this time.

Nevertheless, various ancient appraisals of grammar break it free from its own internal debates which are wont to ask questions like "How many cases are there, really: 6? 7? 8?!"[113] In fact,

those readers who broke with the tradition of taking scholarly reading too seriously.

113 See F. Murru, "Alcune questioni filologico-linguistiche a proposito dell'octavus casus," *Glotta* 56 (1978): 144–55, and F. Murru, "Due ulteriori definizioni dell'octavus casus nei grammatici latini," *Glotta* 57 (1979): 155–57, on the eighth case in the *Grammatici Latini*. Unusual and/or bold poetic uses can turn into "core features of Latin syntax." Vergil-as-normal means that all rulers should be calibrated to measure (a highly imperfect understanding of) his poetry as if it gave the index of Latin itself. Servius mentions several times Vergil's *it clamor caelo* at *Aeneid* 5.451: it is a problem passage that helps to work through other passages. But if you are unable to decide the case of *caelo* here, you can always invent an eighth one to handle more or less exactly this passage: *caelo* is a dative-that's-an-accusative, i.e., "the eighth case." Servius's position is merely that this sort of thing is figurative: "figuratum est; nam de nominativo transit ad dativum" (Servius, *In Vergilii Aeneidos Libros* 10.322). Why one elects to be "figurative" in one place and not in another is of less interest to him. That is, why, exactly, does

it is perhaps too kind to use the word debate of what one sees. The details are regularly elided, and one is more likely to know that "some say that" something is such or so than one is to hear their reasoning. In contradistinction to the *grammatici* and their adumbrations that give everything a very specifically normative pattern of light-and-shadow, wayward, literary students of the letter generate novelties. They appreciate that dramatizing knowledge at work in the world can generate new configurations that are not necessarily just the same game but are played, this time, at a higher level of social mastery. That last option is always on offer and enticing. But we can see as well the possibilities that emerge for the so-good-he's-bad student.

These new efforts and ectopic texts can expose the game for what it is: a place where *jeux de mots* and *jeux d'esprit* can frolic productively. And, significantly, these paraphilological efforts can open up vistas within which the grammatical apparatus can be deployed as a set of productive possible relationships to words. And then learning can be leveraged to sail through a universe of speech-and-writing that is "novel" in both the empirical and literary senses of the word. These innovations in the name of heteroglossia and against monoglossia unsurprisingly tend to have a comic cast to them.[114] For comedy remains the place where the familiar can be most readily challenged. Comedy revels in short-circuits, overlaps, homophonies, and other paralogisms that in fact reveal something scandalous about *logos* himself, namely that a word like *vox* means too many things for us to take it at its word.[115] Plautus's Sosia decides he might not be Sosia after losing a violent grammatical debate-*cum*-altercation

   Vergil write it "clamor ad alta | altaria" at 4.665–66 and "it clamor caelo" at 5.451? What is the force of the figure?
114 See, of course, M.M. Bakhtin, *Rabelais and His World,* trans. Hélène Iswolsky (Bloomington: Indiana University Press, 1984) and M.M. Bakhtin, *The Dialogic Imagination: Four Essays,* ed. Michael Holquist, trans. Caryl Emerson and Michael Holquist. (Austin: University of Texas Press, 1981).
115 See Slavoj Žižek's forword to Alenka Zupančič, *The Odd One In: On Comedy* (Cambridge: MIT Press, 2008) for a manifesto in the name of the short circuit. And then keep reading Zupančič herself for an account of the radical qualities of comedy relative to the order of the sign.

with someone who says that, no, he is Sosia. In Apuleius, Lucius the asinine schoolboy discovers (and also fails to discover) just how much of a metaphorical ass he was when he got himself transformed into a literal ass. This is the sort of foolishly funny thing that breaks lose when one realizes that wordplay is the thing to prick the conscience of the logocentric king.

Ubu-se-trouve: *Ah! messieurs! si beau qu'il soit il ne vaut pas la Grammaire. S'il n'y avait pas de Grammaire il n'y aurait pas de Grammatistes!*

Bibliography

Adorno, Theodor W. *Minima Moralia: Reflections from Damaged Life*. Translated by E.F.N. Jephcott. London: Verso, 1978.

———. *Prisms*. Translated by Samuel and Shierry Weber. Cambridge: Harvard University Press, 1981.

———. "Über epische Naivetät." In *Noten zur Literatur*, edited by Rolf Tiedeman, 34–40. Frankfurt am Main: Suhrkamp, 1981.

———. *Notes to Literature*. 2 vols. Edited by Rolf Tiedemann. Translated by Shierry Weber Nicholsen. New York: Columbia University Press, 1991, 1992.

———. *Negative Dialectics*. Translated by E.B. Ashton. New York: Routledge, 2004.

Anderson, Stephen R. *Languages: A Very Short Introduction*. Oxford: Oxford University Press, 2012.

Andersson, Daniel C. "Did Diomedes Know Latin? A Problem with His *De optativis*." *Hermes* 139 (2011): 110–11. https://www.jstor.org/stable/25800335.

The Anglo-Saxon Chronicle: A Collaborative Edition, vol. 7: *MS. E*. Edited by Susan Irvine. Cambridge: Brewer, 2004.

The Anglo-Saxon Chronicle. Translated and edited by M.J. Swanton. London: Dent, 1996.

Anonymous. *Nox Philologiae: Aulus Gellius and the Fantasy of the Roman Library*. Edited by Erik Gunderson. Madison: University of Wisconsin Press, 2009.

Armstrong, David. *Horace*. New Haven: Yale University Press, 1989.

Arrowsmith, William. "Nietzsche: Notes for 'We Philologists,'" *Arion* 1, no. 2 (1973): 279–380. https://www.jstor.org/stable/20163328.

Attridge, Derek. *Peculiar Language: Literature as Difference from the Renaissance to James Joyce*. Ithaca: Cornell University Press, 1988.

Augustine, *Confessions*. Translated by Henry Chadwick. Oxford: Oxford University Press, 1992.

Bailey, D.R. Shackelton. *Profile of Horace*. Cambridge: Harvard University Press, 1982.

Bakhtin, M.M. *The Dialogic Imagination: Four Essays*. Edited by Michael Holquist. Translated by Caryl Emerson and Michael Holquist. Austin: University of Texas Press, 1981.

———. *Rabelais and His World*. Translated by Hélène Iswolsky. Bloomington: Indiana University Press, 1984.

Bakker, Egbert J. "*Khrónos, Kléos,* and Ideology from Homer to Herodotus." In *Epea Pteroenta: Beiträge zur Homerforschung. Festschrift für Wolfgang Kullmann zum 75. Geburtstag,* edited by Michael Reichel and Antonios Rengakos, 11–30. Stuttgart: Franz Steiner Verlag, 2002.

Banniard, Michel. "Le Latin classique existe-t-il?." In *Latin vulgaire, latin tardif IX: Actes du IXe Colloque international sur le latin vulgaire et tardif, Lyon, 2–6 septembre 2009,* edited by Frédérique Biville, Marie-Karine Lhommé, and Daniel Vallat, 57–78. Lyon: Maison de l'orient et de la Méditerranée, 2012.

Barchiesi, Alessandro. "*Carmina: Odes* and *Carmen Saeculare.*" In *Cambridge Companion to Horace*. Edited by Stephen Harrison, 144–61. Cambridge: Cambridge University Press, 2007.

———. "Final Difficulties in an Iambic Poet's Career: Epode 17." Translated by Maya Jessica Alapin. In *Horace: Odes and Epodes,* ed. Michèle Lowrie, 232–46. Oxford: Oxford University Press, 2009.

Baudrillard, Jean. *Pataphysique*. Paris: Sens et Tonka, 2002.

Becker, Daniel Levin. *Many Subtle Channels: In Praise of Potential Literature*. Cambridge: Harvard University Press, 2012.

Benjamin, Walter. *Selected Writings*. Edited by M.P. Bullock, M.W. Jennings, H. Eiland, et al. 4 vols. Cambridge: Harvard University Press, 1996–2003.

Benveniste, Émile. *Problems in General Linguistics*. Coral Gables: University of Miami Press, 1971.

Bök, Christian. *'Pataphysics: The Poetics of an Imaginary Science*. Evanston: Northwestern University Press, 2002.

Booth, Alan D. "The Appearance of the 'Schola Grammatici.'" *Hermes* 106 (1978): 117–25. https://www.jstor.org/stable/4476045.

Braune, Sean. "From Lucretian Atomic Theory to Joycean Etymic Theory." *Journal of Modern Literature* 33, no. 4 (2010): 167–81. DOI: 10.2979/jml.2010.33.4.167

———. *Language Parasites: Of Phorontology*. Earth: punctum books, 2017.

Brisset, Jean-Pierre. *La grammaire logique. Suivi de la science de Dieu*. Paris: Tchou, 1970.

———. *Les origines humaines*. Paris: Baudouin, 1980.

Bronner, Yigal. *Extreme Poetry: The South Asian Movement of Simultaneous Narration*. New York: Columbia University Press, 2010.

Brotchie, Alistair. *Alfred Jarry: A Pataphysical Life*. Cambridge: MIT Press, 2011.

Brown, Wendy. *Edgework: Critical Essays on Knowledge and Politics*. Princeton: Princeton University Press, 2005.

Burgess, Anthony. *A Clockwork Orange*. London: Heinemann, 1962.

———. *Here Comes Everybody: An Introduction to James Joyce for the Ordinary Reader*. London: Faber & Faber, 1965.

———. *Re Joyce*. New York: Norton, 1968.

———. *Joysprick: An Introduction to the Language of James Joyce*. London: Deutsch, 1973.

———. *A Mouthful of Air: Language and Languages, Especially English*. London: Hutchinson, 1992.

Burghini, Julia, and Beatriz Carina Meynet. "Casos equívocos entre barbarismos y solecismos: *scala, scopa, quadriga* en

Quintiliano, Donato, Diomedes, Pompeyo y Consencio." *Argos* 35 (2012): 40–59.

Burnett, D. Graham. *The Sounding of the Whale: Science & Cetaceans in the Twentieth Century*. Chicago: University of Chicago Press, 2012.

Bushur, James G. *Irenaeus of Lyons and the Mosaic of Christ: Preaching Scripture in the Era of Martyrdom*. London: Routledge, 2017.

Candish, Stewart, and George Wrisley. "Private Language." In *The Stanford Encyclopedia of Philosophy*. Fall 2014 edition. Edited by Edward N. Zalta. http://plato.stanford.edu/archives/fall2014/entries/private-language.

Carracedo Fraga, José. "Un capítulo sobre *barbarismus* y *soloecismus* en el códice *CA* 2° 10 de Erfurt." *Euphrosyne: revista de filologia classica* 41 (2013): 245–58.

Carrubba, R.W. *The Epodes of Horace: A Study in Poetic Arrangement*. The Hague: Mouton, 1969.

Cavarzere, Alberto, ed. *Orazio: Il libro degli Epodi*. Venezia: Marsilio, 1992.

Chubb, Ray. *Skeul an Tavas: A Cornish Language Coursebook for Adults in the Standard Written Form*. 2nd edition. Portreath: Agan Tavas, 2010.

———. *Skeul an Tavas: A Cornish Language Coursebook for Schools in the Standard Written Form*. 2nd edition. Portreath: Agan Tavas, 2010.

———. *Skeul an Tavas: A Coursebook in Standard Cornish*. 2nd edition. Westport: Evertype, 2013.

Citti, F. *Studi Oraziani: Tematica e Intertestualità*. Bologna: Pàtron Editore, 2000.

Classen, Carl Joachim. "Principi et Concetti Morali nelle Satire du Orazio." In *Atti del convegno di Venosa: 8–15 Novembre 1992*, edited by Scevola Mariotti et alii, 111–28. Venosa: Edizioni Osanna Venosa, 1993.

Coletti, Maria Laetitia. "Il barbarismus e il soloecismus nei commentatori altomedievali di Donato alla luce della tradizione grammaticale greco-latina." *Orpheus* 4 (1983): 67–92.

Colman, D.S. "Confessio grammatici." *Greece and Rome* 7, no. 1 (1960): 72–81. DOI: 10.1017/S0017383500014030

Conley, Tim, and Stephen Cain. *Encyclopedia of Fictional and Fantastic Languages*. Westport: Greenwood, 2006.

Conte, Gian Biagio. *The Hidden Author: An Interpretation of Petronius' Satyricon*. Berkeley: University of California Press, 1996.

Dalí, Salvador. "Interprétation Paranoïaque-critique de l'Image obsédante 'L'Angélus' de Millet." *Minotaure* 1: (1933): 65–67.

———. *The Unspeakable Confessions of Salvador Dali*. As told to André Parinaud. Translated by Harold J. Salemson. New York: William Morrow, 1976.

D'Angour, Armand. *The Greeks and the New: Novelty in Ancient Greek Imagination and Experience*. Cambridge: Cambridge University Press, 2011.

Daston, Lorraine, and Glenn W. Most. "History of Science and History of Philologies." *Isis* 106 (2015): 378–390. DOI: 10.1086/681980

David, Sylvain-Christian. "Pataphysique et Psychanalyse." *Europe: Revue Litteraire Mensuelle* 623–624 (1981): 52–61.

De Man, Paul. "The Rhetoric of Temporality." In *Blindness and Insight: Essays in the Rhetoric of Contemporary Criticism*, 187–228. 2nd revised edition. Minneapolis: University of Minnesota Press, 1983.

De Paolis, Paolo. "Cicerone nei grammatici tardoantichi e altomedievali." *Ciceroniana* 11 (2000): 37–67.

Derrida, Jacques. *Of Grammatology*. Translated by Gayatri Chakravorty Spivak. Baltimore: Johns Hopkins University Press, 1976.

———. "Structure, Sign, and Play in the Discourse of the Human Sciences." In *Writing and Difference*, translated by Alan Bass, 278–93. Chicago: University of Chicago Press, 1978.

———. *Limited Inc*. Evanston: Northwestern University Press, 1988.

Didi-Huberman, Georges. "The Surviving Image: Aby Warburg and Tylorian Anthropology," *Oxford Art Journal* 25, no. 1 (2002): 59–70. https://www.jstor.org/stable/3600420.

———. "Artistic Survival: Panofsky vs. Warburg and the Exorcism of Impure Time," Translated by V. Rehberg and B. Belay. *Common Knowledge* 9, no. 2 (2003): 273–85.

Durkheim, Émile. *Suicide: A Study in Sociology.* Translated by John A. Spaulding and George Simpson. New York: Free Press, 1951.

Eburne, Jonathan P. *Surrealism and the Art of Crime.* Ithaca: Cornell University Press, 2008.

Edwards, Catherine. *The Politics of Immorality in Ancient Rome.* Cambridge: Cambridge University Press, 1993.

Fabian, Johannes. *Time and the Other: How Anthropology Makes Its Object.* New York: Columbia University Press, 1983.

Fitzgerald, William. "Power and Impotence in Horace's *Epodes*." In *Horace: Odes and Epodes*, edited by Michèle Lowrie, 141–59. Oxford: Oxford University Press, 2009.

Foucault, Michel. *L'archéologie du savoir.* Paris: Gallimard, 1969.

———. *The Care of the Self: The History of Sexuality, Vol. 3.* Translated by Robert Hurley. New York: Vintage, 1986.

Fowler, Roger. *Literature as Social Discourse: The Practice of Linguistic Criticism.* London: Batsford, 1981.

Franzen, J. "Mr. Difficult." *The New Yorker* 78, no. 29 (September 30, 2002): 100–11.

Gagné, Renaud. "A Wolf at the Table: Sympotic Perjury in Archilochus." *Transactions of the American Philological Association* 139, no. 2 (Autumn 2009): 251–74. https://www.jstor.org/stable/40651972.

Geertz, Clifford. *The Interpretation of Cultures.* New York: Basic Books, 1973.

Ginzburg, Carlo. *Clues, Myths, and the Historical Method.* Translated by John and Anne C. Tedeschi. Baltimore: Johns Hopkins University Press, 1989.

Gioseffi, Massimo. "A Very Long Engagement: Some Remarks About the Relationship Between Marginalia and Commentaries in the Virgilian Tradition." *Trends in Classics* 6, no. 1 (2014): 176–91.

Glynos, Jason, and Yannis Stavrakakis. "Postures and Impostures: On Lacan's Style and Use of Mathematical Science." *American Imago* 58, no. 3 (2001): 685–706. https://www.jstor.org/stable/26304722.

Gordin, Michael D. *The Pseudoscience Wars: Immanuel Velikovsky and the Birth of the Modern Fringe.* Chicago: University of Chicago Press, 2012.

———. "What to Say after Nuclear War." *Histories of the Future.* http://histscifi.com/essays/gordin.

Gowers, Emily. *The Loaded Table: Representations of Food in Roman Satire.* Oxford: Oxford University Press, 1993.

Grafton, Anthony. *Forgers and Critics: Creativity and Duplicity in Western Scholarship.* Princeton: Princeton University Press, 1990.

Greene, Brian. *The Elegant Universe: Superstrings, Hidden Dimensions, and the Quest for the Ultimate Theory.* New York: Norton, 1999.

Gurd, Sean. *Dissonance: Auditory Aesthetics in Ancient Greece.* New York: Fordham University Press, 2016.

———. "David Melnick's *Men in Aïda*." *Classical Receptions Journal* 8, no. 3 (July 2016): 295–316. DOI: 10.1093/crj/clv007.

Hadot, Pierre. *La citadelle intérieur: Introduction aux Pensées de Marc Aurèle.* Paris: Fayard, 1992.

Hagner, Michael. "Bye-Bye Science, Welcome Pseudoscience? Reflexionen über einen beschädigten Status." In *Pseudowissenschaft: Konzeptionen von Nichtwissenschaftlichkeit in der Wissenschaftsgeschichte,* edited by Dirk Rupnow, Veronika Lipphardt, Jens Thiel, and Christina Wessely, 21–50. Frankfurt am Main: Suhrkamp, 2008.

Halliday, M.A.K. "Anti-Languages." *American Anthropologist* 78 (1976): 570–84.

Halmi, Nicholas. *The Genealogy of the Romantic Symbol.* Oxford: Oxford University Press, 2007.

Hawkins, Julia Nelson. "The Barking Cure: Horace's 'Anatomy of Rage' in *Epodes* 1, 6, and 16." *American Journal of Philology* 135, no. 1 (Spring 2014): 57–85. DOI: 10.1353/ajp.2014.0006.

Hawkins, Tom. "This Is the Death of the Earth: Crisis Narrative in Archilochus and Mnesiepes." *Transactions of the American Philological Association* 139, no. 1 (Spring 2009): 1–20. https://www.jstor.org/stable/40212094.

Hellegouarc'h, J. *Le vocabulaire latin des relations et des partis politiques sous la république.* 2nd edition. Paris: Les Belles Lettres, 1972.

Heller-Roazen, Daniel. *Dark Tongues: The Art of Rogues and Riddlers.* New York: Zone, 2013.

Henderson, John. *The Medieval World of Isidore of Seville: Truth from Words.* Cambridge: Cambridge University Press, 2007.

———. "Horace Talks Rough and Dirty: No Comment (*Epodes* 8 and 12)." In *Horace: Odes and Epodes,* edited by Michèle Lowrie, 401–17. Oxford: Oxford University Press, 2009.

Hoban, Russell. *Riddley Walker.* Expanded edition. Bloomington: Indiana University Press, 1998.

Horkheimer, Max, and Theodor W. Adorno. *Dialectic of Enlightenment: Philosophical Fragments.* Translated by Edmund Jephcott. Edited by Gunzelin Schmid Noerr. Stanford: Stanford University Press, 2002.

Homer. *The Odyssey of Homer.* Translated by Richmond Lattimore. New York: Harper, 1965.

Jarry, Alfred. *Gestes et opinions du docteur Faustroll, pataphysicien: Roman neo-scientifique.* Édition annotée. Paris: Cymbalum Pataphysicum, 1986.

———. *Exploits and Opinions of Doctor Faustroll, Pataphysician: A Neo-Scientific Novel.* Translated by Simon Watson Taylor. Boston: Exact, 1996.

———. *Ubu Roi.* Translated by Beverly Keith and G. Legman. New York: Dover, 2003.

———. *Œuvres.* Paris: Robert Laffont, 2004.

———. *Gestes et opinions du docteur Faustroll pataphysicien.* Édition annotée. Paris: La Différence, 2010.

Johnson, Timothy S. *Horace's Iambic Criticism: Casting Blame (Iambikē Poiēsis).* Leiden: Brill, 2012.

Kaiser, David. *Drawing Theories Apart: The Dispersion of Feynman Diagrams in Postwar Physics.* Chicago: University of Chicago Press, 2005.

Kaster, Robert A. "Servius and Idonei Auctores." *American Journal of Philology* 99 (1978): 181–209. DOI: 10.2307/293646.

———. *Guardians of Language: The Grammarian and Society in Late Antiquity.* Berkeley: University of California Press, 1988.

Katz, Joshua T. "*Nonne lexica etymologica multiplicanda sunt?*" In *Classical Dictionaries: Past, Present and Future,* edited by Christopher Stray, 25–48. London: Duckworth, 2010.

———. "Etymological 'Alterity': Depths and Heights," In *Deep Classics: Rethinking Classical Reception,* edited by Shane Butler, 107–26. London: Bloomsbury, 2016.

Keane, Catherine. *Figuring Genre in Roman Satire.* Oxford: Oxford University Press, 2006.

Kennedy, Duncan. *The Arts of Love: Five Essays in the Discourse of Roman Love Elegy.* Cambridge: Cambridge University Press, 1993.

Kiessling, Adolf, and Richard Heinze, *Q. Horatius Flaccus: Satiren.* Zurich: Weidmann, 1999.

Kingsnorth, Paul. *The Wake.* London: Unbound, 2014.

Krebs, Christopher B. *A Most Dangerous Book: Tacitus's Germania from the Roman Empire to the Third Reich.* New York: W. W. Norton, 2011.

Lacan, Jacques. "Le Problème du Style et la conception psychiatrique des formes paranoïaques de l'expérience." *Minotaure* 1 (1933): 68–69.

———. "Motifs du Crime Paranoïaque: Le Crime des Sœurs Papin." *Minotaure* 3–4 (1933): 25–28.

———. *Seminar XI: The Four Fundamental Concepts of Psychoanalysis.* Edited by Alain Miller. Translated by Alan Sheridan. New York: Norton, 1981.

———. *The Seminar of Jacques Lacan: Book III, The Psychoses 1955–1956.* Edited by Jacques-Alain Miller. Translated by Russell Grigg. New York: Norton, 1997.

———. *Écrits: The First Complete Edition in English*. Translated by Bruce Fink, with Héloïse Fink and Russell Grigg. New York: Norton, 2006.

Lana, Italo. "Le Guerre civili et la pace nella poesia di Orazio." In *Atti del convegno di Venosa: 8–15 Novembre 1992*, edited by Scevola Mariotti et alii, 59–74. Venosa: Edizioni Osanna Venosa, 1993.

Latour, Bruno. *We Have Never Been Modern*. Translated by Catherine Porter. Cambridge: Harvard University Press, 1993.

Launoir, Ruy. *Clefs pour la 'Pataphysique*. Paris: Seghers, 1969.

Leonard, Miriam. *Socrates and the Jews: Hellenism and Hebraism from Moses Mendelssohn to Sigmund Freud*. Chicago: University of Chicago Press, 2012.

Macey, David. *Lacan in Contexts*. London: Verso, 1988.

Maltby, Robert. "The Role of Etymologies in Servius and Donatus." In *Etymologia: Studies in Ancient Etymology: Proceedings of the Cambridge Conference on Ancient Etymology, 25–27 September 2000*, edited by Christos Nifadopoulos, 103–18. Münster: Nodus Publikationen, 2003.

Mankin, David. *Horace: Epodes*. Cambridge: Cambridge University Press, 1995.

———. "The *Epodes*: Genre, Themes, and Arrangement." In *A Companion to Horace*, edited by Gregson Davis, 93–104. Malden: Wiley-Blackwell, 2010.

Mankoff, Stacey. "Wankers, Burds, and Skag: Heteroglossia in Trainspotting." *Empty Mirror*. http://www.emptymirrorbooks.com/features/literature/wankers-burds-and-skag-heteroglossia-in-trainspotting.html.

Marani, Diego. *Las adventures des inspector Cabillot*. Paris: Mazarine, 1999.

———. *Las adventures des Inspector Cabillot*. Sawtry: Dedalus, 2012.

McNeill, R.L.B. *Horace: Image, Identity, and Audience*. Baltimore: Johns Hopkins University Press, 2001.

Melnick, David J. *Men in Aïda*. San Francisco: Uitgeverij, 2015.

Miller, Gérard. *Rendez-vous chez Lacan.* Paris: Éditions Montparnasse, 2011. Film.

Miller, Paul Allen. *Lyric Texts and Lyric Consciousness: The Birth of Genre from Archaic Greece to Augustan Rome.* London: Routledge, 2014.

———. "Discipline and Punish: Horatian Satire and the Formation of the Self." In *Texts and Violence in the Roman World,* edited by Monica R. Gale and J.H.D. Scourfield, 87–109. Cambridge: Cambridge University Press, 2018.

Mitchell, David. *Cloud Atlas.* New York: Random House, 2004.

———. "On Reading *Riddley Walker* in Hiroshima." In Russell Hoban, *Riddley Walker,* 223–25. London: Orion, 2012.

Mullan, John. "So to Speak." *The Guardian.* May 30, 2008. https://www.theguardian.com/books/2008/may/31/irvinewelsh.

Munz, Tania. *The Dancing Bees: Karl von Frisch and the Discovery of the Honeybee Language.* Chicago: University of Chicago Press, 2016.

Munzi, Luigi. "Per il testo dei grammatici latini." *Bollettino dei classici, a cura del Comitato per la preparazione dell' Edizione nazionale dei Classici greci e latini* 21 (2000): 103–14.

Murphy, Patricia. "Rabelais and Jarry." *The French Review* 51, no. 1 (October 1977): 29–36. https://www.jstor.org/stable/389604.

Murru, F. "Alcune questioni filologico-linguistiche a proposito dell' octavus casus." *Glotta* 56 (1978): 144–55.

———. "Due ulteriori definizioni dell' octavus casus nei grammatici latini." *Glotta* 57 (1979): 155–57.

Nichol, B.P. *The Martyrology, Books 3 & 4.* Toronto: Coach House Press, 1976.

Nietzsche, Friedrich W. *Kritische Gesamtausgabe: Werke.* Edited by G. Colli and M. Montinari. Berlin: De Gruyter, 1967 to present.

———. *Sämtliche Werke. Kritische Studienausgabe in 15 Einzelbänden.* Edited by G. Colli and M. Montinari. 2nd edition. Berlin: De Gruyter, 1988.

———. *Untimely Meditations.* Edited by D. Breazeale. Translated by R.J. Hollingdale. Cambridge: Cambridge University Press, 1997.

O'Brien, Flann. *At Swim-Two-Birds.* London: Longmans, Green, 1939.

Okrent, Arika. *In the Land of Invented Languages: Esperanto Rock Stars, Klingon Poets, Loglan Lovers, and the Mad Dreamers Who Tried to Build a Perfect Language.* New York: Spiegel & Grau, 2009.

Olender, Maurice. *The Languages of Paradise: Race, Religion, and Philology in the Nineteenth Century.* Translated by Arthur Goldhammer. Cambridge: Harvard University Press, 1992.

Oliensis, Ellen. *Horace and the Rhetoric of Authority.* Cambridge: Cambridge University Press, 1998.

———. "Erotics and Gender." In *Cambridge Companion to Horace,* edited by Stephen Harrison, 221–34. Cambridge: Cambridge University Press, 2007.

———. "Canidia, Canicula, and the Decorum of Horace's Epodes." In *Horace: Odes and Epodes,* edited by Michèle Lowrie, 160–87. Oxford: Oxford University Press, 2009.

Parry, Adam. "The Language of Achilles." *Transactions of the American Philological Association* 87 (1956): 1–7.

Paz, Octavio. *Conjunctions and Disjunctions.* Translated by Helen R. Lane. New York: Viking, 1974.

Peirano, Irene. *Persuasion, Rhetoric, and Roman Poetry.* Cambridge: Cambridge University Press, forthcoming.

Peterson, David J. *The Art of Language Invention: From Horse-Lords to Dark Elves, the Words behind World-Building.* New York: Penguin, 2015.

Pinker, Steven. *The Language Instinct.* New York: Morrow, 1994.

Pirovano, Luigi. "Deformare e deformatio nel lessico di Tiberio Claudio Donato." In *E io sarò tua guida: raccolta di saggi su Virgilio e gli studi Virgiliani,* edited by Massimo Gioseffi, 217–38. Cambridge: Cambridge University Press, 2000.

Plaza, Maria. *The Function of Humour in Roman Verse Satire: Laughing and Lying.* Oxford: Oxford University Press, 2006.

Poliakov, Léon. *The Aryan Myth: A History of Racist and Nationalist Ideas in Europe.* Translated by Edmund Howard. New York: New American Library, 1974.

Pollack, Sheldon, Benjamin Elman, and Ku-ming Kevin Chang, eds. *World Philology.* Cambridge: Harvard University Press, 2014.

Pollitt, J.J. *The Ancient View of Greek Art: Criticism, History, and Terminology.* New Haven: Yale University Press, 1974.

Porphyry. *On the Cave of the Nymphs.* Translated by Robert Lamberton. Barrytown: Station Hill Press, 1983.

Porter, James I. "Content and Form in Philodemus: The History of an Evasion." In *Philodemus and Poetry,* edited by Dirk Obbink, 97–147. Oxford: Oxford University Press, 1995.

———. *The Invention of Dionysus: An Essay on The Birth of Tragedy.* Stanford: Stanford University Press, 2000.

———. *Nietzsche and the Philology of the Future.* Stanford: Stanford University Press, 2000.

———. "Foucault's Ascetic Ancients." *Phoenix* 59, no. 2, Special issue: "Interrogating Theory—Critiquing Practice: The Subject of Interpretation," edited by William Batstone (2005): 121–32. https://www.jstor.org/stable/25067743.

———. "Erich Auerbach and the Judaizing of Philology," *Critical Inquiry* 35 (2008): 115–47. DOI: 10.1086/595631.

———. "Odysseus the Wandering Jew: The Dialectic of Jewish Enlightenment in Adorno and Horkheimer." *Cultural Critique* 74, "Classical Reception and the Political," edited by Miriam Leonard and Yopie Prins (Winter 2010): 200–13.

———. "Nietzsche's Genealogy as Performative Critique." In *Conceptions of Critique in Modern and Contemporary Philosophy,* edited by Ruth Sonderegger and Karin de Boer, 119–36. London: Palgrave-Macmillan, 2011.

———. "Philology in Exile: Adorno, Auerbach, and Klemperer." In *Brill's Companion to the Classics, Fascist Italy and Nazi Germany,* edited by Helen Roche and Kyriakos Demetriou, 106–29. Leiden: Brill, 2017.

———. "Nietzsche's Untimely Antiquity." In *The New Cambridge Companion to Nietzsche,* edited by Thomas Stern. Cambridge: Cambridge University Press, forthcoming.

Radick, Gregory. *The Simian Tongue: The Long Debate about Animal Language.* Chicago: University of Chicago Press, 2007.

Rasula, Jed, and Steve McCaffery, eds. *Imagining Language: An Anthology.* Cambridge: MIT Press, 1998.

Reckford, Kenneth. *Recognizing Persius.* Princeton: Princeton University Press, 2009.

Relihan, Joel C. "The Confessions of Persius." *Illinois Classical Studies* 14 (1989): 145–67.

Reynolds, L.D., and N.G. Wilson. *Scribes and Scholars: A Guide to the Transmission of Greek and Latin Literature.* 3rd edition. Oxford: Oxford University Press, 1991.

Reynolds, Sean. "Hospitality of the Mouth and the Homophonic Kiss: David Melnick's *Men in Aïda*." *Postmodern Culture* 21, no. 2 (January 2011). DOI: 10.1353/pmc.2011.0003.

Riess, Werner. *Paideia at Play: Learning and Wit in Apuleius.* Groningen: Barkhuis, 2008.

Roche, Helen, and Kyriakos Demetriou, eds. *Brill's Companion to the Classics, Fascist Italy and Nazi Germany.* Leiden: Brill, 2017.

Romaine, Suzanne. "Revitalized Languages as Invented Languages." In *From Elvish to Klingon: Exploring Invented Languages,* edited by Michael Adams, 185–225. Oxford: Oxford University Press, 2011.

Ronell, Avital. *Stupidity.* Urbana: University of Illinois Press, 2002.

Rossetti, Cezaro. *Kredu min, sinjorino!* [Scheveningen]: Heroldo de Esperanto, 1950.

Roudinesco, Elisabeth. *Jacques Lacan.* Translated by Barbara Bray. New York: Columbia University Press, 1994.

Sayers, Dave. "Standardising Cornish: The Politics of a New Minority Language." *Language Problems & Language Planning* 36 (2012): 99–119. DOI: 10.1075/lplp.36.2.01say.

Schafer, R. Murray. *Dicamus et Labyrinthos: A Philologist's Notebook*. Indian River: Arcana, 1984.

Schiller, Friedrich. "On Naïve and Sentimental Poetry." In *German Aesthetic and Literary Criticism: Winckelmann, Lessing, Hamann, Herder, Schiller, Goethe,* edited by H.B. Nisbet, 179–232. Cambridge: Cambridge University Press, 1985 [1795].

Schlegel, Catherine M. *Satire and the Threat of Speech: Horace's Satires Book 1*. Madison: University of Wisconsin Press, 2005.

Schwerner, Armand. *The Tablets*. Orono: National Poetry Foundation, 1999.

Sedley, David. "Etymology as *techne* in Plato's *Cratylus*." In *Etymologia: Studies in Ancient Etymology: Proceedings of the Cambridge Conference on Ancient Etymology, 25–27 September 2000,* edited by Christos Nifadopoulos, 21–32. Münster: Nodus Publikationen, 2003.

Serafini, Luigi. *Codex Seraphinianus*. Milan: Franco Mario Ricci, 1993.

Simons, Gary F., and Charles D. Fennig, eds. *Ethnologue: Languages of the World*. 20th edition. Dallas: SIL International, 2017. https://www.ethnologue.com/language/api.

Smolin, Lee. *The Trouble with Physics: The Rise of String Theory, the Fall of a Science, and What Comes Next*. Boston: Houghton Mifflin, 2006.

Sokal, Alan, and Jean Bricmont. *Fashionable Nonsense: Postmodern Intellectuals' Abuse of Science*. New York: Picador, 1998.

Starr, Raymond. "The Flexibility of Literary Meaning and the Role of the Reader in Roman Antiquity." *Latomus* 60 (2001): 433–45.

Stillman, Linda Klieger. "The Morphophonetic Universe of Ubu." *The French Review* 50, no. 4 (March 1977): 586–95. https://www.jstor.org/stable/389379.

Taylor, M.A. Carey. "Le Vocabulaire d'Alfred Jarry." *Cahiers de l'Association Internationale des Études Françaises* 11, no. 1 (1959): 303–22.

Thurston, Luke. "Specious Aristmystic: Joycean Topology." In *Lacan: Topologically Speaking*, edited by Ellie Ragland and Dragan Milovanovic, 314–27. New York: Other Press, 2004.

Tomasello, Michael. *Constructing a Language: A Usage-Based Theory of Language Acquisition*. Cambridge: Harvard University Press, 2003.

Treharne, Elaine. *Living through Conquest: The Politics of Early English, 1020–1220*. Oxford: Oxford University Press, 2012.

Turner, James. *Philology: The Forgotten Origins of the Modern Humanities*. Princeton: Princeton University Press, 2014.

Wallis Budge, E.A., ed., *The Papyrus of Ani: A Reproduction in Facsimile*. 3 vols. London: The Medici Society Ltd. & New York: G.P. Putnam's Sons, 1913.

Warwick, Andrew. *Masters of Theory: Cambridge and the Rise of Mathematical Physics*. Chicago: University of Chicago Press, 2003.

Watson, Lindsey. *A Commentary on Horace's Epodes*. Oxford: Oxford University Press, 2003.

———. "The *Epodes*: Horace's Archilochus." In *Cambridge Companion to Horace*, edited by Stephen Harrison, 93–104. Cambridge: Cambridge University Press, 2007.

Welsh, Irvine. *Trainspotting*. London: Secker & Warburg, 1993.

———. "Introduction." In Anthony Burgess, *A Clockwork Orange*, xi–xix. London: Folio Society, 2014.

Winckelmann, Johann Joachim. "Thoughts on the Imitation of the Painting and Sculpture of the Greeks," in *German Aesthetic and Literary Criticism: Winckelmann, Lessing, Hamann, Herder, Schiller, Goethe*, edited by H.B. Nisbet, 29–54. Cambridge: Cambridge University Press, 1985.

Wright, Roger. "Even Priscian Nods." In *Latin vulgaire, latin tardif VI: actes du VIe Colloque international sur le latin vulgaire et tardif, Helsinki, 29 août–2 septembre*, edited by Heikki Solin, 577–88. Hildesheim: Olms, 2003.

Yerushalmi, Yosef Hayim. *Zakhor: Jewish History and Jewish Memory*. Foreword by Harold Bloom. With a New Preface and Postscript by the Author. Seattle: University of Washington Press, 1989.

Zetzel, James E.G. "The Bride of Mercury: Confessions of a 'Pataphilologist." In *World Philology,* edited by Sheldon Pollock, Benjamin Elman, and Ku-ming Kevin Chang, 45–62. Cambridge: Harvard University Press, 2014.

Zupančič, Alenka. *The Odd One In: On Comedy.* Cambridge: MIT Press, 2008.

Contributors

Steve McCaffery was born in 1947 at the age of 69 in Sheffield England. A founding member of the sound ensemble the Four Horsemen, the Toronto Research Group (TRG), the Canadian College of 'Pataphysics, and the international Institute for Creative Misunderstanding, he is the author of over 45 books, chapbooks and collaborations. His essay "The Pataphsyics of Auschwitz" can be read in his critical gathering *Darkness of the Present: Poetics, Anachronism and the Anomaly* (University of Alabama Press, 2012). A long-time pataphysican in Toronto he is now David Gray Chair endowed Professor of Poetry and Letters at the State University of New York at Buffalo where he remains aged 69.

Sean Gurd is professor of classical studies at the University of Missouri, Columbia. He has written *Iphigenias at Aulis: Textual Multiplicity, Radical Philology* (Cornell University Press, 2006); *Work in Progress: Literary Revision as Social Performance in Ancient Rome* (Oxford University Press, 2012), and *Dissonance: Auditory Aesthetics in Ancient Greece* (Fordham University Press, 2016). He also edited *Philology and its Histories* (Ohio State University Press, 2010).

Vincent W.J. van Gerven Oei is a philologist, publisher, and co-director of independent open-access publishing platform punctum books. He is a specialist of the Old Nubian language and co-editor-in-chief of *Dotawo,* the imprint of the Union for Nubian Studies. His recent publications include *Cross-Examinations* (MER. Paper Kunsthalle, 2015), and the edited volumes *Going Postcard: The Letter(s) of Jacques Derrida* (punctum books, 2017) and with Mihnea Mircan, *Allegory of the Cave Painting* (Mousse, 2015). His three-volume work *Lapidari* (punctum books, 2015) provides the first complete overview of socialist monumentality in Albania. As a translator, Van Gerven Oei works mostly with anonymous Medieval Nubian scribes and more recent authors such as Jean Daive, Hervé Guibert, Dick Raaijmakers, Avital Ronell, and Nachoem M. Wijnberg. His scholarly work has appeared in *ArtPapers, Glossa, postmedieval, Theory & Event,* and *tripwire,* among other venues.

Michael D. Gordin is Rosengarten Professor of Modern and Contemporary History at Princeton University, where he specializes in the history of the modern physical sciences. He is the author of several books, including *Scientific Babel: How Science Was Done before and after Global English* (University of Chicago Press, 2015) and T*he Pseudoscience Wars: Immanuel Velikovsky and the Birth of the Modern Fringe* (University of Chicago Press, 2012). With his colleague and co-author, Joshua T. Katz, he has twice taught a course titled "Imagined Languages," which explored linguistic and philological phenomena on the border of the pata.

Joshua T. Katz is Cotsen Professor in the Humanities, Professor of Classics, and member (and former Director) of the Program in Linguistics at Princeton University. Recent publications consider such matters as wordplay in Vergil, sex in the Old Norse Prose Edda, the prehistory of the Greek pluperfect, and the Proto-Indo-European background of Homeric and Hesiodic poetry. With his colleague and co-author, Michael D. Gordin, he has twice taught a course titled "Imagined Languages," which explored linguistic and philological phenomena on the border of the pata.

James Porter is Chancellor's Professor of Rhetoric and Classics at the University of California, Berkeley. His research interests include the development of Nietzsche's thought and models of aesthetic sensation, perception, and experience in ancient

Greece and Rome. He is author, most recently, of *The Sublime in Antiquity* (2016) and editor of *Time, History, and Literature: Selected Essays of Erich Auerbach* (2016). He is currently working on a book titled *Homer: The Very Idea*.

Sean Braune holds a PhD from York University. His academic articles have appeared in *Journal of Modern Literature, symplokē, Postmodern Culture, Canadian Literature,* and elsewhere. When not writing philosophy, he writes poetry: his poems have appeared in numerous poetry journals and his first poetry chapbook, the vitamins of an alphabet, was published by above/ground press in 2016. Between 2012–14, he guest lectured on experimental writing and storytelling at Yale University. He is the author of *The Parasite: On Phorontology* (punctum books, 2017).

Paul Allen Miller is Vice Provost and Carolina Distinguished Professor at the University of South Carolina. He received his PhD in Comparative Literature from the Unviersity of Texas in 1989. He has held visiting appointments at the University of the Ruhr (Bochum), the University of Paris 13, and Beijing Language and Cultural University. Dr. Miller is the former editor of *Transactions of the American Philological Association*. He is the author of *Lyric Texts and Lyric Consciousness* (1994), *Latin Erotic Elegy* (2002), *Subjecting Verses* (2004), *Latin Verse Satire* (2005), *Postmodern Spiritual Practices* (2007), *Plato's Apology of Socrates* (2010) with Charles Platter, *A Tibullus Reader* (2013), and *Diotima at the Barricades: French Feminists Read Plato* (2015). His *Understanding Horace* is forthcoming from I.B. Tauris. He is currently at work on a book on Foucault's late lectures on antiquity.

Erik Gunderson is Professor of Classics at the University of Toronto. He focuses on the literature and culture of the Roman era with an emphasis on the relationship between the self and institutions. He is the author of monographs on antiquarianism, declamation, rhetorical theory, Plautus, and Seneca.

www.ingramcontent.com/pod-product-compliance
Lightning Source LLC
Chambersburg PA
CBHW071002160426
43193CB00012B/1877